Study Guide

Management of Business Unit 2

for CAPE®

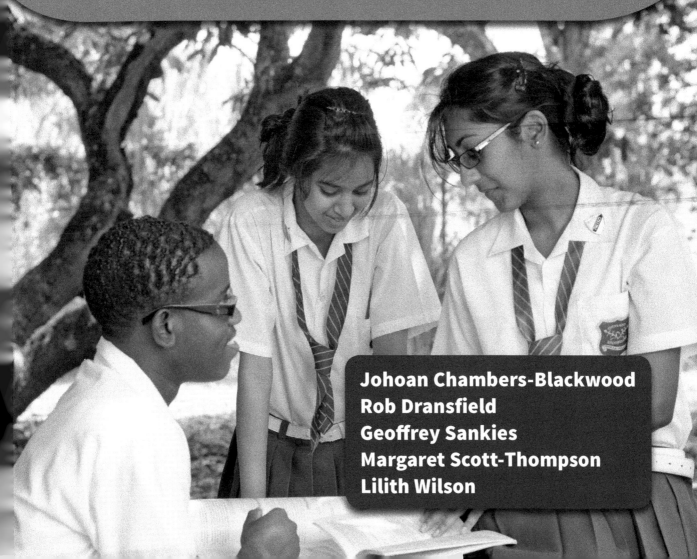

Johoan Chambers-Blackwood
Rob Dransfield
Geoffrey Sankies
Margaret Scott-Thompson
Lilith Wilson

OXFORD
UNIVERSITY PRESS

Great Clarendon Street, Oxford, OX2 6DP, United Kingdom

Oxford University Press is a department of the University of Oxford.
It furthers the University's objective of excellence in research, scholarship,
and education by publishing worldwide. Oxford is a registered trade mark of
Oxford University Press in the UK and in certain other countries

Text © Rob Dransfield, Johoan Chambers-Blackwood, Geoffrey Sankies, Margaret Scott-Thompson and Lilith Wilson 2014
Original illustrations © Oxford University Press 2015

The moral rights of the authors have been asserted

First published by Nelson Thornes Ltd in 2014
This edition published by Oxford University Press in 2015

British Library Cataloguing in Publication Data
Data available

978-1-4085-2098-7

7

Printed and bound by CPI Group (UK) Ltd, Croydon, CR0 4YY

Acknowledgements

Cover photograph: Mark Lyndersay, Lyndersay Digital, Trinidad
www.lyndersaydigital.com
Illustrations: Tony Forbes of Sylvie Poggio Artist Agency, Rory O'Neill of Graham Cameron Illustration and
Tech-Set Ltd, Gateshead
Page make-up: Tech-Set Ltd, Gateshead

The author and the publisher would also like to thank the following for permission to reproduce material:

Text
p49, Abstracted by permission from: Boppana V. Chowdary and Damian George (2012) 'Cost cutting and high quality
in pharmaceuticals production: A Trinidadian drugs manufacturer radically re-engineers its product packing process'.
Strategic Direction, Vol. 28(5), pp.12-15. http://www.emeraldinsight.com/journals.htm?articleid=17026963&show
=html; p67, Red Bull Company Ltd; pp98-99, Adapted from The BCG Portfolio Matrix from The Product Portfolio
Matrix,©1970,The Boston Consulting Group; p122, SM Jaleel & Company Ltd; p129, Digicel Group; p141, GraceKennedy;
p143, Caribbean Harvest Foundation; p145, We would like to extend our greatest appreciation and thanks to Eddy
Grant, Ice Records Limited and its Associated Labels. Please visit IceRecords.com the home of Classic Calypso, Soca and
Ringbang Music.; p150, Reproduced with permission from: Ministry of Industry, Investment and Commerce (2012) 'Table
3: Jamaica's MSME Definition', MSME and Entrepreneurship Policy.; p151, Reprinted by permission of the Inter-American
Development Bank.

Images
p4: (clockwise from top left): Paul Matthew Photography/Shutterstock, AfriPics.com/Alamy, Walter Bibikow/JAI/
Corbis, moodboard/Alamy, Tetiana Vitsenko/Alamy; p6: Thomas Cockrem/Alamy; p8: AFP/Getty Images; p10: travenian/
iStockphoto; p14: JoeClemson/iStockphoto; p16: Jeff Greenberg/Alamy; p18: OJO Images Ltd/Alamy; p40: TP/Alamy;
p52: Small Town Studio/Fotolia; p64: Vespasian/Alamy; p66: Ewing Galloway/Alamy; p72: scorpion56/iStockphoto; p88:
pixeldigits/iStockphoto; p90: Julia Waitring (NT); p93: Africa Media Online/Alamy; p96: Lenscap/Alamy; p100: rainmax/
iStockphoto; p104: Julia Waitring (NT); p105: Magic Martian Green Crush; p107: moodboard/Alamy; p112: sharply_done/
iStockphoto; p114: Alan Novelli/Alamy; p120: frinz/iStockphoto; p126: Redferns/Getty Images; p128: AFP/Getty Images;
p136: David Fisher/Rex Features p138: Chubby, cartoon character from SMJ, Trinidadian drinks co; p141: GraceKennedy;
p142: Friedrich Stark/Alamy; p145: Picture Alliance/Photoshot; p146: onfilm/iStockphoto; p148: Edgar Rogers/fotolibra;
p150: Peter Phipp/Travelshots.com/Alamy; p159: Richard E. Aaron/The Hell Gate/Corbis.

Although we have made every effort to trace and contact all
copyright holders before publication this has not been possible in all
cases. If notified, the publisher will rectify any errors or omissions at
the earliest opportunity.

Contents

Introduction		1

Module 1 Production and operations management   2

1.1	The nature of the production process	4
1.2	Production methods	6
1.3	The location of production: qualitative factors	8
1.4	The location of production: quantitative factors	10
1.5	Forecasting techniques	12
1.6	Product design strategies	14
1.7	Value analysis and the value chain	16
1.8	CAD and CAM	18
1.9	Capacity planning	20
1.10	Improving capacity utilisation	22
1.11	Economies of scale	24
1.12	Layout strategies	26
1.13	Costs of production	28
1.14	Absorption costing and contribution	30
1.15	The break-even point and margin of safety	32
1.16	Marginal costing	34
1.17	Make or buy	36
1.18	Inventory management: order quantities	38
1.19	Inventory management: just-in-time	40
1.20	Importance of quality management	42
1.21	Techniques for improving quality 1	44
1.22	Techniques for improving quality 2	46
1.23	Lean production	48
1.24	Productivity	50
1.25	Factors impacting on productivity	52
1.26	Project management 1: critical path method	54
1.27	Project management 2: decision trees	56
1.28	Practice exam-style questions: Production and operations management	60

Module 2 Fundamentals of marketing   62

2.1	Marketing 1: defining the concept	64
2.2	Marketing 2: concepts explained	66
2.3	Marketing 3: the marketing concept	68
2.4	Composition of the marketing environment	70
2.5	The macro-marketing environment	72
2.6	Market research	74
2.7	Stages of market research 1: identifying a problem	76
2.8	Stages of market research 2: sampling	78
2.9	Stages of market research 3: primary research techniques	80
2.10	Stages of market research 4: secondary research techniques	82
2.11	Stages of market research 5: presentation of results	84
2.12	Market segmentation	86
2.13	Bases of segmentation 1: demographic and geographic	88
2.14	Bases of segmentation 2: behavioural (psychographic)	90
2.15	Consumer buying behaviour	92
2.16	The concept of product	94
2.17	Dimensions of the product mix	96
2.18	The Boston Matrix	98
2.19	New product development	100
2.20	The product life cycle	102

2.21 Branding and packaging   104

2.22 Marketing goods and services   106

2.23 Introduction to pricing   108

2.24 Factors influencing price   110

2.25 Pricing strategies 1: competition
      pricing   112

2.26 Pricing strategies 2: cost-plus pricing   114

2.27 Pricing strategies 3: other strategies   116

2.28 The role of distribution   118

2.29 Factors influencing distribution
      decisions   120

2.30 Logistics strategies   122

2.31 Introduction to promotion   124

2.32 Promotional tools 1: advertising   126

2.33 Promotional tools 2: personal selling,
      sales promotion and publicity   128

2.34 Internet marketing 1: development   130

2.35 Internet marketing 2: opportunities
      and challenges   132

2.36 Practice exam-style questions:
      Fundamentals of marketing   134

Module 3 Small business management 136

3.1 Entrepreneurship   138

3.2 Corporate entrepreneurship   140

3.3 Social entrepreneurship   142

3.4 Successful entrepreneurs   144

3.5 Economic systems and their impacts
     on business decisions   146

3.6 The size of a business   148

3.7 Measuring business size:
     the limitations   150

3.8 Small firms versus large firms   152

3.9 Opportunities for growth   154

3.10 Small businesses: challenges and
      opportunities 1   156

3.11 Small businesses: challenges and
      opportunities 2   158

3.12 Assistance for small business   160

3.13 Business planning   162

3.14 Elements of a business plan 1:
      executive summary and business
      description   164

3.15 Elements of a business plan 2:
      environment analysis   166

3.16 Elements of a business plan 3:
      market and competitor analysis 168

3.17 Elements of a business plan 4:
      the marketing plan   170

3.18 Elements of a business plan 5:
      operations plan   172

3.19 Elements of a business plan 6:
      financial planning 1   174

3.20 Elements of a business plan 7:
      financial planning 2   176

3.21 Elements of a business plan 8:
      financial planning 3   178

3.22 Practice exam-style questions:
      Small business management   180

Glossary   182

Index   186

Introduction

This Study Guide has been developed exclusively with the Caribbean Examinations Council (CXC®) to be used as an additional resource by candidates, both in and out of school, following the Caribbean Advanced Proficiency Examination (CAPE®) programme.

It has been prepared by a team with expertise in the CAPE® syllabus, teaching and examination. The contents are designed to support learning by providing tools to help you achieve your best in CAPE® Management of Business and the features included make it easier for you to master the key concepts and requirements of the syllabus. *Do remember to refer to your syllabus for full guidance on the course requirements and examination format!*

Inside this Study Guide is an interactive CD that includes the answers to practice exam-style questions and electronic activities to assist you in developing good examination techniques:

- **On Your Marks** activities provide sample examination-style short answer and essay type questions, with example candidate answers and feedback from an examiner to show where answers could be improved. These activities will build your understanding, skill level and confidence in answering examination questions.

- **Test Yourself** activities are specifically designed to provide experience of multiple-choice examination questions and helpful feedback will refer you to sections inside the Study Guide so that you can revise problem areas.

This unique combination of focused syllabus content and interactive examination practice will provide you with invaluable support to help you reach your full potential in CAPE® Management of Business.

1   Production and operations management

General objectives

On completion of this module, you should be able to:

- understand the operations involved in the production of goods and services
- have a developed awareness of the importance of productivity and quality in production
- appreciate the importance of tools and techniques required for production and operations management
- be aware of the impact of the external environment on the production and operations function.

Operations

Module 1 begins with a focus on operations in an organisation. Operations are the processes and acts, often practical, that an organisation performs to satisfy customers. For example, your hairdresser may wash, colour, cut and dry your hair, while holding an entertaining conversation with you – all of these are operations. They will take place in a particular physical location, in this example in a hairdressing salon. To meet customer requirements efficiently, an organisation must organise its methods of production.

The nature of operations depends on the good or service being produced. Operations in restaurants take place in the kitchens and in serving at the tables, and include the preparation and drawing up of menus, preparation and cooking of food, serving it and responding to customers' requests. In a bottling factory, operations include filling the bottles with liquid, checking that the right quantity is contained, sealing the bottles, putting them into boxes, crates and other containers, storing them and moving them ready for transport.

The nature of production

Production is the process of using resources to add value to a good or service in order to meet the customer's needs. In a manufacturing company, this involves buying in raw materials and transforming them into finished products that can be distributed to the market.

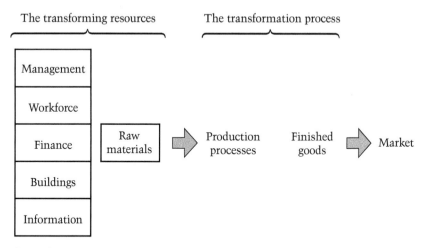

The production process

Operations management

Module 1 also looks at the function of operations managers, who organise the operations of a company, both day to day and in the long term. Their skills are essential for efficient production. A good manager aims to achieve this efficiency by maximising the value-adding processes and minimising the waste-creating processes in the organisation. Value analysis is used to identify the activities that add most value to production, and to indicate to managers how to organise the physical layout of plant and equipment to maximise efficiency. Operations managers work closely with other managers, such as with sales managers in forecasting sales. Efficient operations management is important in every industry, from organising bus routes and timetables, so that buses arrive and depart on time, to manufacturing garment fabric in the clothing industry, providing the most attractive colours and designs.

Costing techniques

Operations managers need to be familiar with a range of different approaches to calculating the costs of individual units of output as well as total costs of production. You will be introduced to a range of costing techniques, including absorption costing and marginal costing.

Inventory management

Key production decisions relate to the efficient management of stocks, making sure that inventory is supplied internally to production units within a company, and that finished goods are supplied on time to the end consumers.

Productivity

The concept of productivity is closely associated with efficiency. The productivity of factors of production is the output that can be produced with a given quantity of factors (land, labour, raw materials, etc.). Higher productivity occurs when a greater volume of output can be produced with the same or a smaller quantity of resources.

Quality

The module also considers how an emphasis on quality is a good way to increase productivity. 'Quality' relates to a product or process that does what is expected of it: it is fit for purpose. Quality is an important focus for modern operations management, and is the responsibility of everyone that works for a company. A good operations manager will design systems that enable all employees to contribute to quality improvement.

Tools and techniques to improve operations

The module will outline the many different tools and techniques that can be employed by the operations manager. Charts can be created to show the time taken for operations. A critical path analysis diagram can identify the most important operations that need to be completed and the time required to complete them. Stock (inventory) levels can be measured to identify when inventory needs to be replenished.

The external environment and its impact on operations

Finally, the module looks at how a good operations manager is aware of the external environment in which operations are performed. Managers should be aware of new and emerging technologies that may change production processes. They should be aware of the economic cycle: for example, to identify when and how production costs can be reduced in order to be more competitive in a period of recession. They also need to be aware of the legal environment: for example, how health and safety legislation impacts on how production can be carried out.

The module concludes with a consideration of decision-making techniques that can be employed by operations managers to support the planning process.

Specific objective

On completion of this section, you should be able to:

■ describe the major decisions involved in the production process, with reference to input (factors of production), throughput (production process) and output (finished goods and services).

KEY TERMS

Operations: converting inputs into finished outputs.

Did you know?

Often operations at the end of the chain of production add more value than those at the start. For example, branding clothes often significantly increases the price that consumers are willing to pay for them.

Figure 1.1.1 *Operations management transforms inputs into finished goods*

Operations

Operations involve converting inputs into finished outputs. Figure 1.1.1 shows how operations management facilitates this process by successfully transforming inputs into desired goods and services.

This can be illustrated by the manufacture of garments from home-grown Sea Island cotton in Jamaica, Antigua, Barbados and Nevis. Named after the Sea Islands in the US states of South Carolina and Georgia where it was first grown, this type of cotton has the longest fibres of any cotton plant and provides a luxurious crop. The cotton bolls (the protective capsules that grow round the seeds) mature at different times, so they need to be harvested by hand. The harvested cotton is packed into bales. Many of the bales are exported, often to European and US markets, but some is bought by local garment manufacturers. The cotton is so luxurious that it trades for several times the price of cotton grown in other parts of the world.

Table 1.1.1 shows the number of inputs, and many processes, that lead to the output.

Table 1.1.1 *The production process for Sea Island cotton goods*

Inputs (materials)	Throughputs (transformation processes)	Outputs
Cotton plants	Tending and harvesting by farm workers	Cotton bales
Sea Island cotton Energy (to work machines) Labour Capital Information	Carding Spinning Designing Cutting, sewing, shaping, marketing, selling	Cotton garments: shirts, dresses, scarves, etc.

Sea Island cotton provides employment for people at the different stages of production. In the primary sector, agricultural workers grow and harvest the raw cotton. In the secondary sector, fashion designers and textile workers make up the raw cotton into a desirable finished product. In the tertiary sector, distribution workers transport the product, marketers engage in marketing activities across the world and retailers engage in selling the product. Sea Island cotton is a premium cotton product, commanding a high price in domestic and international markets.

Transforming and transformed products

A useful distinction can be made between transforming resources and transformed resources.

- Managers, employees, machinery and equipment are transforming resources.
- The resources that they transform are the materials and information that they process.

Key decisions

Key operational decisions include:

- What resources will we employ in the production process?
- What quantities of resources will we use?
- How will we organise the production processes (that is, the operations)?
- What steps will we take to maximise quality?
- How can we minimise costs in relation to the quality of our product?
- How can we make best use of our plant and equipment?
- What sorts of technologies will yield the best results?
- What steps do we need to take to make sure that our products are those required by the market?

Did you know?

You may hear the expression that production is at the 'sharp end' of business activity. This means that if production does not produce the right goods, the organisation will fail. Targets have to be met and standards maintained. Failure to meet targets and standards can lead to falling orders and profits for a company.

Summary table

Inputs	Throughputs	Outputs
What goes into producing a product	The processes involved in production	The end product
Resources such as energy, materials, labour, capital and information	Tasks and processes such as transporting, storing, forming, shaping, cutting and checking	A good or service
Transforming resources	Transformation processes	The final output
Operations managers decide which inputs to use	Operations managers decide what processes to employ	Production managers work with marketing to identify customer requirements

Summary questions

1 Identify the inputs, throughputs and outputs in:
   a a hotel business
   b a clothing manufacturer
   c a bank.

2 What are the main types of decision that an operations manager would need to take in a factory producing shoes? Which of these decisions relate to inputs and which to throughputs?

3 How can an operations manager make sure that the output that a business produces is based on using the most effective throughputs?

On completion of this section, you should be able to:

- identify and outline the features of the four main production methods.

Figure 1.2.1 *Job production involves providing a specific job of work for a particular customer: for example, cutting and braiding someone's hair*

Did you know?

Another example of job production is where a producer in a recording studio works with a particular recording artist to produce a recording of their music.

Methods of production

Most businesses use one of the following methods of production:

- job production
- batch production
- line/continuous flow production
- cell production.

The method chosen depends on the demand for the product and the extent to which specific attention needs to be paid to the different needs of customers.

Job production

Job production is where an organisation produces one or a small number of items for a specific customer, such as a wedding cake. Job production is also relevant in producing large infrastructural projects, such as building a port facility. Often the product will be made on the premises of the producer, as with the wedding cake at a bakery. In some situations a job may need to be completed on site, as in the case of a construction project.

The producer may work on several jobs at the same time: for example, supplying wedding cakes to several couples who are getting married on the same day. Firms engaging in job production need to make sure that they keep building up orders for new jobs to replace the ones nearing completion.

Job production enables attention to be given to the specific needs of customers, so it involves a lot of discussion and listening to customer requirements. The producer is able to build a strong relationship with the customer, which can lead to repeat business. Profit margins tend to be higher because of the uniqueness of the task and the time needed to do each job well.

Batch production

In batch production, a number of identical or similar items are produced in a set or batch. The items need not be for any specific customers but are made at regular intervals in specific quantities. Batch production involves work being passed from one stage to another. Each stage of production is highly planned.

A simple example is the production of loaves of bread in a bakery. Every day 200 brown loaves, 100 white loaves and 500 small buns are produced. First the dough is made for the brown loaves. While this is rising, the dough is made for the white loaves. While this is rising, the dough for the brown loaves is kneaded – and so on.

A key feature of batch production is that every now and then you have to stop the production process and reset it for a different product (which can be viewed as a waste of time).

Line production

This involves products passing down a line. The production process is a repeating one, with identical products going through the same sequence of operations. Car assembly lines are a classic example of line production. The work comes down the production line to the worker, who carries out a set operation. Nowadays humans have been replaced by robots in many production lines.

Line production produces identical products. The disadvantage of this is that many customers, such as car buyers, want their purchase to be differentiated or distinctive in some way, but line production makes these tailored products difficult to achieve. However, line production enables economies of large-scale production.

Continuous flow production takes line production a step further. Here a production line can be run for 24 hours a day: for example, in three sequential eight-hour shifts. Examples of companies that employ a continuous flow process in the Caribbean are oil refineries, paper mills and confectionery manufacturers. Machinery plays a key part in continuous flow production – particularly automatically programmed machines.

Cell production

Cell production has become popular in recent times. Workers, machines and materials are grouped together in a particular production space. The team of workers and other production resources is termed a **cell** and it focuses on a family of related tasks, products or component assembly. The workers in the cell have access to all the tools and machines required. The benefits of cellular working include providing a group of workers (cell members) with shared responsibility for carrying out a series of related operations. Together, they are able to identify best working practices and improvements to reduce waste.

Cell production is a key element of **lean production**. Inventory store, manufacturing and **work in progress** all take place within the same area of a factory, which speeds up processes, and reduces the distances and time involved in moving components, materials and people.

Summary table

	Advantages	Disadvantages
Job production	Concentrates on individual requirements of customers	Costly to implement Typically takes longer to complete
Batch production	Unit costs lower than for job production Enables longer production runs	Time wasted – with cost implications when resetting machinery for new runs
Line production	Focus on scale production enables large quantities to be manufactured for low unit costs – based on automated factory processes	Less scope for differentiation around individual customer requirements
Cell production	Cells can focus on eliminating waste and creating value for customers	Training required More skilled workers needed who can run different processes and take more responsibility

KEY TERMS

Cell: a group of workers, machines and resources focused on producing families of related components and products.

Lean production: concentrating on creating value in manufacturing by eliminating all forms of waste (e.g. wasted materials and time).

Work in progress: partly assembled goods and processed raw materials part way through the manufacturing process.

Summary questions

1 Which production methods would be most suitable in the following situations? Give reasons for your answers.
   a Bottling popular soft drinks
   b Pedicure
   c Producing complex engines for motor vehicles
   d Processing cinema goers visiting a multiplex cinema
   e Producing fast food
   f Home tutoring
   g Book publishing
   h Food processing

2 A pharmaceutical company currently produces a range of patent medicines using a production line method. However, there are frequent delays and errors. It has been suggested that the company switches to cell production. Why might this be a good idea? What would be the best alternative?

1.3 The location of production: qualitative factors

Specific objective

On completion of this section, you should be able to:

■ describe the major decisions involved in the production process, with reference to location of production (qualitative factors).

Figure 1.3.1 *Countries with a good infrastructure of roads and other transport links, and reliable energy supplies, are most likely to attract businesses of all types*

Qualitative and quantitative factors

An important decision for a business is choosing the most cost-effective location. Factors that influence this decision are both quantitative and qualitative. Quantitative factors involve calculations: these will be discussed in 1.4. Qualitative factors are based on value judgements and opinions.

Qualitative location factors

The most significant qualitative factors are:

■ suitability of infrastructure

■ environmental considerations

■ planning considerations

■ management preferences.

In 1.3 and 1.4 we are interested not only in where to locate within the whole Caribbean region, but also in where to locate within a particular territory.

Suitability of infrastructure

Before deciding to set up an enterprise in a particular location, all companies look very carefully at the infrastructure of the country or region. The infrastructure is the foundation of capital resources on which the economy is based. It includes:

■ energy supplies and distribution systems

■ transport networks – road, rail and air links

■ water supplies

■ information technology and internet systems

■ education systems.

Countries with a well-developed infrastructure provide more attractive locations for business. Barbados, for example, has abundant sources of energy and fresh water, good schools and reliable internet services. Entrepreneurs can be confident that the infrastructure will be of high quality and reliable. This may not be true of rural areas, which may have marked contrasts in development. An example of a territory with a weak infrastructure is Haiti: for various reasons there is a poor road and transportation system, lack of ready access to water supplies, limited internet connections and poor systems of primary, secondary and higher education.

Environmental considerations

There are two main aspects of environmental considerations:

■ **The impact of the company on the environment:** companies that create **pollution** will need to locate away from centres of population. For example, an airport or noisy factory should not be sited close to densely populated residential areas. Similarly, a company that causes air or water pollution should not be situated upstream or upwind from urban areas, where the **spillover effect** of its activities will impact negatively on human populations.

KEY TERMS

Pollution: the introduction of harmful substances or products into the natural environment.

Spillover effect: a secondary result of an activity that affects those who are not directly involved in it.

- **The impact of the environment on the company:** hotel and leisure resorts will prefer to set up in countries and areas where the air, sea, rivers and beaches are clean and unpolluted.

Planning considerations

Planning considerations involve the guidelines and regulations that impact on where a company can set up and the nature of the plant that it is allowed to build. To build a new factory a company requires planning permission from the local government planning board. Authorities impose restrictions such as the size of a plant, what can be produced and how waste must be disposed. Acquiring planning permission can be a lengthy process, particularly for activities with an element of danger, such as mining operations, and those that will affect the environment, such as drilling for oil. Key considerations for a company are therefore:

- What are the planning laws?
- How long will it take to get planning permission?
- How costly will it be to get planning permission?
- How will planning approval curtail intended business plans?

Management preferences

Another qualitative factor that impacts on the choice of location is management preferences. Studies show that for family firms, choosing a business location is similar to choosing a family home. Determining factors include the quality of life: availability of good schools, recreational facilities, clean air and a pleasant living environment. High-quality managers with families prefer to live and work in pleasant environments where they can bring up their children with a good quality of life. Many parts of the Caribbean today focus on tertiary (service) business activity as opposed to primary (e.g. farming) and secondary (e.g. manufacturing) activity. Managers of companies in the tertiary sector are more likely to choose areas where there is access to good-quality housing and other amenities, and where crime rates are lower.

Summary table

Key qualitative factors impacting on location decisions in the Caribbean		
Factor	**Description**	**Suitable territories**
Infrastructure	Transport links, energy supplies, access to clean water	Barbados, Bahamas, some urban rather than rural areas
Environment	Areas favoured that have a cleaner environment and less pollution	Barbados, St Lucia
Planning	Elaborate planning regulations act as a deterrent to setting up a company in a territory, as it can be a costly process	Countries with fewer restrictions
Management preferences	Particularly in the tertiary sector, managers and owners choose locations with a better quality of life for family	Countries with better leisure, recreational and educational facilities

Did you know?

A key qualitative factor impacting on location decisions in the Caribbean is climate and the possibility of natural disasters. Areas that are more susceptible to hurricanes (e.g. some of the Windward Islands) and volcanic activity (e.g. Haiti) are less likely to attract inward and foreign direct investment (FDI).

Summary questions

1 Carry out an internet search for the Ease of Doing Business Index.
  a Which Caribbean countries have the fewest planning regulations?
  b How might this impact on choice of location?

2 a Why might companies not choose to set up in areas with the fewest planning regulations?
  b What other factors will impact on how they choose a location?

1.4 The location of production: quantitative factors

Specific objective

On completion of this section, you should be able to:

- describe the major decisions involved in the production process, with reference to location of production (quantitative factors).

KEY TERMS

Least-cost location: a site where, after taking all costs into account, the cost of manufacturing or distribution is lowest.

Figure 1.4.1 *A key consideration in choosing a location for an oil refinery is to find a low-cost site away from centres of population*

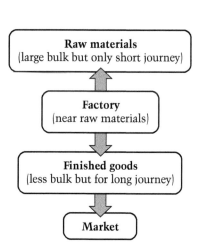

Figure 1.4.2 *Bulk-decreasing industries are better placed near their source of raw materials*

KEY TERMS

Bulk-decreasing industry: an industry with output that is cheaper to transport than its input.

Quantitative location factors

In the past, quantitative factors were significant in determining business location, particularly where the impact of location on cost could be shown. A business would seek to achieve the **least-cost location**.

A number of factors affect the choice of least-cost location, principally the costs of moving:

- materials
- products
- people.

These costs can be measured in terms of miles (or kilometres), money and/or time. In each case the lowest figures are the best. Other costs that can be measured include the cost of storing materials and goods, and government taxes in different locations.

Locating close to raw materials (materials costs)

Some businesses require heavy and bulky raw materials in their manufacture, although the finished products may be much smaller and lighter. For example, finished steel is a lot lighter than the ore, limestone and other materials that have gone into its manufacture. If the raw materials are bulky and expensive to transport, it makes sense to locate near their source. Industries like this are known as **bulk-decreasing industries**, as their output is much cheaper to transport than their input (Figure 1.4.2).

Locating close to market (transport costs)

Many businesses need to be close to their market: that is, their customers. Restaurants need to be near the dining-out population, while taxi ranks need to be close to airports and town centres.

Service industries such as entertainment and banking also have to locate near their markets to be available for their customers. Manufacturing industries producing bulky, or fragile, items that are expensive to transport also locate close to market. Large centres of population, such as Kingston and Port of Spain, attract **bulk-increasing industries**. These are industries where the output is more expensive to transport than the raw materials. They need to be close to their market in order to minimise transport costs.

Locating at a low-cost site (site costs)

Land costs vary from area to area. Some firms, such as oil refineries, deal with large quantities of goods and require a lot of space. Other businesses need to check that a site has the right geology to support heavy weights, or the right climate for producing certain goods.

Location where labour is cheapest (labour costs)

A business may not necessarily find the sorts of labour and skills it needs locally. If a firm moves to an area that does not have the right sort of labour, it will have to pay employees for **relocation**, or train new people in the skills it needs. This costs money. In some areas there may be a tradition of work in a particular industry and there will be a large pool of workers with the right skills already available. Barbados has many skilled IT professionals, attractive to new businesses needing these skills.

Footloose industries do not require any particular location. These industries are therefore attracted to areas where labour is cheap.

Locating where revenue is highest relative to cost (revenue costs)

A key location consideration is where revenue will be highest relative to costs. In simple terms:

high revenues and low costs → high profits

A business should therefore choose a location where revenue is likely to be high (close to a market with wealthy consumers) and costs are lower (where transport costs are low, or there are government incentives to set up and run a business).

Summary questions

1. How can a quantitative approach be used to choose the most suitable location for establishing a company producing packaging for food manufacturers?

2. Why might a company choose not to locate close to the market for the finished product? Give examples.

3. What types of company are most likely to be bulk increasing and which bulk decreasing? How does this impact on location decisions?

Summary table

Consideration	Description	Example
Materials costs	Locate close to bulky materials	Metal extraction and refining
Transport costs	Locate close to market	Fresh vegetables and perishable products
Site costs	Locate where land is cheap	Oil refineries on spacious and safe sites
Labour costs	Locate where the right labour is cheap	IT industries in Barbados where trained IT professionals are plentiful
Revenue costs	Locate where costs are low as a proportion of revenue	Any location decision with the right balance between low costs and high revenues

Specific objective

On completion of this section, you should be able to:

- explain techniques involved in forecasting including sales force composite, the Delphi method, consumer surveys, jury of experts and moving average.

KEY TERMS

Forecasting: making a prediction of what will happen in the future, usually based on identifying a pattern from past and current data.

Did you know?

Other disadvantages of the sales force composite method include:

- sales people may not be able to differentiate between what customers want and what they will actually do

- sales people are sometimes overly influenced by recent experiences. Thus, after a period of low sales, their estimates may tend to be too low.

KEY TERMS

Consumer survey: a consumer research technique in which a questionnaire is used to research a particular topic, such as consumers' opinions about a specific product or issue. The survey typically involves a sequence of questions.

Forecasting

Forecasting the level of demand for a product helps to determine production levels. Five important forecasting techniques are discussed below.

Sales force composite

The sales force composite method involves a composite, or total, of the expected sales of each member of the sales team in their particular sales area. Sales staff working in the various territories are able to use their experience of selling conditions to estimate future sales. These figures can then be fed back into production decisions. An advantage of the sales force composite method is that sales staff are in direct contact with customers and are often aware of plans they may have for the future. Disadvantages of using this approach are possible over-estimation by sales staff and lack of use of data that are external to the organisation (see 2.10).

Delphi method

With the Delphi method, people who have relevant experience are asked to examine, for example, future consumer spending patterns. They usually answer a questionnaire. They do not meet, so their views are independent and uninfluenced by the others. After each round of questions a facilitator provides an anonymous summary of the forecasts. The experts are then encouraged to revise their previous answers. This should lead to a convergence of ideas, so that a more refined picture emerges of the future market.

The process stops at a predetermined point, say after a given number of rounds or when a consensus forecast has been reached. The key benefit of this technique is the use of independent views. Disadvantages are the cost and time required to assemble a specialist group and facilitate the process.

Consumer surveys

Consumer surveys are one of the most frequently used methods of forecasting. They may take the form of a face-to-face interview with a trained interviewer who fills in the answers, or questionnaires may be sent out. The key benefit of this approach is direct engagement with potential and actual customers, where one gathers information that might not be available elsewhere. Drawbacks include the time and cost required to create a suitable questionnaire. Surveys are covered in more detail in 2.9 in the context of market research.

Jury of experts

Unlike in the Delphi method, a jury of experts meets together. Often this involves particular managers with specialist knowledge in an organisation: it may be called a jury of executive opinion. Each expert opinion throws some light on likely future trends, which in turn leads to informed forecasting. A disadvantage of the method is that a strong personality in the group may enforce his/her opinion on others, leading to a biased and possibly inaccurate forecast. Another disadvantage is that responsibility to finalise a forecast is diffused throughout the group, resulting in less pressure to make a decision.

Time series and moving averages

Time-series analysis involves forecasting by examining past and present relationships between sales and time to predict future sales pattern. A moving average shows how the average of sales moves over time.

Imagine a firm, on an island where tourism is popular, which supplies petroleum products. The firm faces its highest demand in peak tourism periods and its lowest demand when visitors are few. To find out the long-term trend in demand for its product, the business needs to eliminate seasonal variation from its demand picture. It does this by creating a moving average, which smooths out demand for the four seasons of the year (peak, mid, low and high season).

The first step is to calculate the average for the first group of four seasons. Then an average is taken for a second group of four seasons, starting with mid-season, and so on. The demand pattern and resulting moving averages are shown in Figure 1.5.1.

	Demand for fuel (000 litres)		Moving average (000 litres)
Year 1	Peak season: 100		
	Mid-season: 80		
			85
	Low season: 70		
			87.5
	High season: 90		
			90
Year 2	Peak season	110	
			92.5
	Mid-season	90	
			95
	Low season	80	
	High season	100	

Figure 1.5.1 Demand pattern and moving average for fuel

You can see from the table that in each of the seasons in Year 2, values have risen by 10 from the previous year. Having removed the seasonal variation, it is possible to identify a steady upward movement.

Summary questions

1 a What are the most significant differences and similarities between the Delphi method and a jury of experts?

 b Which approach is likely to yield the most useful sales forecasting data?

2 In what ways is a 'moving average' likely to provide the following?

 a A good picture of future sales trends

 b A poor picture of future sales trends

3 Why is sales forecasting important for operations management?

Summary table

Method	Description	Examples of advantages	Examples of disadvantages
Sales forecast composite	Aggregate of sales staff forecasts	Based on local knowledge	Relies on internal rather than external data
Delphi method	Facilitated review of expert opinions	Uses expert views	Time and cost to set up
Consumer survey	Questionnaire of consumer opinions	Engages directly with customers	Time and cost of preparing and delivering
Jury of experts	Brings together experts to produce shared forecast	Enables sharing of knowledge	Experts may influence each other's views
Moving average	Forecasted change in sales based on average changes	Uses statistical approach based on past and current trends	Lacks human opinions and relies on historical data

Figure 1.6.1 *Modular offices enable a combination of customisation with the benefits of mass production*

Product design

Product design involves a number of processes, including the generation of ideas, concept development, testing alternatives and product manufacture or service implementation. This section examines three widely used production strategies: modularisation, integration and miniaturisation.

Modularisation

Modules are product systems made up of a number of components that can be assembled in a flexible way: modular buildings are assembled from components such as window and door frames, walls and furniture units. The modules are transported to a construction site and assembled to form structures such as a school, part of a hospital, or construction site cabins. The modules can be configured according to customer needs yet producers can still benefit from standardised manufacturing processes.

Modularisation enables the management and development of complex products and processes by decomposing them into simpler **sub-assemblies**. Modularisation is particularly significant in a complex international economy: separate modules can be assembled in different countries and transported for assembly in an assembly plant.

The main benefits of modularisation are:
- It enables mixing and matching of modules.
- It enables differentiation around customer requirements.
- It reduces labour, inventory and waste in operations.
- It reduces costs of operations.
- It enables improved quality and productivity (through standardisation).

Integration

In contrast to modularisation, integration of product design involves designing each component so that it works specifically (often exclusively) with other components in a tightly integrated system. The emphasis is on creating an integrated whole, considering how each product component and process fits together into a single (often unique) system. For example, in creating a parliament building for a Caribbean country, the designers will consider how they can build into the design specific lighting, visual imagery, temperature control or seating features that are uniquely associated with that building (and the distinctive nature of the country). The end result is a tightly coupled system. Inevitably, integration is more costly than modularity, but more differentiated.

Miniaturisation

Miniaturisation is one of the most exciting new developments in operations management in the 21st century. Large sums of money have been invested, particularly by the Japanese and US governments. Miniaturisation involves reducing products and processes to a minute scale. For example, **micromachines** are tiny intelligent machines powered by the latest laser technology. They can be programmed to perform a number of key operations, such as working inside other machines. Micromachines are also able to enter a mechanical device that is too small for human hands. Eventually, micromachines may be able to enter the human body to perform complex surgery.

CASE STUDY

Nanotechnology

The term 'miniaturisation' was first used by Richard Feynman in 1959. He showed that biological cells contain the complex information that determine human characteristics. He envisaged the possibility that humans would be able to make things as small as human cells that do what we want (i.e. microscopic systems). Computer technology was seen as providing the brain power to control such tiny systems. Feynman suggested that what we now refer to as 'nanotechnology' could be used to combine biological and chemical processes in order to manufacture miniaturised devices.

There are many benefits from miniaturised manufacturing processes, including:

- smaller space requirements
- fewer resource requirements
- mass production in batches
- low cost of production and transportation.

Examples of micro products include optical, pressure and chemical sensors, grippers, valves, pumps and motors.

1 What do you see as the principal benefits of nanotechnology?

2 What difficulties are likely to arise in the development of nanotechnology?

Increasingly, we have seen the development of smaller and smaller products, such as hand-held computers and smartphones, which still have the equivalent power of much larger devices. In the consumer field, miniaturisation is particularly evident in the field of consumer electronics. In the field of manufacturing, it is evident in the development of medical equipment and in developments in the aviation, chemical and pharmaceutical industries.

Summary table

Product design strategy	Description	Benefits
Modularisation	Design and development of sub-assemblies in the form of modules that can be combined into final assemblies	■ Combines flexibility with large-scale production ■ Differentiation coupled with low cost
Integration	Designing components to work specifically (often exclusively) with other components in an integrated whole	■ Creates tailor-made products targeted at specific customer requirements
Miniaturisation	Designing tiny products and processes	■ Takes up small space ■ Uses small quantities of resources

Summary questions

1 Identify products that are manufactured locally to you using modularised systems. How can the modules be combined in different configurations?

2 Identify some local products that are manufactured using integrated systems. How do the components of the integrated system support each other?

3 Identify products that you use that are smaller today than 10 years ago. Have the products become more or less sophisticated? How would you explain this change?

On completion of this section, you should be able to:

- discuss the strategies involved in product design, with reference to value analysis and the value chain.

Figure 1.7.1 *As consumers we carry out a value analysis when buying a product such as a car: we compare its usefulness to us with the cost of its purchase*

Value analysis

All customers want value from the products that they use: a good level of performance, and aspects such as style – for example the appearance of the product and perhaps its texture. These positive aspects will be compared with the cost of purchasing the product. In simple terms, the consumer compares the usefulness of the product (to them) with its cost.

For the producers the challenge is therefore to create as much value as possible compared with the cost of production. This is 'value analysis'.

Every product provides a set of primary functions (the most important aspects that the customer is looking for) and a set of secondary functions (less-important aspects that still add to the product's usefulness).

To provide a competitive product, therefore, a producer needs to identify the cost of providing each primary, and secondary, function. Each primary function will be essential but it might be possible to omit some of the secondary functions: those that provide the least value relative to cost.

In value analysis the producer needs to consider:

- **what** needs to be provided
- **how** it will be provided.

In making decisions about basic functions, the producer must provide these functions but has some choice about how the functions will be provided.

In making decisions about secondary functions, the producer can choose whether or not to provide these functions. If he or she decides to provide them then they will have some choice about how to provide them (see Table 1.7.1).

Table 1.7.1 *Considerations in value analysis*

	WHAT functions	HOW to provide those functions
Basic functions	Producer must provide	Producer chooses how to provide
Secondary functions	Producer chooses whether or not to provide	Producer chooses how to provide

There are therefore a number of questions associated with value analysis that help to determine production decisions:

- Can we do without that process or function? Some secondary functions can be eliminated.
- Does the process or function do more than is required by the customer? If so, eliminate it.
- Does the process or function cost more than it is worth? There is a possibility of cutting out these functions.
- Is it possible to use less-costly materials, tools and methods?

The value chain

The concept of the **value chain** was developed in the 1980s by Michael Porter from a study of top-performing companies in the US. The value chain provides an analysis of how value is added in the production process, that is, the steps involved in making products more desirable. Porter identified primary and secondary activities. Primary activities follow in sequential steps: acquiring materials, components and equipment (inbound logistics), processing the goods (operations), distributing them (outbound logistics), finding out what customers want and providing them with their requirements (marketing and sales), and providing additional service (such as repairs). Secondary activities also add value that enables some companies to be more effective than others. These include a focus on technological development, human resource management, the way the organisation is structured (infrastructure) and relationships with suppliers (procurement). Figure 1.7.2 shows this as a diagram. Note that both primary activities (the bottom half of the diagram) and secondary activities (the top half of the diagram) contribute to generating a profit margin.

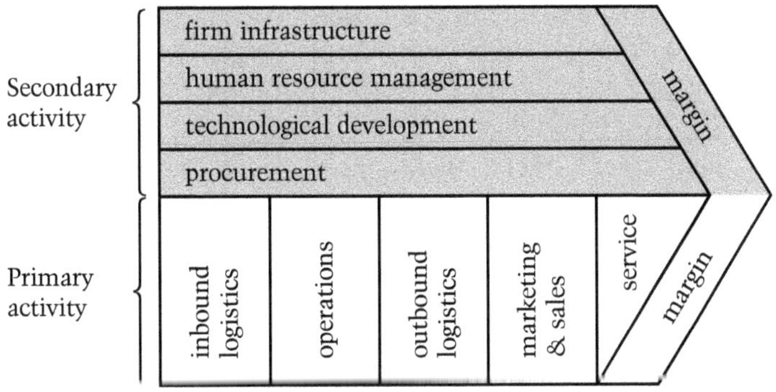

Figure 1.7.2 *The value chain*

Analysis of the activities enables the producer to identify the best ways to create value for the consumer. Producers should identify not only the value-creating processes, but also how they combine to provide value for consumers.

In summary, the importance of the value chain concept lies in its demonstration that the creation of value lies not just in the efficient management of operations, but in all the primary and secondary activities in an organisation.

Did you know?

When we think of how a company adds value we tend to focus on primary activities. However, secondary activities are just as important in moving an organisation forward. If you take care of your employees they will interact with your customers better; if you employ more effective technologies you will be able to produce more efficiently.

Summary table

Term	Relevance	Implication for operations
Value analysis	Used to assess the relationship between the value and cost of various functions provided by the producer for consumers.	Producers can identify **what** function an activity or process provides for consumers and **how** that function can be provided. It enables decision making about what functions to provide.
Value chain	Used to identify all processes involved in adding value in a particular industry.	Producers need to focus on all activities that create value and how they combine together.

Summary questions

1 In what ways do both value analysis and value chain analysis focus on the needs of the consumer?

2 A value analysis might lead some car manufacturers to build more functions into their design while others might take some out. Why do you think this might be the case?

Specific objective

On completion of this section, you should be able to:

- discuss the strategies involved in product design, with reference to CAD and CAM.

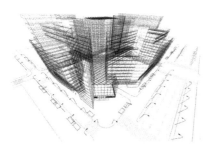

Figure 1.8.1 *A CAD drawing*

Figure 1.8.2 *Designers used to spend a lot of time at drawing boards*

Did you know?

Some of the best opportunities for CAD-related jobs in the Caribbean are in the Trinidad oil industry, e.g. pipeline designers.

Computer-aided design (CAD)

Forty years ago designers spent a lot of time at drawing boards. The skills brought to the job included:

- creativity: for example, thinking up ideas and styling
- analysis: for example, calculating strengths or quantities
- mechanical drawing: putting the ideas on paper.

Although the central role of the designer was to carry out creative and analytical work, much of the time was spent on drawing and redrawing. Today, with the development of sophisticated computers, it is possible to use a computer screen instead of a drawing board. This saves considerable time and effort.

A designer employing a CAD program uses a keyboard (or mouse), a screen, an electronic drawing pencil and a graphics pad. The designer programs the computer to perform many quick calculations of angles, volumes or dimensions, as well as uploading pre-drawn designs from the computer's memory bank.

Having drafted the design, the designer can view the item on the screen as if from different positions, and view it three-dimensionally, as a solid object instead of just a series of lines. The computer can then be set to calculate all the important features of the design, and to show how these change when, for example, one dimension is altered.

In industry, CAD has revolutionised almost every area of design, from wedding dresses to supertankers.

Benefits of CAD include:

- speed and accuracy
- reduction in the cost of the design process
- ability to draw on millions of existing designs and drawings
- ability to convert projections instantaneously to show a range of views
- ability to visualise a finished product from a sketch or initial design.

Costs of CAD include:

- initial investment in sophisticated CAD packages
- time taken to train users new to CAD applications.

Computer-aided manufacturing (CAM)

Over recent years many developments have taken place in production industries. As well as CAD, there have been developments in machine tools, allowing the use of computers to control machinery – CAM. Many are now controlled numerically or digitally by computer numerical control (CNC).

Benefits of CAM in mass production include:

- Where plants have large throughputs (volumes of outputs), small savings through efficient computerised control can lead to significant cost savings.
- Where the manufacturing process is frequently disrupted (for example a change in the environmental conditions in a factory, such as

temperature, which impacts on the ability to manufacture certain products), CAM enables a quick response.

- Where the manufacturing process is particularly complex, computers can be far more effective than human operators because of their ability to make complex calculations quickly.
- Where batch production takes place, computers can quickly reprogram the manufacturing process to produce different types of batches.

Developments have also taken place in robotics – the use of machines that have been programmed to perform often complex production operations. Robots are now so sophisticated that they can carry out complex and intricate tasks.

With CAM, computers play a key role in organising and supervising the manufacturing process, ensuring that production is carried out to specified standards. Computers can check standards, alter production runs and processes, and carry out other operations much more quickly and with a greater degree of accuracy than human operators. Its high level of **quality control** means that CAM has been one of the driving forces behind just-in-time manufacturing (see 1.19).

With CADCAM (computer-aided design combined with computer-aided manufacturing), data from the CAD system is used to drive machines, making the CAD system part of the manufacturing process.

KEY TERMS

Quality control: ensuring that goods meet the requirements of the end user.

Summary table

Technique	What does it involve?	Benefits
CAD	Using computers to design products and processes	Saves time, enables greater accuracy, enables visualisation of the end product, reduces design costs
CAM	Using computers to control machinery	Enables more-complex manufacturing, supports quick change of production line including batch production, reduces costs and increases quality of manufacturing output
CADCAM	Combining the design and manufacturing process using computers	All of the above plus integration of design and manufacturing processes

Summary questions

1 Why might a large Caribbean bottling plant employ computer-aided manufacturing techniques? How could the manufacturer offset the costs of investing in building a CAM plant?

2 In what fields might small businesses benefit from the application of CAD? Give a reason for your answer. Why might they be discouraged from investing in CAD?

3 Identify local companies that employ CADCAM approaches. Why do they do so?

Capacity utilisation

The productive **capacity** of a business is the total level of output that it can produce in a given period of time.

Capacity utilisation is defined as the percentage of a firm's total production capacity that is actually being employed at a given time.

$$\text{Capacity utilisation} = \frac{\text{Actual output per time period}}{\text{Maximum possible output in that period}} \times 100$$

For example, if an oil company in Trinidad can produce 100,000 barrels of oil in time period X with its existing capacity and only produces 50,000, then its capacity utilisation is:

$$\frac{50,000}{100,000} \times 100 = 50\%$$

One of the key benefits of high-capacity utilisation is that a business can spread its **fixed costs** over a higher level of output. For example, if the Trinidadian oil company has fixed costs of $1m in the time period considered in the above calculation, then by working at full capacity it is spreading these fixed costs at $10 per barrel. In contrast, if it produces 50,000 barrels, then the average fixed cost per barrel is higher at $20 per barrel. This is a significant difference.

However, there are issues with working at full capacity, including:

■ not having time to stop the **plant** for essential maintenance

■ working other resources, including manpower, at full capacity, which may lead to stress and errors

■ inability to meet new demand as it arises.

Capacity planning

Capacity planning enables a business to meet the changing demand for its products. A company should aim to avoid both **overcapacity** (too much plant and production resources relative to demand) and **undercapacity** (insufficient plant or other resources to meet the demand). An efficient organisation will have enough capacity to meet the current demand for its product and be able to adjust it to meet future demand patterns.

Ways to improve capacity include:

■ investing in more plant, equipment and other resources (for example, taking on more employees)

■ using more effective technology and techniques (methods) of production

■ working existing plant for longer hours (for example, through operating a shift system).

Capacity planning strategies

Operations managers identify three main types of capacity planning strategy:

■ **Matching strategy:** adding or reducing capacity (typically in small amounts) according to changes in the level of demand.

- **Leading strategy:** increasing capacity (typically building up more stock) in anticipation of future increases in demand.
- **Lagging strategy:** the business is a follower rather than a leader of market trends. It adopts a cautious approach that waits to see how the demand pattern for its product changes before increasing or reducing capacity. Applying this approach enables a company to cut down on waste (in the case of overproduction), but might also mean loss of potential and actual customers by not having enough product in stock.

Did you know?

Capacity planning is useful for the hotel industry, where effectiveness is measured by the room occupancy rate (the percentage of rooms occupied in a given period compared with the number of rooms available). A given occupancy rate is required to break even.

CASE STUDY

Production strategy in book publishing

The Caribbean book publishing market has recently seen an increase in the demand for literary works by Caribbean-based authors. Caribbean Publishers Inc. focuses on this market and is currently able to produce 50,000 books a year, although it is actually producing only 40,000 books. It anticipates that sales will increase by 10 per cent a year for the next five years. It is therefore increasing its production capacity so that it can produce 60,000 books.

1 What is the current production capacity of Caribbean Publishers Inc.?

2 What is the current capacity utilisation of Caribbean Publishers Inc.?

3 Comment on the capacity planning strategy of Caribbean Publishers Inc.

4 If Caribbean Publishers Inc. is to adopt a 'matching strategy', what will be the implications for changes in its production capacity?

Ethical considerations and capacity planning

There are a number of issues to be considered when using plant beyond its maximum capacity. Think of a public transport bus that has a maximum capacity of, say, 64 passengers. If 80 people are allowed to board, all the passengers' safety is put at risk and everyone will be uncomfortable. Similar logic can be applied to areas of industry. Where machinery and factory equipment is used beyond the manufacturer's recommended limit and is not maintained, the result can be increased risk for everyone.

Summary table

Concept	What it means
Capacity	The output that a company can produce in a given time period
Capacity utilisation	The percentage of total capacity actually produced in a given period
Capacity plan	The plan in place determining the production capacity in current and future time periods
Capacity matching	Matching capacity to demand patterns

Summary questions

1 How might a company be more efficient in its capacity utilisation even though it produces less than a rival company?

2 How can a company gain competitive advantage over a rival by engaging in a higher capacity utilisation.

3 How might a company that engages in a capacity matching strategy gain an advantage over the following?

  a A company that engages in a capacity lagging strategy

  b A company engaging in a capacity leading strategy

On completion of this section, you should be able to:

- explain the concept of capacity planning, with reference to efficiency and capacity, design capacity and methods of improving capacity utilisation.

KEY TERMS

Sustainable growth: growth of a business (e.g. by growing capacity) in such a way that growth can be maintained steadily over the long term.

Design capacity: maximum amount of work that an organisation is capable of completing in a given period of time.

Effective capacity: maximum amount of work that a company can actually achieve in a particular period of time.

Using capacity efficiently

Capacity planning is a long-term process intended to make sure that a company has the right quantity and quality of resources in place to supply products efficiently, in line with the demand from customers.

In 1.9 we saw that a business needs to have high levels of capacity utilisation in order to spread fixed costs over a larger output and make use of existing resources. We saw, however, that producing at maximum capacity gives rise to a number of problems, such as not having time to maintain plant and equipment effectively and putting too much pressure on human resources.

The challenge for production managers, therefore, is to identify levels of capacity utilisation that allow for the **sustainable growth** of the business and meeting orders in an efficient way.

Design capacity and effective capacity

Design capacity refers to the maximum amount of work that an organisation is capable of completing in a given period of time.

Effective capacity refers to the maximum amount of work that a company can actually achieve in a particular period of time, bearing in mind constraints such as delays and problems in handling materials. Effective capacity is therefore lower than design capacity. By improving production efficiency it is possible to increase effective capacity to levels that are closer to design capacity.

Ways to improve capacity utilisation

The methods that a production manager can employ to improve capacity utilisation depend on the current level of production.

When production is close to or at capacity the following methods can be used to improve capacity utilisation:

- Increasing the quantity of plant, equipment, machinery, labour and other resources available to the company. This involves investment in new resources.
- Increasing the quality of plant, equipment, machinery, labour and other resources available to the company. This involves investment in new technology (for example, more advanced automated equipment) and training staff to work more efficiently.

When production is below the level needed to meet customer demand, and there is excess capacity the following methods can be used to improve capacity utilisation:

- Increasing the efficiency with which existing plant and equipment is used, making better use of existing resources. This can be achieved by improving production processes and training labour to use existing equipment more effectively.
- Working existing resources for longer: for example, by increasing the length of time that existing plant is used, perhaps by working an additional shift.

Capacity utilisation and throughput

It is important to understand that higher levels of capacity utilisation do not always lead to higher levels of throughput (processing jobs through the production system). Think of cars moving along the highway in your territory: if there are not many cars on the highway, capacity utilisation will be low. However, the more cars that are on the road (increasing levels of capacity utilisation) – for example, at rush hour with drivers dodging from lane to lane – the greater the chance of hold-ups and traffic jams. As capacity utilisation increases, **wait time** (that is, delays) will also increase.

This is illustrated in Figure 1.10.1.

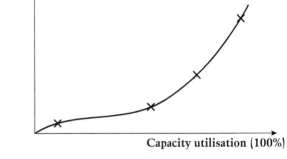

Figure 1.10.1 *Capacity utilisation*

Production planning for efficiency

Operations managers therefore face three challenges:

- to use production capacity efficiently. Typically, this involves high levels of production capacity utilisation (between 80 and 90 per cent in many industries)

- to organise production to avoid wait time. A challenge here is to ensure a steady flow of resources into the production system, and to have sufficient production capacity to use available inputs of raw materials and labour

- to combine high levels of throughput with levels of production capacity appropriate to meeting customer demand in such a way as to minimise **unit costs**.

In the Caribbean, production efficiency can be seen in short-haul budget flights to the US. The planes operate with most of their seats full, to tight turnaround schedules, while at the same time having sufficient time for aircraft maintenance.

Did you know?

Ferries between Caribbean countries operate in an efficient way when the ferry runs on time and has sufficient passengers for the ferry to be well loaded but not overcrowded.

KEY TERMS

Wait time: delays.

Unit costs: the cost of producing one unit of output.

Summary table

Methods to improve capacity utilisation	<ul><li>Where plant is being underutilised: work plant for longer, use better production methods, cut out waste</li><li>Where plant is already operating near to full capacity: organise production more efficiently, expand production capacity</li></ul>
Methods to improve productive efficiency	<ul><li>Increase capacity utilisation to an optimum level</li><li>Use plant, equipment and other resources efficiently</li><li>Maximise throughput by reducing wait time</li></ul>

Summary questions

1 Examine the capacity utilisation for a service that you use regularly, such as a ferry service, bus service, cinema or restaurant:

   a What factors influence the production capacity for the service?

   b What is the typical level of capacity utilisation for the service?

   c How could capacity utilisation be improved?

   d What issues are associated with capacity utilisation of the service?

2 How could wait time for a service that you use be reduced through more effective production planning?

On completion of this section, you should be able to:

■ explain the concept of capacity planning, with reference to economies and diseconomies of scale.

Did you know?

Scale of operations is usually measured by the number of units produced over a period of time.

KEY TERMS

Economies of scale: benefits from operating on a larger scale that enable a business to produce at lower unit costs than smaller firms.

Diseconomies of scale: the disadvantages from having higher production capacity, resulting in rising unit costs of production.

Long-run average cost curve: a curve showing unit costs at different levels of output in the long term.

Internal economies of scale: benefits from the growth of an individual firm, resulting in lower unit costs for that firm.

Economies and diseconomies of scale

Large organisations can spread their fixed costs over a greater output than small businesses, enabling them to produce their goods and services at competitive prices. If the volume of production increases, average unit costs over most production ranges are likely to fall: the organisation is said to benefit from **economies of scale** – the advantages it gains from being larger.

Organisations aim for the scale of production that best suits their line of activities. This is achieved when unit costs are at their lowest for the output produced. Beyond this point an organisation starts to find that inefficiencies or **diseconomies of scale** (the disadvantages of being too large) push costs up.

When a company increases its production capacity, it increases the scale of production. By doing so it can spread its fixed costs over a larger output, enabling it to benefit from economies of scale directly associated with production capacity. If, however, it increases its production capacity too much, so that there is considerable under-utilisation of capacity, this will lead to rising fixed costs per unit of output, resulting in diseconomies of scale.

The term 'returns to scale' refers to the benefits (increasing returns) of increasing the scale of operations, or drawbacks (diminishing returns) of increasing the scale of production. The outcome of these benefits or drawbacks is either falling cost per unit of output (as a result of increasing returns) or rising cost per unit of output (diminishing returns).

Figure 1.11.1 presents a **long-run average cost curve** showing unit costs at different levels of output.

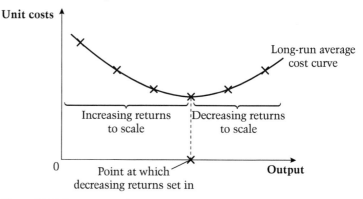

Figure 1.11.1 *Returns to scale*

Internal economies of scale

Internal economies of scale result from firms increasing the scale on which they produce. By doing this firms are able to benefit from improved production techniques: for example, using larger, automated, sophisticated equipment capable of high levels of production at low unit cost. Labour and managerial economies, such as employing specialist or more highly trained employees, can be made.

Firms can also benefit from commercial economies associated with buying and selling on a larger scale: for example, buying raw materials and components at discounted rates, and spreading marketing and selling overheads over larger volumes of output. Larger companies are also able to raise finance more cheaply, as they incur lower interest rates on loans. They can also diversify their product portfolio to spread their risks.

Internal diseconomies of scale

Increasing production capacity can also lead to **internal diseconomies of scale** and rising unit costs of production. Reasons for this include:

- **Having too much spare capacity:** for example, where production levels are only 50 per cent of production capacity, this leads to higher fixed costs per unit (compared, for example, with operating at 80 per cent of production capacity).
- **Management and process inefficiencies:** the size of the plant may become too large for existing managers and skilled employees to run efficiently. This might lead to breakdowns in production and increasing waste and errors, all of which lead to rising unit costs.

External economies of scale

Businesses can also benefit from **external economies of scale**. These occur when the industry in which they are operating grows, leading to a reduction in unit costs. Reasons for this include:

- **Concentration:** if similar organisations develop in the same geographical area, a number of benefits arise – for example, a skilled labour pool, a reputation for the quality of the work in the area, local college and university courses tailored to meet the needs of a particular industry, and better social amenities. An example of this is the high reputation of the tourism industry in the Caribbean, benefiting most Caribbean companies operating in this field.
- **Information:** larger industries have information services and employers' associations designed to benefit their members. An example is the Caribbean Hotel and Tourism Association.
- **Disintegration:** in areas where certain industries develop (for example, the music industry in Kingston), component or service industries develop to provide maintenance and support activities. For the music industry this means provision of, for example, session musicians or skilled sound technicians.

KEY TERMS

Internal diseconomies of scale: drawbacks from the growth of an individual firm, resulting in higher unit costs.

External economies of scale: benefits from the growth of an industry that enable all (or most) firms in that industry to produce with lower unit costs.

Disintegration: in business and economics, breaking down into component parts. Disintegrated elements are usually smaller businesses that serve the needs of larger organisations at the heart of a particular industry.

Did you know?

External diseconomies of scale refer to the over-expansion of an industry in a particular area, e.g. where too many hotels in an area result in overcapacity and competition, driving down prices.

Summary table

Type of economy	Impact on capacity	Impact on unit costs
Internal economies of scale	Firms expand production to increase production capacity	Individual firms benefit from falling unit costs (up to a certain point – where diseconomies set in)
External economies of scale	Industry production capacity increases	Most firms benefit from falling unit costs

Summary questions

1 **a** How might an increase in production capacity for a commercial fishing company lead to internal economies of scale?

   b How might it lead to diseconomies of scale?

2 A hotel increases its production capacity but finds that its unit cost of production has increased. How would you explain this situation?

Specific objective

On completion of this section, you should be able to:

- examine various strategies involved in the production layout process, with reference to process layout, product layout, fixed position layout and cellular layout.

Layout

An important aspect of efficient production is the organisation of plant (see p20). The design of a plant and the positioning of equipment should enable it to function smoothly. Specialist engineers help to design the plant, giving consideration to the availability of power sources, maintenance requirements and layout in order to maximise efficient throughput. Plant layout tends to follow one of a number of basic designs, outlined here.

Process layout

In process layout, all operations of the same type are performed in the same area: for example, in vehicle manufacture, spot welding may be in one location, riveting in another and stapling in a third. Using the process layout, different types of product can pass through the system. For example, in Figure 1.12.1 Products A and B are different but they both need to be processed by X-type machines and Y-type machines. While passing from stage X to stage Y, both Products A and B will need to be placed in a storage area, where they can be referred to as work in progress.

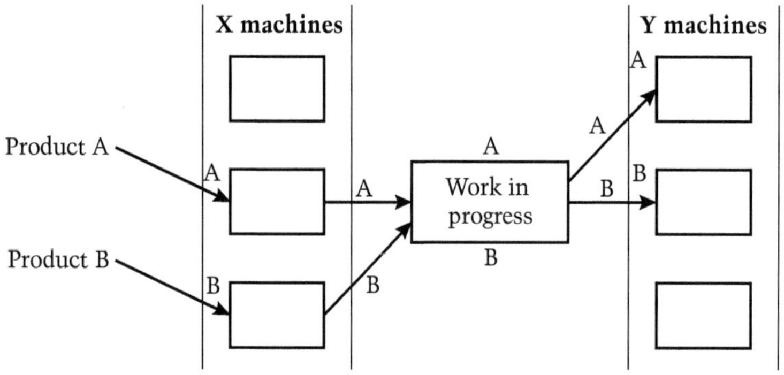

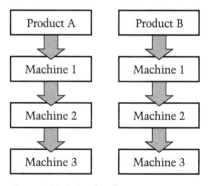

Figure 1.12.1 Process layout

Product layout

Product layout is also referred to as 'line layout'. Plant is laid out according to the requirements of the product in a line of production. Products 'flow' from one machine or stage to another. Control is simplified because paperwork, material handling and inspections procedures are reduced. Figure 1.12.2 shows that with this layout Product A and Product B have their own separate area and line which focus specifically on the needs of the product. Specialist workers may work exclusively on their own production line.

Figure 1.12.2 Product layout

Fixed position layout

In layout by fixed position, the machinery and equipment is located, as the name suggests, in fixed positions. When operations need to be carried

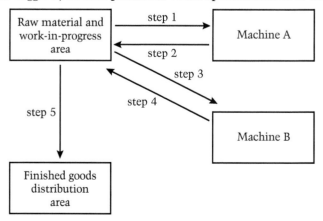

Figure 1.12.3 Fixed position layout

out, the raw materials or work in progress is taken to the machinery for processing. In Figure 1.12.3 you can see that the raw materials and work in progress are taken to Machine A, then returned to where they are being prepared, then taken to Machine B and then returned to the preparation area. When the good is completed it will be taken to a loading bay for distribution to a storage area or delivered to a wholesaler or retailer.

Cellular layout

Cellular production is an important innovation in modern engineering (see 1.2). A cell typically consists of multi-skilled workers who work in a team to produce complete products, or significant components of a complete product. The cell works in an area that is larger than a traditional workstation but smaller than a production department. Its production tasks are related to the skills that the workers have, using a range of equipment that they are competent to use. The components that are assembled can be seen as families of parts (that is, they are closely related). Cells take up less space than is required for other forms of production layout, and typically lead to higher production levels and greater accuracy. As production workers are multi-skilled, working in cells can give greater work satisfaction.

In Figure 1.12.4 a cell of employees and machines receives supplies (for example, components) which they then process through a series of operations within the cell. When the cell has completed the required operations, the assembly or finished product is passed to the customer

In cellular production, suppliers and customers may be external to the company or internal. An internal cell might consist of providers of other sub-assemblies, which are passed on to further cells.

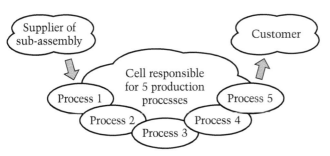

Figure 1.12.4 *Cellular production layout*

Summary questions

1 To what extent does cellular working combine the best aspects of process and product layouts?

2 How does cellular production help to save some of the time and space required for fixed position layouts?

Summary table

Type of layout	Description	Advantage
Process layout	All operations of the same type carried out in same area regardless of product	Enables focus on effective process specialisation
Product layout	Each product has its own production line	Enables specialisation on specific products
Fixed position layout	Work is taken backwards and forwards to specific machines	Enables machine work to be handled by specialists in that area and machines are in fixed positions
Cellular layout	Family of related tasks and components worked on by multi-skilled cells of machines and workers	Enables focus on related activities and encourages ownership of the tasks involved in specific cells of workers producing a specific product

Did you know?

Some costs (e.g. labour costs) are difficult to tie down to a specific unit. If we know it takes a worker 15 minutes to make a product and they are paid $10 an hour, the direct labour cost of making the product is $2.50 (one-quarter of 10). In contrast, the wages of a labourer who maintains a machine are much more difficult to tie into a specific unit of output. These wages are therefore indirect costs, and accountants have to devise a method of apportioning (dividing) them between the various products that a company makes.

Importance of costing

An understanding of costing is particularly important to operations managers, who should know exactly how much it costs to produce units of output. They should also have an understanding of where savings can be made.

Direct and indirect costs

A key distinction is made between direct and indirect costs. This is outlined below.

Direct costs

Direct costs can be allocated to a particular item or unit of production. Management accountants can calculate with some accuracy the cost of materials used to make an item and the time spent by a production operative in making that unit.

For example, to produce a can of beans the costs of the direct materials needed are:

- the cost of the beans
- the cost of the can
- the cost of the labelling.

On top of this is the direct labour cost. For many manufactured items it is possible to calculate the cost of labour that goes into making the product: how many hours or minutes, at the labour rate per hour or minute.

Indirect costs

Indirect costs cannot be allocated in the same way as direct costs. They are items such as the factory manager's salary, rent of a property or the cost of electricity to light the factory. The indirect expenses are likely to be the most significant indirect costs, although indirect labour is also important. Indirect labour costs include wages and salaries paid to employees while they are not making cost units. This includes payments to staff engaged in areas such as general management, marketing and transport.

An example is book production: the management accountant knows that some of the total cost of marketing books needs to be calculated into the cost of producing, for instance, this book. The accountant therefore needs to share out the total marketing cost between each of the different books that the company produces, including calculating the indirect cost of producing this particular book.

Fixed and variable costs

Another important way of classifying costs is as fixed or variable.

Variable costs

Variable costs, as the name suggests, vary with the output (or sales) of goods. Examples of variable costs are materials and direct labour costs.

For example, a street vendor may sell hot patties. The costs that go into making each unit of product are:

- raw materials – flour, filling and packaging
- staff wages, which are based on how many products each employee sells.

Assuming that it costs $2 in variable cost for each patty sold, then:

- the variable cost of one patty = $2
- the variable cost of two = $4
- the variable cost of three = $6 etc.

Fixed costs

Fixed costs do not vary with the level of output or sales. For the patty seller, fixed costs might include the rent of the stall, local business taxes, insurance and the manager's salary. If the fixed costs are $20,000 a year in total, this will not vary with the number of patties sold.

If only one patty is sold in the year, the fixed cost will be $20,000. If 100,000 patties are sold, the fixed cost is still $20,000.

Total cost of production

The total cost of producing different levels of output (or sales) can be calculated by combining the fixed cost and the variable cost of production. For example, if the patty seller produces 5,000 patties, his total variable cost will be 5,000 × $2 = $10,000. If we add this to the total fixed cost of $20,000, the total cost of production will be $10,000 (variable cost) + $20,000 (fixed cost) = $30,000.

Did you know?

Indirect costs are not directly accountable to a cost object (e.g. a specific product or project). Indirect costs can be either fixed or variable.

☑ *Exam tip*

Remember that total cost increases as the quantity of goods produced increases. Each additional unit of output incurs an additional cost.

Summary table

Direct costs	Costs that can be allocated to a specific item (product) or project
Indirect costs	Costs that cannot be allocated to a specific item or project
Variable costs	Costs that vary with the level of output or sales
Fixed costs	Costs that do not vary with the level of output or sales

Summary questions

1 A dressmaking company in your territory makes ball gowns for special events such as dance evenings. To make one gown takes 3 metres of material at $5.00 per metre. It takes one person five hours to make the gown with wages at $8 per hour. Designers' and management salaries and other fixed costs come to $1,000. Calculate the fixed cost of running the business and the variable cost of producing:

   a five gowns

   b 10 gowns

   c 20 gowns.

2 Why are direct costs likely to increase as a business increases its level of output or sales? Why might indirect costs also increase when a business increases its level of output or sales?

Absorption costing

In 1.13 you learned that it is important to be able to calculate the cost of producing individual units of a product, and that while it is easy to calculate the direct cost of producing a cost unit, this is not so easy for indirect costs. **Absorption costing** is a process that charges fixed as well as variable overheads to cost units. Through this process it becomes possible to calculate the costs of producing an individual unit of output, taking account of the factory overheads required to produce that product as well as the variable costs.

For example, in a factory producing cotton garments, you not only include the cotton and the labour that goes into producing each garment (the variable costs), but also 'absorb' a proportion of the total factory overhead into that garment when costing out the production of the garments.

Management accountants use simple but logical approaches to absorb overheads. For example, if the total factory overhead comes to $100,000 and machines in the factory are running for 10,000 hours in that period, a simple method of absorbing the overhead is by machine hour:

$$\frac{\$100,000 \text{ (factory overhead)}}{10,000 \text{ hours (machine hours)}} = \$10 \text{ per hour}$$

If we know that an individual garment includes $5-worth of cotton (direct materials) and takes two hours' labour time to produce at $10 per hour ($20 wages) then the variable cost is $25. We can also absorb two hours-worth of factory overheads (two machine hours) – that is, $20 – into the garment.

Using the absorption cost method, we can then cost the garment at:

$5 (materials) + $20 (labour) + $20 (factory overhead) = $45 (cost of garment)

Absorption costing is a technique superior to variable costing because it takes account of overheads as well as variable costs. The main methods of absorption are:

▣ direct machine-hour rate (as used in the illustration above, which is based on the number of hours that machines run for)

▣ direct labour-hour rate (based on the number of hours of labour time employed in a factory).

Contribution

The concept of **contribution** helps us to understand how sales of individual products help a business to cover its fixed costs. A business manufacturing or selling items obviously needs to cover costs to avoid making a loss. If the variable cost of producing an item is higher than the revenue received for it, a company will make a loss on that sale. To make a profit, however, a company needs to cover not only its variable costs, but also its fixed costs.

This is best illustrated through an example. In 1.13 we gave the example of a hot-patty seller with variable costs of $2 per patty and annual fixed costs of $20,000.

Now let us assume that the hot-patty seller sells patties for $4 each.

Variable cost per patty = $2

Revenue per patty = $4

From these figures you should be able to see that each patty sold is contributing $2 to paying off the fixed costs of the business. We refer to this $2 as the contribution that the item being sold is making to fixed costs, so:

Revenue per patty – variable cost per patty = contribution per patty

$4 – $2 = $2

Applying common sense, you should now be able to see that the patty-selling stall needs to sell 10,000 patties in the year to achieve **break-even** – that is, cover all of its costs with its revenues.

Note that a possible limitation of using the contribution concept is where it might be difficult to accurately calculate the variable cost.

Did you know?

Whereas costs involve an outlay for a company, revenues represent an inflow of income to a company.

KEY TERMS

Break-even: to exactly match costs with revenues received.

Summary table

Costing methods	Description	Calculation	Importance
Absorption costing	Method of accounting for manufacturing overheads as well as variable costs in costing out production	To absorb the overhead, use a technique such as working out the number of machine hours required to produce a product as a percentage of total machine hours	Allows a company that produces multiple products to allocate some of the overall cost to different product lines
Contribution	Method of accounting used to identify how much individual units of output or sales contribute to covering the fixed costs of a business	To calculate the contribution, subtract variable cost per unit from the sale price	Helps to identify how many individual units of production contribute to paying off fixed costs Helpful in calculating break-even

Summary questions

1 A company's machinery runs for 50 hours per week. The total manufacturing overheads per week are $25,000. One of the company's products, shirts, takes up 10 hours of machine time and produces 1,000 shirts in this time.

   a How much of the overall factory overhead should be absorbed by the overall product line of shirts?

   b How much of the factory overhead should be allocated to each shirt produced?

2 Using the contribution method, calculate the break-even point for a taxi driver who charges an average of $10 per customer, when the cost per trip is $4 and the fixed costs are $25,000 per year.

Specific objective

On completion of this section, you should be able to:

■ assess the importance of costing in production, with reference to the break-even point and margin of safety.

Did you know?

Break-even output is the number of sales required to cover all of the costs of a business.

Calculating the break-even point

The break-even point is the point at which sales levels are high enough not to make a loss, but not high enough to make a profit. At break-even, sales just cover costs.

The break-even point can be calculated as:

$$\text{Break-even point in sales units} = \frac{\text{Fixed costs}}{\text{Contribution per unit}}$$

where

$$\text{Contribution per unit} = \text{Selling price} - \text{Variable cost}$$

Illustrating break-even

A graph or chart can help to identify the break-even point. This is shown in the following case study.

CASE STUDY

Ramesh's car repair business

In order to raise finance for his car repair business, Ramesh is preparing a business plan to present to his bank manager. He wants to know how many customers he needs to attract each week in order to break even. Fixed costs are estimated to be $400 per week and a typical repair at $120 will incur material costs of $40.

Contribution per customer = $120 − $40
= $80

Break-even point = $400/$80
= 5 customers per week

Sales value at break-even = number of
customers ×
sales price
= 5 × 120
= $600

Step 1 – the first step is to quantify costs and revenues at different volumes of sales:

Customer numbers	Fixed cost ($)	Variable cost ($)	Total cost ($)	Sales value ($)
2	400	80	480	240
4	400	160	560	480
6	400	240	640	720
8	400	320	720	960

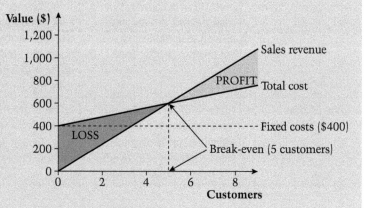

Figure 1.15.1 *Illustrating break-even*

Step 2 – the next step is to plot fixed costs, total cost and sales revenue against business activity – in this case, numbers of repairs (see Figure 1.15.1).

The point at which the lines for sales revenue and total cost intersect is the break-even point. To the left of the break-even point, the vertical gap between the sales and total cost lines represents the loss made. To the right of the break-even point, the gap between the two lines represents profit.

1 If fixed costs fall to $320, what will be the impact on break-even?

2 If Ramesh increases the price he charges for a typical repair to $200, what will be the impact on the following?

   a Contribution per repair

   b The break-even point (assuming the original cost schedule shown in the table)

The margin of safety

The break-even point can be compared with anticipated volumes of sales to test the viability of a business plan, and with actual activity to monitor business performance.

The difference between planned or current volumes and the break-even point represents the margin of safety. This can be expressed as a percentage.

$$\text{Margin of safety} = \frac{\text{Actual sales} - \text{Break-even sales}}{\text{Actual sales}} \times 100$$

Continuing the example for Ramesh, if he anticipated seven customers per week, the margin of safety would be: $\frac{7-5}{7} = 29\%$

This shows that Ramesh's actual sales would exceed the break-even point by 29 per cent.

CASE STUDY

Kemal's Spices: margin of safety

Kemal's Spices currently produces 5,000 packets of mixed spice per month. Using figures for cost and revenue, it can be seen that the business will break even at 2,500 units. The margin of safety is therefore:

$$\frac{5,000 - 2,500}{5,000} = 50\%$$

The margin of safety for Kemal's Spices can also be illustrated graphically by the horizontal difference in Figure 1.15.2.

1 If Kemal's Spices alters its plans so as to increase the actual volume produced and sold by 10 per cent, what will happen to the margin of safety?

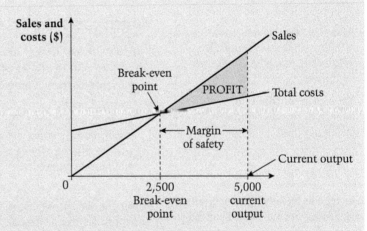

Figure 1.15.2 Margin of safety for Kemal's Spices

Summary table

Concept	Description	Formula
Break-even	Point where sales revenue = total cost	$\dfrac{\text{Fixed cost}}{\text{Contribution per unit}}$
Margin of safety	Difference between planned or actual volumes and break-even point	$\dfrac{\text{Actual sales} - \text{Break-even sales}}{\text{Actual sales}}$

Summary questions

1 A beauty salon charges an average of $12.50 per customer. It has a cost per visit of $5 and fixed costs of $100,000 per year. What is the break-even point?

2 A recording studio charges $25 per customer per hour. It has a variable cost of $7.50 per hour and an annual fixed cost of $50,000. What is the break-even point?

3 A hairdresser plans to service 200 customers a week. The break-even point is calculated at 150 customers a week. What is the margin of safety? What would happen if the stylist only serviced 120 customers a week?

Specific objective

On completion of this section, you should be able to:

- assess the importance of costing in production, with reference to marginal costing.

KEY TERMS

Marginal cost: change in total cost resulting from producing one additional unit of output.

Marginal revenue: change in total revenue resulting from producing one additional unit of output.

Change in contribution: marginal revenue minus marginal cost.

Did you know?

If a cost has already been incurred, it is not relevant to a marginal costing decision – it is referred to as a 'sunk cost'. For example, when a house builder has built the foundations of houses, and started other construction activities, these costs are already 'sunk' into the project and cannot be retrieved.

Unavoidable costs (i.e. costs that will be incurred irrespective of the decision to be made) are also not relevant.

Marginal cost

In a business, the 'margin' refers to additional units of output. If a business increases output from 100 units to 101, the marginal unit is the 101st. The **marginal cost** is thus the cost of producing the 101st unit, and the **marginal revenue** is the revenue from this unit. The difference between the marginal cost and the marginal revenue is the **change in contribution**.

Marginal costing is a tool for short-term decision making. It looks at how additional output contributes to fixed costs and profits. Provided that the marginal revenue from the additional unit is higher than the marginal cost, the additional unit will contribute to covering fixed costs.

Which costs should be included in marginal costing?

Any item of cost that is likely to change as output changes must be taken into account in marginal costing. These include:

- **variable costs**, which vary directly with the level of output (see 1.13)
- **stepped costs**, which are fixed for a range of business volume, but jump to a new level when volume increases beyond a certain point (examples are supervision wages, planning costs and equipment costs – as production levels increase, plant and equipment may have to be added to or upgraded).

Consider a tour bus company that has to accommodate an extra passenger. We can measure marginal cost in terms of the fuel needed to transport the extra passenger (variable cost). Fixed costs are irrelevant to marginal costing as long as there are extra seats on the bus.

If, however, the bus is at full capacity and the company is obliged to meet the demand from additional passengers, an extra bus must be put on to the route, with its additional fixed costs. The marginal cost of the extra passenger is much higher as a result. In this case the marginal cost consists of both the variable cost and the stepped cost of employing an additional bus.

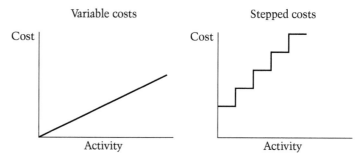

Figure 1.16.1 *The difference between variable and stepped costs*

It is important not to overlook opportunity costs: the benefits that have to be sacrificed in choosing one course of action rather than another. You will remember that you learned about these earlier in your studies (see Unit 1, 3.26): how, for example, the purchase of a new MP3 player might mean that you were unable to buy books and equipment for your studies.

Contribution from selling an additional unit

If a sports equipment shop selling in-line skates can sell 10 units for $100 or 11 units at $95, the marginal revenue for the 11th unit is just $45: $(11 \times \$95) - (10 \times \$100)$.

In this case, if the marginal cost is less than $45, selling the extra unit will increase contribution.

1 If the marginal cost of producing the 11th unit is $30, what will be the contribution of this unit?

2 Why is it important for a business to understand the relationship between marginal costs and marginal revenue?

When is marginal costing useful to a business?

Marginal costing enables managers to make business decisions: for example, whether to drop an existing product, charge a special sale price for a product, or make changes in business activity to increase or reduce contribution at the margin.

Marginal costing is also often used to help with decision making in the following situations:

■ **Make or buy** (1.17): when a business needs to decide whether to manufacture a product in-house or subcontract to a supplier.

■ **Terminating a business activity:** part of a business or a particular product line may be reporting losses under the absorption costing system (see 1.14). The business needs to find out how closure or termination will affect total business profits. What costs will be saved and what revenues will be lost?

■ **Setting the selling price:** a business needs to know where to pitch the selling price of its products.

Summary table

Definition	Explanation	Uses
Marginal cost	Total additional cost of producing one more unit	■ Determining whether it is worthwhile producing extra outputs ■ Helping in make or buy decisions ■ Deciding whether to terminate an activity ■ Setting selling prices

Summary questions

1 a What will be the impact on contribution if marginal revenue is lower than marginal cost?

   b How will this impact on the decision about how much to produce?

2 How might marginal cost differ from the variable cost of production?

3 In which of the following instances should a firm produce an addition unit of output?

   a The marginal cost of producing an additional unit is 20 cents; the marginal revenue from selling that unit would be 22 cents.

   b The marginal cost of producing an additional unit is $1 and the marginal revenue would also be $1.

   c The marginal cost of producing an additional unit is 15 cents whereas the marginal revenue would be 14 cents.

Make or buy

A company can produce – 'make' – products or carry out activities, or it can subcontract the work to other suppliers – 'buy' it. This is usually done for activities and products that are not core lines for the business. A company might **outsource** the warehousing and distribution of its products to a subcontractor, or outsource the production of spare parts.

Two factors to consider relating to make or buy are:

- whether the company has **spare capacity** to make the part itself
- the costs of making the part compared with the costs of buying it in.

As you learnt in 1.16, marginal costing can be used in a make or buy situation. The procedure for making the decision involves:

1 calculating the cost of **in-house production** of the good or service

2 calculating the cost of buying in from an external supplier/outsourcing

3 comparing the costs to establish which is lower.

Other considerations in make or buy

The main consideration so far in a make or buy decision is the cost. Other factors that might encourage a company to 'make' are:

- availability of spare plant capacity
- control of production and particularly quality
- maintainance of design secrecy and protect intellectual property rights
- avoidance of working with unreliable suppliers
- preservation of the current workforce in employment
- the quantity may be too small to interest an outside supplier.

Factors other than cost that might influence the decision to buy externally include:

- lack of technical skills in making the product in-house
- only a small volume of the product is required
- lack of spare capacity to make the product
- the item required is not core to the company's main lines of production.

Did you know?

Emotional reasons, such as pride in the company making its own components, may also be a factor in encouraging a company to 'make'.

CASE STUDY

Make or buy?

A manufacturing company is deciding whether to buy in a component from an outside supplier or produce the part itself. Buying from an outside supplier will cost $90 per unit. The company accountant has produced a list of costs in the following table.

	Total cost (for 5 components) ($)	Cost per unit ($)
Direct costs		
Materials	200	40
Labour	120	24
Manufacturing overheads		
Variable	30	6
Fixed	80	16
General overheads	60	12
Total cost	490	98

These figures indicate that it is cheaper to buy in the component at $90 rather than manufacture it at $98. However, the accountant points out that only 50 per cent of the fixed manufacturing cost is related to this specific component (i.e. $40 rather than $80 total manufacturing overhead cost, or $8 rather than $16 unit costs). The general overheads should also be taken out of the calculation as they are not related to the decision.

We therefore need to restate our calculation in the following way:

	Make ($)	Buy ($)
Purchase costs of 5 components		450
Direct costs		
Materials	200	
Labour	120	
Product-specific manufacturing overheads		
Variable	30	
Fixed	40	
Total cost	390	450

1 What decision should the company make based on these cost calculations: should it make or buy?

2 Why should some of the manufacturing overheads be taken out of the calculation in the way shown?

3 In what situations might it be not appropriate for the firm to make the components itself rather than buy them in? What factors other than cost should be taken into account?

Summary table

What is make or buy?	Deciding whether to carry out an activity, or produce a product, within the company or buy in from outside.
Key determinants	■ Additional (marginal) cost of making or buying the good ■ Whether spare capacity exists
Examples of other determinants	■ Capability of the company to make the product ■ Extent of the requirement (how many?) ■ Company's desire to maintain quality and control of production

Summary questions

1 How does marginal costing help in the decision-making process about making or buying a product?

2 Seadrift Computing designs and manufactures most of the items used to assemble its state-of-the-art laptop computers. It is agreed that the next product development should include an updated disk drive to speed up data transfer. The table indicates the cost of developing and manufacturing 20,000 of the new drives.

The 3,000 hours of research and development time could otherwise be contracted out to clients at $50 an hour. Of the factory overheads, 60 per cent comprises fixed costs.

	Total ($)
Research and development – 3,000 hours at $30	90,000
Direct materials	150,000
Direct labour	50,000
Factory overheads	150,000

Should Seadrift Computing make or buy, assuming that comparable disk drives could be purchased for $19 each?

Specific objective

On completion of this section, you should be able to:

- examine the concept of inventory management, with reference to stock control management and its importance and EOQ (economic order quantity).

Inventory/stocks

A key decision for nearly all organisations is how much stock, or inventory, to hold. Controlling the amount of stock held is called **inventory control**. An organisation may choose to store just a few items, or millions. In manufacturing, a production-inventory system is concerned with effective management of the total flow of goods, from the acquisition of raw materials to the delivery of finished products to the final consumer.

There are three main types of inventory in a manufacturing business:

- finished stocks waiting to be dispatched
- raw-material stocks held in stores for use in product manufacture
- work in progress – that is, partly assembled goods and processed raw materials in the middle of the manufacturing process.

Reasons for holding stocks

Stocks are held for several purposes:

- as an insurance against higher-than-average demand, to make sure that customer demands can be met
- as an insurance against uncertain supplier delivery times (lead times)
- to enable an organisation to take advantage of price fluctuations – a company might buy in extra stock when prices are lower
- to take advantage of discount – on bulk orders this can sometimes offset the cost of storing inventories
- to minimise production delays resulting from shortages.

Organised reordering

The aim of any stock control system is to provide enough stocks to cater for current demand and uncertainties, while keeping stock levels to a minimum so that working capital is not wasted. Too high a stock level can result in stock loss (for example, through wastage, deterioration or pilfering), as well as stock items becoming obsolete. The cash tied up in stock might also be used more profitably for other purposes. Too low a stock level can mean an inability to satisfy customer demand and loss of business.

In an ideal situation, stocks should never fall below the **minimum stock level** set, or rise above the **maximum stock level** set (Figure 1.18.1).

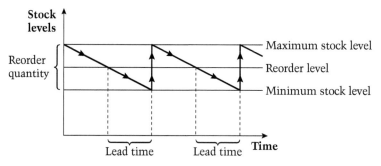

Figure 1.18.1 Managing stock levels

Stocks should be reordered when the minimum stock level is about to be breached. The amount to be reordered (**reorder level**) should take stock back up to the maximum required. If new stocks are ordered at this point, they will be delivered (after a given lead time) just in time to prevent the stock falling below the minimum acceptable level.

Economic order quantity (EOQ)

The **economic order quantity** is the number of units that a company should add to stock with each order so as to minimise the total costs of inventory, such as the cost of holding stock and the cost of ordering it. Identifying EOQ is part of a continual review process of inventory that makes it possible to determine how much should be ordered. Accurately calculating EOQ enables an organisation to minimise costs, while having enough stock to run the business efficiently.

When ordering new stock, a business is faced by two costs in addition to the costs of the stock itself.

- **The ordering cost** (sometimes referred as the set-up cost): the cost you have to pay the supplier to make a new order. This is given the letter S in the formula that follows.

- **The holding cost**: the cost of holding stock in storage (for example, paying someone to store inventory for you when you do not have sufficient space). This is given the letter H in the formula.

You need to get a balance between having more stock (which increases H) and having less stock (which increases S because you have to make more orders). The economic order quantity is the quantity that minimises these costs and it is calculated using the following formula:

$$EOQ = \sqrt{\frac{2 \times D \times S}{H}}$$

The letter D in the formula refers to the company's overall demand for new stocks in the year.

For example, a small bookshop purchases stocks of 1,200 books per year from publishers for resale ($D = 1,200$). The cost of making individual orders for books is $90 (the cost of setting up each order, $S = \$90$). The cost of storing the books is $3 per book ($H = \$3$ per unit). So:

$$EOQ = \sqrt{\frac{2 \times 1,200 \times \$90}{\$3}}$$

The EOQ is thus the square root of 72,000 which works out at 268.33 books per order. The EOQ as a whole number would then be either 268 or 269 books (depending on whether you round down or round up the figure). This is the stock order quantity that results in the lowest cost of ordering stock.

Summary table

Reorder level: quantity of stock required to replenish stock from minimum to maximum stock level.

Economic order quantity: the number of units a company should add to stock with each order so as to minimise the total costs of inventory.

Summary questions

1. In what situations might a company want to upgrade or increase the amounts involved in calculating reorder quantities and economic order quantities?

2. How might inventory control calculations help a shoe retailer to calculate appropriate levels of stock?

3. Why might overstocking be as serious a problem for a company as understocking?

What is inventory?	Examples	How can it be controlled?	How much inventory should be ordered?
Stocks stored, the quantity of goods and materials ready (or soon to be ready) for sale	■ Finished goods ■ Work in progress ■ Raw materials	Inventory management systems	■ Reorder quantity ■ Economic order quantity

Specific objective

On completion of this section, you should be able to:

■ examine the concept of inventory management, with reference to just-in-time.

KEY TERMS

Just-in-time: producing in response to demand from consumers, only supplying when demand is signalled and delivering just in time to meet the order.

Just-in-case: producing to ensure that there is enough inventory to meet additional demand from consumers – typically by operating with inventories of finished goods, raw materials and work in progress.

Did you know?

A disadvantage of JIT is that the business does not build up stockpiles, so if stock suddenly runs out because of disruption to production, for example an earthquake or hurricane, then the production line has to close down. This is an issue in Japan, a country which relies heavily on JIT systems.

KEY TERMS

Bottlenecks: hindrances to the flow of production, usually a point of congestion in the production process. Here workloads arrive more quickly than can be handled by that section of the system, resulting in the congestion. This causes the entire process to slow down or stop.

Figure 1.19.1 *The Japanese car company Toyota best captures the concept of just-in-time manufacturing in its Toyota Manufacturing System (TMS)*

Just-in-time and just-in-case

The traditional approach to inventory management was to have enough stock to meet customer requirements. This often led to a build-up of stocks that incurred costs of storage, deterioration and, when stock became out of date, obsolescence. The emphasis is now on a **just-in-time**, or JIT, approach to secure more effective inventory management.

JIT is traditionally associated with Japanese manufacturing techniques but over the last 25 years has become part of the wider production landscape worldwide, including the Caribbean. The idea of JIT is simple:

■ Finished goods are produced just in time for them to be sold, rather than months, weeks or even days ahead.

■ The parts that go into a finished product arrive just in time to be put together to make the final product, rather than being stored at some cost in a warehouse.

Just-in-case is the opposite, traditional, approach, in which large inventories of raw materials and components necessary for production are maintained, in case sudden consumer demand cannot be met. This might happen if, for example, there are delays in transport and delivery of components. The approach is more common in less-industrialised countries.

To run a company according to JIT, with the smallest possible levels of stock and work-in-progress, needs careful planning:

■ All sources of uncertainty must be removed from the manufacturing process. There must be absolute reliability of production targets, supplies and levels of output achieved.

■ The time to set up machines must be reduced to a minimum so that components and finished products can be produced in small batches as and when required.

■ **Bottlenecks** must be eliminated.

Using a JIT system requires complete reorganisation of the traditional factory. Factories were traditionally organised into 'shops', each working on a particular stage in producing a final product. With a JIT system, people are grouped together around the products they produce. They may need to have access to a 'family' of machines, such as a lathe, a milling machine, a drill and a grinder.

A JIT car manufacturing system

Many car manufacturing companies adopt JIT and 'lean' production methods in which workers operate in cells around specific related processes.

In a JIT manufacturing system, the speed at which plants operate is determined by customer demand. If demand goes up, so does the speed of production. If demand goes down, the production line slows down so that there is no need for extra parts, and there are no cars standing unsold in the car parks. The rate at which cars pass along the production line is therefore timed carefully to correspond to demand, which fluctuates with the economic cycle in different countries.

Working together in their teams or production cells, employees take great responsibility for managing their own affairs. The site where a cell works is clean and uncluttered – they do not have spare parts and stores lying around. If new parts are needed, workers press a cord or other signal for the parts they want and these are delivered either by a forklift driver or by an automatic line, just in time for the parts to be used. In this way the company does not need large areas of storage space, and does not have to order parts from suppliers until it needs them.

Employees are encouraged to work 'smarter' (that is, to come up with better ways of carrying out production). Employees feel more motivated and work harder for the company and for themselves because they are involved in the decision-making process.

1 What do you see as being the principal benefits of the JIT system employed by some car manufacturing companies?

2 What do you understand by cell production?

3 How could these ideas, which have been borrowed from Japanese companies, be more widely applied in the Caribbean?

Did you know?

A just-in-time approach focuses on both internal and external customers of a business. Internal customers include people at the next stage of a manufacturing process. External customers are people outside the organisation supplied by the business.

Summary table

Just-in-case	Traditional approach to inventory management	Involves creating a surplus or buffer stock of goods to supply customers – an excess of supply relative to demand. Goods are pushed into the manufacturing system
Just-in-time	Newer approach to inventory management, most famously pioneered and developed by Japanese companies	Involves responding to demand by providing stocks only when they are required. Goods are pulled through the manufacturing system

Summary questions

1 How is a just-in-time approach likely to reduce manufacturing costs?

2 How might an online book retailer adopt a just-in-time approach to serving customers?

3 Which Caribbean industries with which you are familiar do you think might benefit from applying a more effective just-in-time approach?

Specific objective

On completion of this section, you should be able to:

■ explain the concept of quality management, with reference to the importance and dimensions of quality (performance, features, reliability, conformance, durability, serviceability, aesthetics and perceived quality).

KEY TERMS

Fitness for purpose: when a good or service does what a customer wants it to do.

Total quality management: developing a quality culture within an organisation so that everyone inside the organisation sees themselves as having a responsibility for satisfying customers and for making improvements to quality.

Quality and its importance

In his widely acclaimed book *Thriving on Chaos* (1987), Tom Peters argued that consumers' perception of the quality of a product or service is the most important factor in determining its success. Quality as defined by the consumer, he argued, is more important than price in determining the demand for most goods and services. Quality should therefore be viewed as '**fitness for purpose**' in the eyes of the consumer. This means that the good provides the benefits that the consumer wants.

It is important to note that if an organisation develops a reputation for poor quality of its goods and/or services, it can have a negative impact in the following ways:

■ loss of business
■ liability costs – due to damages or injuries incurred
■ lower productivity
■ increased operational costs such as failure costs, appraisal costs and prevention costs.

Quality management

Quality management is the process through which managers ensure that the products they supply are indeed fit for purpose. Successful organisations consist of people and processes that are built around satisfying customer requirements.

Total quality management (TQM) is a philosophy that aims to involve all organisation members in a serious effort to attain quality of goods and services; this involves suppliers as well as customers, with the customer being the focal point (1.21).

Dimensions of quality

There are eight main dimensions to quality. Some of them overlap, but they are features that are immediately recognised by manufacturers, operatives and customers:

1 **Performance:** the product should do what it claims to do. A sound system should provide quality sound, an eraser should rub out marks on a page, a pair of spectacles should enable the wearer to see more effectively. A company whose products perform poorly will lose sales and gain a poor reputation.

2 **Features:** these are the additional benefits that a user will look for in a product: for example, a sunroof on a car, an air conditioning system, assisted parking or warning sounds that come on when the seat belt is not fastened.

3 **Reliability:** the product should perform consistently over its lifetime. The purchaser of a new pair of jeans wants them to be wearable even after washing and not lose shape after only a few months.

4 **Conformance:** does the product conform to, or meet with, the required specifications: for example, health and safety standards? Does it include all the specified features?

5 **Durability:** how long does the product last? Ideally it will retain its value over a long period of time. Warranties and service agreements are important in durability because they help to guarantee the ongoing performance of the product or service.

6 **Serviceability:** is the product easy to service? Is service support provided by the producer or seller in a desirable way? For example, is after-sales care helpful and are staff friendly?

7 **Aesthetics:** does the product look good? Is it well designed to meet the requirements of the user?

8 **Perception:** the quality of a product is ultimately determined by customers' perception – do they feel that the good or service is a quality product?

CASE STUDY

Quality holidays in the Caribbean

A range of Caribbean companies provide quality holidays. Providers of premium holidays like Sandals offer performance in the form of high-end service in beautiful beach locations with features including top-quality cuisine and entertainment. Holidaymakers returning to a particular holiday provider find reliability, in that the service has been maintained or improved, and conformance, in that the holiday meets the highest standards expected by Caribbean tourism boards.

These and other dimensions of the holiday all help to create the perception of a quality holiday. However, it is not just premium holidays that can be seen as quality holidays. In the Caribbean there are also many budget holiday providers who give their customers performance in the form of an enjoyable and relaxing holiday experience, combined with additional features, a personal and friendly service and conformance to standards set by the Caribbean tourism boards, as well as aesthetics in the form of fine beach fronts. So there is a range of pricing points at which holiday customers in the Caribbean can perceive that they are buying into a quality product.

1 Choose a product that you buy regularly and to which you are loyal, in order to demonstrate how it provides the dimensions of quality.

2 Show how a low-price and a high-price version of a product can provide quality for different groups of consumers of that product.

Summary table

Quality	<ul><li>Refers to fitness for purpose in the eyes of customers</li><li>Important for the success of a product</li><li>Requires quality management to ensure products are fit for purpose</li></ul>
Dimensions of quality	<ul><li>Performance – a product doing what it is supposed to do</li><li>Features – add to the main performance characteristics</li><li>Reliability – the extent to which the product continues to deliver expected performance</li><li>Conformance – with the design specification</li><li>Durability – length of time for which the product delivers, and toughness in use</li><li>Serviceability – ease of maintenance and repair and other characteristics of service (e.g. friendliness)</li><li>Aesthetics – visual appearance and impression given</li><li>Perception – the customer's overall impression of the product's quality</li></ul>

Summary questions

1 What is the relationship between the performance of a product and the customer's perception of the quality of a product?

2 Identify a product that you consider to be of poor quality. Why might someone else believe that this is a quality product?

3 Which of the dimensions of quality do you see as being the most important and why? Relate your answer to a specific product.

Specific objective

On completion of this section, you should be able to:

- explain the difference between quality control, quality assurance and total quality management.

Figure 1.21.1 *Customer quality standards*

KEY TERMS

Quality control: ensuring that goods meet the requirements of the end user.

Quality assurance: checking work in progress during the production process and final goods at the end in order to supply goods with zero defects.

Culture of quality: established patterns, values and norms focusing on meeting, exceeding and delighting internal and external customers.

Development of quality

Figure 1.21.1 highlights what is meant by quality standards from the customer's point of view. It shows that the ultimate aim is not just to satisfy the customer but to delight them so that they become an advocate of the good or service.

There are three main stages in the development of quality:

1   quality control (QC)

2   quality assurance (QA)

3   total quality management (TQM).

Quality control

The aim of **quality control** is to detect and remove components or products that fall below set standards. The process takes place after these products have been produced. Most commonly, quality control inspectors carry out the check by examining and testing the product. The main benefit of quality control is that it prevents defective or substandard parts and products from being released at the end of the production pipeline. The disadvantage is that quality control involves a layer of cost at the end of the production process, as this is the point when defective products are identified and scrapped.

Quality assurance

The aim of **quality assurance** is to produce goods with 'zero defects'. Checks are made both during and after the production process in order to eliminate faults where they arise.

Quality assurance is the responsibility of the workforce, working in cells or teams, rather than an inspector (although inspection will also take place). The key benefit is that faults are cut out at source. The main disadvantage and cost is that training is required to make sure that all staff can participate in the process.

Total quality management

Total quality management goes beyond quality assurance. It is concerned with creating a **culture of quality**, so that every employee will seek to delight customers: the customer is at the centre of the production process. Some of the top Caribbean companies, such as SM Jaleel, Sandals and Blue Mountain Coffee, have been following this policy for a long time. It involves providing customers with what they want, when and how they want it. It involves closely integrating the marketing and production functions of a company and moving with changing customer requirements and fashions to design products and services that meet, and exceed, their requirements. Satisfied customers will pass the message on to their friends.

Under TQM everyone in an organisation is expected to see themselves as working for customers both internal and external to the organisation. All employees are encouraged to make suggestions and implement customer-focused improvements in their work practices. TQM is the most complete form of operations management. It encourages all the staff in the workplace to think about quality in everything they do. Every employee sets out to satisfy customers, placing them at the heart of the production process.

The Japanese term 'kaizen' is closely associated with TQM. Kaizen means 'continuous improvement' and is a process of continually seeking small changes and improvements in production methods as a continuous flow of new ideas and practices. Kaizen is often a product of quality circles (examined in 1.22).

In summary, quality control focuses on inspection and detection, while quality assurance seeks to prevent errors and faults. Total quality management is concerned with continuously improving quality standards. Figure 1.21.2 shows the steps in moving towards total quality management.

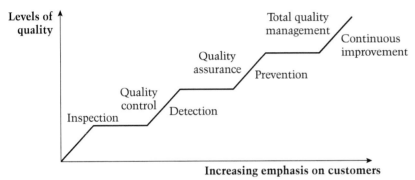

Figure 1.21.2 *Increasing emphasis on meeting customer requirements*

Summary table

Quality control (QC)	Focuses on inspection and detection	Prevents end-of-pipeline faults
Quality assurance (QA)	Focuses on preventing faults and lack of quality through quality assurance systems	Assures the quality of production
Total quality management (TQM)	Gives everyone in the organisation responsibility for quality as part of a quality culture	Focuses on continuous improvement to delight customers

Summary questions

1 You have been told that a total quality management system is very expensive to set up, as this requires extensive training of staff. How would you counter this argument?

2 It has been argued that quality control is more suitable for small companies whereas total quality management is more suitable for larger companies. How would you counter this argument?

Specific objective

On completion of this section, you should be able to:

- explain the concept of quality management, with reference to the techniques for improving quality (quality circles, ISO standards, benchmarking and outsourcing).

KEY TERMS

Brainstorming: discussion process whereby members of a group are encouraged to suggest ideas and solutions to problems based on the first ideas that come into their heads. These ideas are refined by working with ones that are useful and eliminating those that cannot be taken further.

Randomised sampling of product units: examining what has been produced to identify strengths, weaknesses and areas for development.

Cause-and-effect diagrams: simple illustrations often showing how problems or successes have arisen, with the aim of achieving a fuller understanding of operational processes.

Did you know?

One area of ISO is environmental management, with stringent standards concerning waste reduction and pollution control.

There are four further techniques that can be used for improving quality:

- quality circles
- ISO standards
- benchmarking
- outsourcing.

Quality circles

Quality circles (QCs) are an important way of increasing participation in organisational activities. A study group of 5–15 volunteers meets regularly to discuss operational and employee problems. The volunteers are ordinary employees and their immediate supervisors and managers. A supervisor or manager usually operates as the circle leader.

Quality circles are concerned with putting ideas into action. This involves in-depth analysis, proposals for action and presentations to management of ideas to improve operations. There are four main components of a quality circle framework:

- a steering committee (one per organisation), staffed by senior managers, who make general policy and set up the framework and resources for the circles
- a facilitator who supports the discussion process, providing guidance if required
- a circle leader – often the unit supervisor – who stimulates discussion within the circle without dominating it. Leaders need to be familiar with problem-solving techniques and group dynamics
- the members of the circle.

The circles meet during company time, perhaps for one hour a week. The discussion uses **brainstorming**, graphs showing the frequency of problems, **randomised sampling of product units** produced and **cause-and-effect diagrams**.

ISO standards

ISO is the International Organization for Standardization, a standard-awarding body representing the quality of production and its processes or management systems.

International set standards have a number: ISO 9000 indicates to potential customers that a company's quality procedures are reliable, and by implication that the company is capable of delivering consistently the promised quality product or service. ISO 9001 indicates that companies have in place environmental management systems of a sufficient standard to minimise the impact of business activity on the environment.

Within specific Caribbean nations there are standard-setting bodies: the Bureau of Standards in Jamaica, for example, establishes quality standards that producers must meet for products to be provided in the Jamaican context and to be fit for export.

Benchmarking

Best practice **benchmarking** (BPB) is a method many organisations use to help them discover the 'best' methods available for carrying out processes, and then using them in their own organisations. An organisation can benchmark either internally, to find out the best practice within it, or externally, by looking at other organisations. Many organisations set themselves the objective of becoming the 'benchmark for the industry'. BPB involves:

- what customers consider excellent practice
- setting standards for business processes based on best practice
- finding out how the best companies create best practice
- creating standards within an organisation that meet or exceed the best currently available.

Figure 1.22.1 illustrates the process of benchmarking.

KEY TERMS

Benchmarking: the continuous process of measuring products, services and practices against the toughest competitors of those companies, regarded as industry leaders.

Outsourcing

As you learned in 1.17, many businesses outsource by contracting out a process or production activity. A company can benefit by buying in from companies that have more effective quality processes. A company with little experience of quality management may also outsource its quality function: for example, using an outside contractor to take responsibility for quality management in the supply chain. There is a risk for a company with high internal quality procedures in subcontracting to one with inferior processes. A company planning to outsource should give careful attention to potential quality issues.

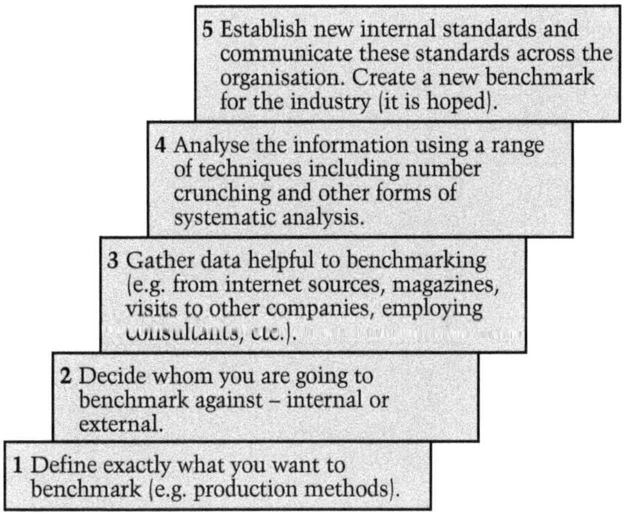

5 Establish new internal standards and communicate these standards across the organisation. Create a new benchmark for the industry (it is hoped).

4 Analyse the information using a range of techniques including number crunching and other forms of systematic analysis.

3 Gather data helpful to benchmarking (e.g. from internet sources, magazines, visits to other companies, employing consultants, etc.).

2 Decide whom you are going to benchmark against – internal or external.

1 Define exactly what you want to benchmark (e.g. production methods).

Figure 1.22.1 *The process of benchmarking*

Summary table

Quality circle	Work-based group that focuses on practical issues associated with improvement of quality
International standards	Independent standards set by international bodies that act to certify that a company is employing quality operational processes
Benchmarking	Exercise to identify the best possible processes and procedures so that a company can seek to emulate best practice and set the benchmark itself
Outsourcing	Contracting out business processes or manufacture of products to outside contractors. Companies need to be careful when outsourcing to ensure that quality is maintained or improved

Summary questions

1 a How do you think that quality circles can contribute to a kaizen process?

b Give an example of how a quality circle of people on your course, or at your place of work, might contribute to making suggestions for work-based improvements.

2 A supermarket has decided to outsource the transportation and delivery of goods to its stores.

a What might be the implications of this for quality management?

b Give examples of how the store's quality management might:
i be improved
ii deteriorate.

1.23 Lean production

Specific objective

On completion of this section, you should be able to:

- explain the concept of lean production including the link between inventory management, quality and capacity and employee roles.

Did you know?

For most production operations, only a fraction of the total time and effort spent actually adds value for the end customer.

> Cleverly designing manufacturing processes to focus on value-adding activities

> Minimising the use of inventory by just-in-time production

> Reusing materials

> Using more-effective materials

> Using CAD and CAM (see 1.8) to focus on the most efficient use of resources

> Engaging employees in the lean process through quality circles and other direct decision-making activities

> Recycling activity, with waste management teams focusing on the issue and staff trained to think continually about recycling and avoiding waste.

Figure 1.23.1 *Ways to achieve lean manufacturing*

What is 'lean' production?

Lean production is based on the principle that any use of resources that does not create value for the consumer is 'waste'. A 'lean' company makes best use of resources by cutting out waste. Lean production is therefore an important aspect of quality management. In lean production, a quality system is put in place to achieve reductions in labour, materials, inventories, and space and time – all by reducing defects and eliminating waste. Where lean production works effectively, production processes should involve 'zero defects'.

Reducing waste

Reducing waste involves identifying production activities that do not add value to the customer. Quality circles (see 1.22) are used to identify improvements in processes. Members of a quality circle use their knowledge and experience from interactions with their customers to make suggestions on how to create value for their customers.

A quality management system should be the principal driving force for eliminating waste. It works best when it focuses on kaizen (see 1.21) and operates through small steps – 'continuous improvement'. Everyone who works for a lean organisation is encouraged to suggest ways of improving production, from an employee in stores with a good idea about how to improve the management of inventories, to staff in the assembly unit with suggestions for improving manufacturing processes for a particular product component.

International Standards ISO 14001 and 9001 relate to environmental management, and lean manufacturing is part of that. ISO 14001 shows that a company is compliant with high-quality environmental management, including management of waste. A company that meets ISO 9001 has:

- a set of procedures for all key processes in the business, which are checked for efficiency
- outputs that are checked for defects, and corrected where necessary
- a system of continual improvement (kaizen).

Figure 1.23.1 shows how a company can focus on lean manufacturing.

Benefits of lean production

Benefits of lean production that enable a company to increase profit margins include:

- reduction of costs through eliminating waste processes, wasted inventories and wasted time
- reduction of costs by minimising inputs relative to the outputs that can be achieved. Production can take place in a smaller area and in less time
- minimising the lead time between orders being made and orders being delivered (especially through just-in-time)

- ongoing quality management. Quality management systems, employee involvement and kaizen guarantee efficiency at every stage of production
- enhanced company reputation for timeliness and quality of product, which will increase sales, revenues and profits
- increased production capacity because more can be produced from existing, or even fewer, resources. Wasted capacity is eliminated to focus on productive capacity. Machines, manpower and management focus on value added rather than waste.

CASE STUDY

A Trinidadian pharmaceuticals manufacturer radically re-engineers its product packing process

In 2012, two Trinidadian researchers, Boppana Chowdary and Damian George, produced a study of lean manufacturing in the journal *Strategic Direction*. They focused on a Trinidadian producer of pharmaceutical products, looking at the stock-keeping unit on the line with the highest sales revenue in creams and ointments. A focus group was established involving members of the production, distribution and stores sections of this line. The group examined ways of re-engineering (modifying) processes in order to engage in leaner processes, so cutting out waste. They created a value-stream map, identifying where value was being created and then sought to cut out non-value-adding activities in typical processes such as filling, capping, labelling, coding, packing and inspection.

A new cellular working layout was designed around common setting up of equipment, cutting space, handling and inventory management. As a result of the exercise, reductions were made possible in staffing on the line, inventory, work in progress and floor space.

Each of these reductions can be considered as a reduction in waste and represents an increased focus on adding value.

1 What would be the purpose of re-engineering the value creation process?

2 What are the principal benefits of lean manufacturing outlined in the case study?

Summary table

What is lean manufacturing?	■ A focus on value-creating activities at the expense of waste ■ An approach to creating a 'zero defects' manufacturing system
What are the benefits of lean production?	■ Reduction in inventories required for manufacturing so that inventories are just used to add value ■ Focus on quality, i.e. giving customers what they want ■ Increase in production capacity by being able to produce more from less ■ Employees engaged in the process of adding value through quality circles and other employee involvement initiatives ■ All the above lead to reducing costs and increased efficiency/higher margins

Summary questions

1 A company re-engineers its production lines to focus on lean production. What is likely to be the impact on the following?

   a The value of output

   b The time taken to produce goods

   c The amount of waste generated

   d The profitability of the business

   e Employee involvement in decision making

   f Space required to produce a particular level of output

   g Inventory requirement levels

   h Plant capacity

   i Customer satisfaction levels

2 Do you think it would be possible for service industries to be lean to the same extent as manufacturing? Give some examples to illustrate your answer.

1.24 Productivity

Specific objective

On completion of this section, you should be able to:

- explain methods of measuring and improving productivity, with a focus on the definition of productivity.

KEY TERMS

Production: the processes involved in providing goods and services.

Productivity: a measure of the output (or value of output) that can be obtained from using productive resources.

Did you know?

A simple formula for labour productivity is:

$$\frac{\text{Output}}{\text{Time worked}} \times \text{Number of workers}$$

For example, if 2,000 units of output can be produced by 10 workers working for an average of 10 hours, productivity is:

$$\frac{2,000}{10 \times 10} = \frac{2,000}{100}$$

$$= 20 \text{ units of output per employee}$$

Production and productivity

Production is the processes involved in providing goods and services. Each stage in production adds value to the good or service being produced.

Productivity is a measure of the output (or value of output) that can be obtained from using productive resources. For example, if 10 employees can produce 100 units of output in an hour, their productivity is 10 units per employee per hour. Productivity can also be measured in money terms. So if each unit produced is worth $5, the productivity per employee per hour is $50.

So productivity can be measured in real terms, as units of output produced per unit of input, or in money terms, as the financial value of output per unit of input. The productivity of a machine could be measured in two ways (assume that each physical unit is sold for $5):

- the physical output method: for example, 200 units per machine hour
- the revenue output method: for example, $1,000 per machine hour.

Plant or unit productivity

Productivity is calculated to measure the output of particular units. For example, a business wanting to cut costs by closing some stores or factories would use productivity to identify which units were least profitable. It could also identify profitable outlets, which is useful if a business wants to expand its operations in an area.

Productivity can be measured by comparing the operating cost of the plant with revenue achieved. For example, in 2013 production output of a factory was valued at $200,000. Operating costs were $100,000. Productivity was therefore 200 per cent:

$$\frac{200,000}{100,000} \times 100\% = 200\%$$

In 2014 production output of the factory increased to $220,000, with operating costs remaining at $100,000. Productivity has increased to 220 per cent of operating costs.

$$\frac{220,000}{100,000} \times 100\% = 220\%$$

The increase in productivity of the plant in 2014 compared to 2013 is 10 per cent (an increase in 20 per cent from a base of 200 per cent).

Productivity of resources

Productivity can also be calculated to measure specific resources, such as the impact of taking on an additional employee. You looked at marginal costing techniques in 1.16. You will remember that these can be employed to inform decision making about the impact of employing additional resources such as labour, machinery or equipment.

Table 1.24.1 shows the impact of employing increasing numbers of workers on a production line, with total output and marginal output increasing as more employees are employed. Assume that units of output are sold for $10 each.

Table 1.24.1 *Labour productivity with a fixed amount of capital*

Labour input (employees)	Total manufacturing output	Marginal physical product of labour ($)	Marginal revenue product of labour ($)
1	40	40	400
2	90	50	500
3	145	55	550
4	205	60	600
5	255	50	500
6	295	40	400
7	325	30	300
8	345	20	200
9	355	10	100
10	360	5	50

Initially, as more employees are used on the production line, productivity will increase in terms of **marginal physical product of labour** (and **marginal revenue product of labour**). However, using too many people (in this case more than four) will lead to declining marginal physical and marginal revenue product.

The decision about how many employees to take on depends on the marginal cost of employing additional people (**marginal cost of labour**) Assuming that the wage rate is $400, it will pay the firm to employ up to six. The marginal revenue product of the sixth employee will be $400; the marginal cost of employing the sixth worker will be $400. Marginal costing is therefore a useful technique for making resource use decisions. The cost of employing additional resources can be compared with the returns from employing additional resources. Look back to 1.16 if you wish to remind yourself of this topic.

KEY TERMS

Marginal physical product of labour: number of products that can be produced by an additional employee.

Marginal revenue product of labour: value in money terms of the output of an additional employee.

Marginal cost of labour: cost in money terms of employing an additional employee.

Summary table

What is productivity?	The volume or value of output that can be produced with given resource inputs
How do we measure productivity?	$\dfrac{\text{Output}}{\text{Input}} \times 100\%$
What values do we use to measure productivity?	Can be measured in terms of physical units, or revenue per physical unit
What is marginal productivity?	The revenue (marginal revenue product) or output (marginal physical product) from employing an additional unit of labour (or other resource)

Summary questions

1 In a particular production plant, 10 employees produce 100 units per hour, which sell for $5 each. Management is considering investing in new machinery that would enable eight employees to produce 100 units per hour at $5 each. How might knowledge of productivity help managers to make a decision about whether to upgrade the plant?

2 As a production manager you are advised that employing additional workers will increase the level of production but lead to falling levels of productivity. How might this influence your decision about whether to employ more labour?

Specific objective

On completion of this section, you should be able to:

- explain methods of measuring and improving productivity, with a focus on factors that impact on productivity.

Illustrating improvements in productivity

An improvement in productivity occurs when more can be produced with the same or a smaller quantity of resources. Figure 1.25.1 shows how the total revenue product of labour would increase as a result of an increase in productivity.

Figure 1.25.1 *The effect of an increase in productivity*

The lower curve shows the productivity of different quantities of labour before an increase in productivity. The higher curve shows the productivity of labour after an increase in productivity. What factors are likely to lead to this increase, so that a higher value of product can be made with the same quantity of labour?

Increasing productivity

The following factors impact on productivity.

Technology

Introduction of new technology such as automated production machinery and better techniques of production, such as CAD and CAM, can increase labour and plant productivity and lead to higher levels of output per unit of input. Poor and outdated technology can be inefficient and unreliable, leading to a decrease in productivity.

Training

Training employees enables them to become more effective, and hence more productive. They waste less time and resources, and can complete jobs more quickly. Revenue product per employee increases.

Quality of labour supply

The quality of available labour affects productivity. Skilled labour – that is, workers with a reasonable level of education, training and practical experience – is more productive than unskilled. On a national scale,

Figure 1.25.2 *Introducing automated factory equipment can radically increase production capacity*

countries with abundant skilled labour, such as Barbados, are more productive than countries where skilled labour is in short supply.

Demand for and price of outputs

The intensity of demand for products produced by labour and other resources will impact on productivity (where this is measured in terms of revenue product). This takes place through the medium of pricing. For example, if 10 employees produce 100 units that are sold for $5 each, the revenue product per employee is $500/10 = $50 per employee. However, assume that the demand for the product increases so that its price rises to $6 per unit. The 10 employees still produce 100 units of output. However, their revenue productivity increases: $600/10 = $60 per employee.

Table 1.25.1 shows that productivity has risen by 20 per cent because of an increase in the price of the product being made.

Table 1.25.1 *Effect of an increase in price on productivity*

Physical output	Price per product	Revenue product	Increase in productivity
100	$5	$500	
100	$6	$600	20%

Competition

Note that competition between producers may have the impact of lowering productivity as measured by the value of revenue product. For example, if instead of raising prices a producer lowers them (in order to compete), the value of the revenue product of employees will fall.

Eliminating waste

In the previous sections we have seen how processes such as lean manufacturing and quality management can lead to a greater focus on value-adding processes and the elimination of waste. Every time that waste is eliminated or value-adding procedures are built into production, productivity will increase.

Strategies to increase productivity

Strategies by which a business can increase the productivity of its resources include:

- employing more productive resources: for example, investing in better machinery and equipment that increases the productivity not only of the plant and equipment, but of the labour force that works the plant

- employing better-quality labour, that is, employees with higher levels of education, training and experience. This might involve countries with a limited talent pool in growth industries recruiting from overseas

- training existing employees to work with more sophisticated equipment, techniques and production processes

- increasing demand for the product produced by the existing resources, which will immediately impact on the revenue product

- eliminating waste through production strategies such as quality management, just-in-time and lean manufacturing.

Summary table

Ways of increasing productivity
■ Eliminating waste
■ Increasing the capability of existing resources (e.g. plant and labour)
■ Increasing the demand for the end product produced by existing resources

Summary questions

1 A pharmaceutical company engages in a range of production processes including:

   a mixing ingredients

   b bottling ingredients

   c capping bottles

   d labelling bottles

   e storing bottles

   f distributing the bottles to retailers.

   Explain how the company might be able to increase the productivity associated with each of these processes.

2 A factory manager reports that the productivity of the plant has increased this year, even though the quantity being produced in the plant has remained the same. What explanations could you provide for this apparent contradiction?

Specific objective

On completion of this section, you should be able to:

- interpret and draw simple critical path diagrams.

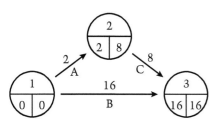

Figure 1.26.1 *Part of a critical path diagram*

Critical path method

The **critical path** method (CPM) is an important decision-making technique used by operations managers in project planning. A diagram is used to set out:

- the sequence of **activities** involved in carrying out a project or producing a good
- the time taken to carry out each activity
- the critical path – that is, the sequence of activities that are most important to the project, and which must not be subject to delays.

Once the critical path has been identified, project managers can monitor the sequence closely to make sure that tasks are being completed on time. If problems arise, it may be possible to pool extra resources into activities along this path.

Critical path analysis is best explained with the use of examples.

Example 1

The network in Figure 1.26.1 shows components at the start of a critical path diagram. Each task is represented by an arrow with a letter denoting the task, A, B, and C. Arrows are drawn from left to right to show the sequence in which activities must be completed.

The diagram also includes circles known as **nodes** – points in time when one or more activities finish or start.

A network links a series of nodes showing the sequence of activities and timescale involved. Each circle can be broken down into two components:

- The top semi-circle gives the number of the node.
- The bottom semi-circle shows the **earliest start** and **latest finish times** (left- and right-hand segments respectively) for the activity. The bottom right-hand section is particularly important, as it shows the latest time that the next activity must start if the project is to be completed on time.

For example, in the set of activities in Figure 1.26.1, the earliest time to complete activity C is 16 days. This is because, although activities A and C can be completed in 10 days (A = 2 and C = 8), it takes a minimum of 16 days to complete activity B, so the earliest time that the project can arrive at node 3 is 16 days.

Note that to work out the latest time that an activity should be finished involves working backwards from the end of the project. To calculate the latest finish time of an activity you would deduct the duration of the next activity from the latest finish time of the next activity (for example in Figure 1.26.1 the latest finish time in node 2 = 16 − 8).

Example 2

Figure 1.26.2 shows the number of days required to finish a project with 12 nodes. Again, dates are calculated by working backwards from the project completion date. Note that the two activities drawn in dotted lines are 'dummy activities' that do not use time or resources. The critical path is shown by the line of thicker arrows.

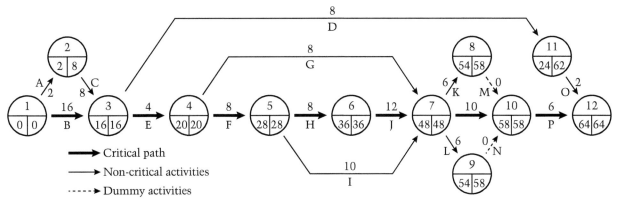

Figure 1.26.2 A 12-node critical path diagram

It is useful to summarise some of the key features of Figure 1.26.2. To help you do this, here are some questions that a project manager would want to answer in building his or her critical path model:

1 Activity D can be completed in a minimum of eight days. Why is activity D not part of the critical path? What would be the implications for the project if activity D actually took 20 days to complete?

2 Activity H is planned to take eight days. What would be the implication for the project if it actually took 10 days to complete?

3 Why is it essential, if the project is to keep on schedule, that activity P only takes six days to complete?

Did you know?

Software packages such as Microsoft Project® are useful as they highlight the times when certain resources need to be employed, including the specific responsibility of the project team members. As well as helping to solve these problems, the software facilitates effective communication of the plan.

Summary table

A critical path diagram	Sets out sequences of end dates for activities necessary for a project to be completed on time
What is in the diagram?	Activities – denoted by letters, and the time required to carry out each activity Nodes – showing the number of each node, the earliest time that an activity can start, and the latest time it should be completed if the project is to finish on time
The critical path	Is the single most important sequence of activities that must be completed on time if the project is to meet its end date

Summary questions

1 Set out a critical path diagram consisting of five activities. A must be completed first and takes six days. It is followed by B and C, which can be carried out simultaneously. B can be completed within five days. C can be completed within 10 days. B is followed by D, which takes six days and must be completed before the final task F. C is followed by E, which takes seven days and must be completed before the final task F. F takes two days to complete and effectively completes the project. Identify the critical path and show the earliest start and latest finish times for each activity.

2 In project planning, why is it important to work back from the end of the project?

Drawing a decision tree

Decision trees are a simple graphic way of setting out alternative courses of action. They are used if a company needs to decide whether, for example, to open a new factory or whether to produce one line of products rather than another. The basic procedure for constructing a decision tree is to set out the alternatives as branches of the tree and then calculate the **probability** of the success of each branch and the likely **financial return**.

Worked example of a decision tree

As a result of taking over another company, a business has acquired an empty factory and is now faced with the following choices:

Option 1: sell the factory immediately for $125,000.

Option 2: retain it for a year in the hope that property prices will rise, and then sell it for $400,000. There is a 10 per cent probability that the company will be able to sell it at this price in a year's time. However, there is a 90 per cent chance that property prices will fall. This would mean having to reduce the price to $100,000.

Option 3: refit the factory and use it for manufacturing. This will cost $200,000. If the business takes this option it will have three further choices:

- Manufacture a new product, but there is a 50 per cent chance that this will make no profit at all.
- Extend production of an existing popular product, with a 40 per cent chance of making a $400,000 profit.
- Produce a modified product, with a 10 per cent chance of making a profit of $1,500,000.

The three alternatives under Option 3 can be set out as in Table 1.27.1. This information is then set out as a decision tree in Figure 1.27.1.

Table 1.27.1 *Possible outcomes from developing the factory now*

Type of production	Probability	Expected profit ($)
New product	5/10 (0.5)	0
Existing popular product	4/10 (0.4)	400,000
Modified product	1/10 (0.1)	1,500,000

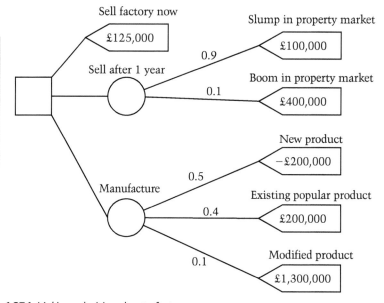

Figure 1.27.1 *Making a decision about a factory*

Steps taken to construct the tree

The following steps show how the tree is constructed.

1 Set out the decision fork

The decision fork is the square on the left of the diagram. Three lines are drawn from it, representing the three possible alternatives: sell now, sell later or manufacture (Figure 1.27.2).

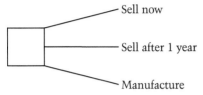

Figure 1.27.2 *The decision fork*

2 Work out the consequences of each course of action

- The consequence of **Option 1** is the easiest to set out. There is only one possible outcome: the proceeds of $125,000 from the sale of the factory.

- **Option 2** yields alternative outcomes because of the chance element. These are shown as lines emanating from a circle. There are two possible outcomes, labelled with their probabilities (0.9 and 0.1).

  How do we know the financial effect of these outcomes? Selling the factory next year has a 90 per cent chance of yielding only $100,000 and a 10 per cent chance of yielding $400,000.

- **Option 3** involves setting out a circle to represent an even more complicated chance fork. In each of the three cases we need to subtract $200,000 (the cost of refitting the factory).

The purpose of the decision tree is to help you to choose the best course of action. To do this, you need to work back from right to left along the decision tree, filling each chance and decision fork (Figure 1.27.3).

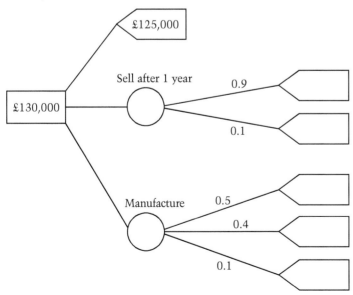

Figure 1.27.3 *Probabilities associated with alternative choices*

Did you know?

In a decision tree a distinction is made between 'points of decision' and 'points where chance and probability come into play'.

Decision forks (points of decision) are represented by squares. Chance forks are represented by circles.

In the example shown, the decision at the fork is whether to sell the factory now, sell it later, or use the factory for manufacturing. Note that the probability lines all come out of the circles.

3 Fill in the chance forks

Each chance fork needs to be averaged:

- **Option 1:** sell now – needs no alteration because it contains only one figure: $125,000.

- **Option 2:** sell in a year's time – needs to be averaged out. We must take the average value by multiplying each outcome against its probability. The average value is referred to as the **expected value (EV)**.

The expected value of selling the factory next year is therefore:

$$EV = 0.9(100,000) + 0.1(400,000)$$
$$= 130,000$$

This figure of 130,000 can now be added to the Option 2 chance fork (in the circle).

- **Option 3:** use the factory for manufacturing – now needs to be calculated (in each option we have deducted $200,000, which is the cost of refitting the factory).

The expected value of manufacturing is:

$$0.5(-200,000) + 0.4(200,000) + 0.1(1,300,000) = 110,000$$

We can now fill in 110,000 in the Option 3 chance fork (in the circle) (Figure 1.27.4).

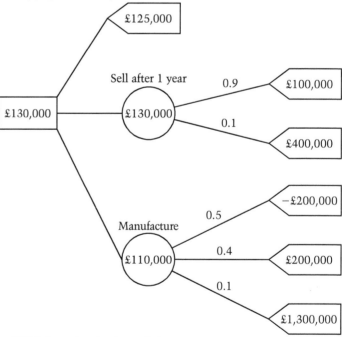

Figure 1.27.4 *Averaging the chance forks*

4 'Prune back' the decision tree

Once the decision forks and chance forks on the decision tree have been filled in, the final step is to 'prune it back' – in other words, eliminate the less attractive options to leave the best course of action. This is done by comparing the expected values of the three options:

- Expected value of selling factory now = $125,000
- Expected value of selling in one year = $130,000
- Expected value of manufacturing = $110,000.

We can now cut off the less attractive branches (Figure 1.27.5).

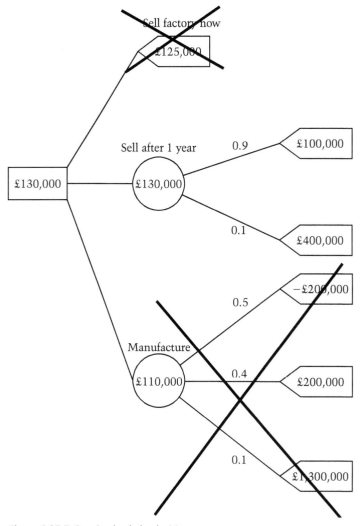

Figure 1.27.5 *Pruning back the decision tree*

Having cut off the less attractive branches, we are left with just one expected value in the decision square: that is, $130,000.

Summary table

A decision tree	A simple graphic way of illustrating the consequences of (and of making) a decision
Step 1	Set out a decision fork to identify the alternative choices
Step 2	Work out the consequences of each course of action
Step 3	Fill in the chance forks to identify expected values
Step 4	Prune back the less attractive options. You are left with the expected value of the best alternative

Summary questions

1 A chain of coffee bars has just lost one of its experienced managers and will be without a full-time manager for one month. Executives of the chain have to decide whether to:

   a close the coffee bar for a month and make a financial loss of $2,000

   b give temporary responsibility (one month) for running the coffee bar to an existing employee with little management experience. The existing employee would need to be paid an extra $2,000. The chance of achieving a healthy profit of $8,000 is 0.2. The chance of achieving a modest profit of $4,000 is 0.8

   c recruit an experienced temporary manager from an agency for the month. This would involve a payment of $8,000, made up of the manager's salary for one month plus the agency commission. The probability of this manager making a good profit of $10,000 is 0.9, while the probability of a modest profit of $6,000 is 0.1.

2 Calculate the EV of each of the three alternatives. Prune back your tree to reveal the most desirable option.

Answers to all exam-style questions can be found on the accompanying CD.

Section 1: Multiple-choice questions

1 A good example of a 'bulk-decreasing' industry would be:

   A steel manufacture

   B furniture manufacture

   C building construction

   D car assembly.

2 A sales forecasting technique that is based on the views of experts who do not physically meet with each other to create a forecast is:

   A calculating a moving sales average

   B the Delphi method

   C a sales force composite

   D a consumer survey.

3 The purpose of 'value analysis' from the perspective of the producer is to:

   A eliminate operations and activities that add most value to production

   B focus on providing benefits to consumers that are easiest to provide

   C concentrate on providing secondary rather than primary functions for consumers

   D create as much value as possible relative to the cost of production.

4 The capacity utilisation of a firm is defined as:

   A the total level of output that a firm can produce in a given period of time

   B the percentage of total production capacity that is being employed at a moment in time

   C the maximum possible output in a specific period of time

   D the output achieved per unit of input employed.

5 Which of the following statements about 'wait time' is the most accurate?

   A 'Wait time' will typically be longer at low levels of capacity utilisation than at high levels of capacity utilisation.

   B As capacity utilisation increases, 'wait time' is also likely to increase.

   C The busier a plant is, the lower the levels of 'wait time' will be.

   D The lower the production capacity of a plant is, the lower the 'wait time' for throughput is likely to be.

6 A company invests in more highly trained employees. This is classified as:

   A an internal commercial economy of scale

   B an external diseconomy of scale

   C an internal labour economy of scale

   D an external economy of concentration.

7 Production in a car plant is clustered around a set of machines and specialist workers who focus on related manufacturing operations. This is referred to as:

   A layout by fixed positions

   B product layout

   C cell production

   D automated production.

8 Which of the following is the best example of a direct cost associated with producing a pair of shorts?

   A The factory overhead

   B Management salary costs

   C Cost of fabric used in the shorts

   D Marketing costs for the shorts

9 The economic order quantity (EOQ) is:

   A the lowest number of goods that can be ordered economically

   B the total inventory cost per year

   C the order quantity that minimises the cost of inventory management

   D the cost of making an order for goods.

10 The series of activities that need to be completed on time in project planning is described as the:

   A critical path

   B decision tree

   C network analysis

   D float time.

Section 2: Structured questions

11 Better Bakers is a small bakery that produces bread, rolls and cakes, which it supplies directly to retailers and caterers.

   a **i** The bakery uses batch production: explain how it does this. [2]

      ii In what way will this production method benefit Better Bakers? [4]

   b Better Bakers wants to forecast likely future sales of different products in order to plan production more effectively. Compare the sales force composite method and a consumer survey as methods of forecasting consumer requirements. [10]

   c Explain how a moving average of sales would help the company to forecast the growth in sales over time. [5]

   d Better Bakers sometimes uses job production for specific customers. Identify a situation in which Better Bakers might engage in job production and why it might do so. [4]

12 Portia Lewis is a fashion designer focusing on the design and manufacture of wedding dresses.

   a How might Portia benefit from using computer-aided design in her business? Explain THREE benefits. [6]

   b What would be the benefits to Portia's business of additionally using elements of computer-aided manufacturing? Explain TWO benefits. [4]

Portia has identified the value chain as an important way of providing her customers with value for money.

   c Identify and explain primary activities in the value chain that would enable her to make more profit from wedding dresses. [6]

   d Identify and explain secondary activities in the value chain that would enable her to make more profit from wedding dresses. [6]

   e How might Portia be able to reduce the direct cost of producing her dresses? [3]

13 Fresh Juice Bottlers is an imaginary bottling plant based in Trinidad. Production managers at the plant are seeking to maximise the operational efficiency of the plant. The company currently runs the plant for eight hours a day.

   a The company is able to maximise production from its existing plant by producing 100,000 bottles per month. Recent figures show that in January it produced 60,000 bottles, in February 50,000 bottles and in March only 40,000 bottles. Comment on the capacity utilisation of the company in these three months. [6]

   b Fresh Juice Bottlers has recently been approached by a large drinks manufacturer with an offer of a contract for Fresh Juice to bottle 80,000 bottles of drink every month of next year. How might Fresh Juice alter its production capacity in order to meet this order? [9]

   c What would Fresh Juice want to know before it accepts the order? [4]

   d How might Fresh Juice Bottlers be able to reduce its costs by operating on a larger scale? [6]

14 An events manager has booked a hotel room at a cost of $2,000 and an inspirational business speaker for a fee of $1,000. The room has space for 200 delegates, who will be charged $90 each to attend the event. Each delegate will be provided with a conference pack, which costs the organiser $5 per pack to put together, and lunch, which costs the organiser $25 per delegate.

   a What is the production capacity available? [2]

   b What is the contribution per delegate to the event? [2]

   c How many delegates will be required for the event to break even? You will need to show your working. [5]

   d How much profit will be made if only 60 delegates attend the event? [6]

   e How might a knowledge of marginal costing enable the organisers to increase the profitability of the event by offering a special discount rate to delegates booking at the last minute? [10]

15 Outboard Engineering is a company producing outboard motors for different types of sea-going boat. It is seeking to maximise the efficiency of its inventory management.

   a Identify THREE types of inventory that Outboard Engineering is likely to hold at any time. [3]

   b The company regularly purchases components from other engineering companies. How will knowledge of the economic order quantity (EOQ) help the company to decide on the size of orders to make? [5]

   c Outboard Engineering seeks to supply customers using a just-in-time approach. What would be involved in supplying just-in-time and how would this differ from a just-in-case approach? [10]

   d Outboard Engineering benchmarks its processes against those of a leading US provider of outboard motors. Explain how this benchmarking exercise might work. [4]

   e How could Outboard Engineering improve its productivity? [3]

Further exam questions and examples can be found on the accompanying CD.

2 Fundamentals of marketing

General objectives

On completion of this module, you should be able to:

- understand the roles and importance of marketing
- assimilate the principles of marketing management
- develop an awareness of the impact of the external environment on marketing.

KEY TERMS

Marketing: the anticipation and identification of consumer wants and needs in order to meet those needs, and to make a profit.

Adding value: making goods and services more desirable for the end consumer.

Did you know?

A helpful way of thinking about marketing principles is to think about them as the marketing strategies and tactics that you can control. In particular, you can control the four key elements of the marketing mix that are outlined on p63: product, price, place and promotion.

Marketing is the process through which an organisation anticipates and identifies the requirements of consumers in order to satisfy them. This enables the business to meet its corporate objectives, such as making a profit. Module 2 begins by explaining four marketing concepts:

1 Marketing – a process that includes anticipating, identifying and meeting customer requirements.

2 Market – any situation in which goods and services are traded and exchanged.

3 Exchange – a process through which trades are made: for example, between a firm supplying goods and consumers buying those goods.

4 Value added – making goods and services more desirable for the end consumer. Any process that does this is referred to as **adding value**. By adding value to goods, businesses are able to sell them at higher prices. The more value they add, the more they can charge.

Marketing is important because it enables an organisation to satisfy and respond to the changing requirements of the markets in which it operates. Market-led companies sell goods easily because they produce what consumers want.

The principles of marketing management

Throughout Module 2 you will learn a number of key principles of marketing management. These include how to identify different groups of customers and their needs (market research), how to target marketing activities at different types of consumer (targeting and positioning), how to carry out effective market research and how to develop a marketing strategy (plan).

The macro- and micro-marketing environment

The marketing department of a company needs to consider two dimensions of the environment in which marketing decisions are made:

1 The micro-environment consists of elements over which the company has some direct influence, such as its relationships with its own customers and suppliers. By building stronger relationships with customers and suppliers, the company can influence the micro-environment.

2 The macro-environment consists of factors that are external to the company and over which it has little control. These include the actions of competitors, and social trends that lead to changing buying patterns among customers. A change in the age structure of the population, for example, is outside the control of the business.

Market research

In order to find out what customers want, a business needs to carry out market research. This means systematically gathering, recording and analysing data about the market for goods and services.

The information needed by the business includes:

- What is the target market?
- Where are the people in this market?
- What do they want?
- When do they want it?
- How can we provide it for them?

Market segmentation

It is useful for marketers to identify groups with similar buying patterns. They can then target their products, promotions and advertising at these groups. Groups of customers with similar characteristics can be further divided into market segments.

The marketing mix

A number of key principles are associated with the **marketing mix**. When marketing products, a company needs to create a successful mix of:

- the right product
- sold at the right price
- sold in the right place
- using the most suitable promotion.

To create the right marketing mix, businesses have to meet the following conditions:

- The **product** has to have the right features – for example, it must look good and work well. This is the principle of product management.
- The **price** must be right. When the price is right, customers will buy in large numbers and the business will realise healthy profits. This is the pricing strategy.
- The goods must be in the right **place** at the right time. Making sure that the goods arrive when and where they are wanted is an important operation. This is the principle of distribution management.
- The target group needs to be made aware of the existence and availability of the product through **promotion.** Successful promotion helps a firm to spread costs over a larger output. There are a number of tools associated with promotion.

The importance of internet marketing decisions

Internet marketing, e-business (electronic business) and e-commerce (electronic trading) have created new business models. Most businesses now involve 'bricks and clicks': that is, a physical presence, such as a store, and a website. Some businesses, however, are just 'clicks' and are carried out only online.

Businesses with a strong internet-based presence need different marketing strategies and tools from traditional 'brick' businesses. The products they sell may be different from traditional businesses. The prices they charge may be lower because they can cut some costs. Typically, they use electronic promotions. But the most obvious change relates to distribution, as the business deals with customers online rather than face to face and distributes through mail and other distribution channels. Distribution channels are discussed in 2.28.

> **KEY TERMS**
>
> **Marketing mix:** the four key elements that businesses must plan to attract customers: product, price, place and promotion (the four Ps). These are the things that customers focus on when making buying decisions.

Did you know?

Sales promotion refers to a set of methods used to encourage customers to buy a product, usually at the point of sale. Sales promotion is used along with advertising, personal selling and publicity. It can include the use of point-of-sale materials (for example, leaflets and brochures), competitions, offers, product demonstrations and exhibitions.

Figure 2.1.1 *A taxi driver is able to keep in close touch with his customers*

What is marketing?

Marketing is the management process responsible for identifying, anticipating and satisfying customer requirements profitably.

Some organisations are physically very close to their customers. For example, a taxi driver at Grantley Adams International Airport in Barbados talks to his customers on a day-to-day basis. For other organisations, consumers may be thousands of miles away: Blue Mountain coffee is produced in Jamaica but is sold worldwide. The principle that the 'consumer is king and queen' is just as relevant to the organisation engaged in international marketing as to the local trader.

There are a number of key words in the definition of marketing given above:

■ **Identifying:** this involves answering questions such as: 'How do we find out what the consumer's requirements are?' and 'How do we keep in touch with the consumer's thoughts, feelings and perceptions about our good or service?'

■ **Anticipating:** consumer requirements change all the time. For example, as people become richer, they may seek a greater variety of goods and services. Anticipation involves looking at the future as well as at the present. What will be the 'next big thing' that people will require?

■ **Satisfying:** consumers want their requirements to be met. They seek particular benefits. They want the right goods, at the right price, at the right time and in the right place.

■ **Profitability:** marketing also involves making a margin of profit. An organisation that fails to do this will have nothing to plough back into the business in future. Without the resources to put into ongoing marketing activities, it will not be able to identify, anticipate or satisfy consumer requirements.

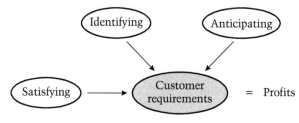

Figure 2.1.2 *The ingredients of marketing*

The market

'Market' refers to any situation where customers interact with suppliers of goods and services. The most obvious example is a street market, but other examples include the stock market, for buying stocks and shares, and the capital market, for borrowing finance over long periods.

Marketers (specialists seeking to find out more about consumers and their preferences) carry out research in different markets to find out about the wishes of consumers.

Exchange relations

The market enables **exchange**: the act of giving or taking one thing in place of another. In the marketplace, this involves the exchange of goods and/or services for money payment. The market is a highly efficient mechanism for making exchanges because means of payment are so widely accepted. For example, a Grenadian company can contract with a Trinidadian oil supplier for the supply of oil in exchange for dollars (or for the transmission of funds from one bank account to another). Power relations are often significant in exchange. The more someone wants what you have to offer, the greater the power you will have in striking a bargain.

Value added

A key aspect of marketing is adding value to a good or service, to make it more desirable. The key benefits of adding value are:

- your product or service becomes more competitive when compared with those of rivals
- you are likely to be able to increase the price of your product.

Marketing activity enables a firm to identify what types of additional value a customer is looking for. The Bahamas imports a large volume of Japanese vehicles (cars, buses, SUVs, minibuses). Many of these are used as taxis. Aspects of value associated with Japanese vehicles are high quality, reliability, durability and comfort. The vehicles are spacious, relatively fuel-efficient (for example, compared with American models) and efficient in a range of terrains. Marketers working for Japanese companies like Toyota, Honda and Nissan have, through market research, identified what particular benefits taxi drivers and other customers are looking for. These features have then been built into the vehicle design to add value in the ways desired by taxi drivers in the Bahamas, across the Caribbean and worldwide.

Summary table

What is marketing?	The process of anticipating, identifying and meeting customer requirements in order to make a profit
Where is the market?	Any situation in which buyers and sellers come into contact to make an exchange
What are exchange relations?	Relationships between buyers and sellers for the trading of goods
How do firms add value?	By making the good or service desirable to the end consumer

Did you know?

Adding value can be illustrated by the process of adding air conditioning (AC) to the design of a car. In the Caribbean, people will pay higher prices for an air-conditioned car than a non-air-conditioned car. A taxi driver with AC is able to charge a higher fare for offering AC as an additional value-added service.

Summary questions

1 Think about the example of barber shops.
   a What is the market for barber shops?
   b How could barbers engage in marketing activities?
   c With whom are they in an exchange relationship?
   d How could barber shops add value to the service they offer?

On completion of this section, you should be able to:

■ assess the implications of various marketing concepts, with reference to the production concept, product concept, selling concept and societal marketing concept.

Figure 2.2.1 *The Ford Motor Company, operating in the early 20th century, focused on marketing standard black motor cars at affordable prices to families across the US*

Did you know?

The view that the 'customer knows best' was adopted by the Ford Motor Company in the US in the early 20th century. The company produced standard black Model T Fords using mass production techniques. Millions of these cars rolled off the production line.

What are marketing concepts?

Marketing concepts are views that companies have about the purpose of marketing. Five concepts shape the way in which different companies build relationships with their customers:

1 the production concept, focusing on producing inexpensive products for customers

2 the product concept, focusing on increasing the quality of products and building in more features and value-added aspects

3 the selling concept, focusing on the sales effort to persuade customers to buy more of the product

4 the marketing concept (outlined in 2.1), which involves interacting with customers to find out what they want

5 the societal marketing concept, which seeks not only to meet customers' needs, but also to take an ethical approach to meeting the needs of wider society.

The production concept

The production concept assumes that the producer knows best what customers want – they want products to be readily available and affordable. The benefit of the production concept is that it encourages large-scale, low-cost manufacturing. It can be successful where buyers are price conscious. For example, many people in the Caribbean, and elsewhere, like to use inexpensive biros and shave with disposable razors. They are content with a functional product at a low price. The French company Bic produces millions of cheap biros and razors, sold as low-cost items all over the world.

The product concept

The focus of the product concept is also on the production side – to produce goods that customers want. The product concept, however, focuses more on high-quality, innovative features and performance. Companies that use the product concept continually seek to develop products that are superior to those of their competitors.

Motor car manufacturers constantly strive to develop new features and gadgets, as well as to improve fuel efficiency and the look and driveability of their vehicles.

The main advantage of the product concept is that companies can develop a strong reputation for producing top-quality products and products that continually improve. The key weakness is that it focuses more on what the company wants and can produce than on the needs and wishes of customers.

The selling concept

The selling concept emphasises sales efforts. Companies may focus on selling if they think that products will not sell without support. They use advertising and promotion to raise the profile of their brand and products.

The main advantage of the selling concept is that it provides support for products that might be less visible to the public. It is particularly useful for selling new products or when a firm has unsold stocks.

The key weaknesses are that applying this concept may temporarily hide weaknesses in the product, and that it leads to a focus on what the company has to sell rather than on what the customer wants to buy.

Red Bull's selling concept

A classic example of the selling concept is the energy drink Red Bull. On a global level, the makers of Red Bull promote the brand at globally-screened sports events, through ownership of a Formula 1 racing team and football teams such as the New York Red Bulls. The company seeks to keep the brand in the public eye by creating international events in sports that

include windsurfing and cliff diving. It also promotes the brand through creating music events such as competitions for DJs in larger territories such as Trinidad and Jamaica.

1 Why do you think Red Bull spends so much money on advertising and promotion?

2 Why do you think the company selects sporting activities and music events to promote itself in the Caribbean?

The marketing concept

The marketing concept is examined separately in 2.3. Its key focus is identifying what the customer wants and needs, using market research.

The societal marketing concept

Societal marketing builds on the marketing concept of taking into account the wishes of consumers. Societal marketers also take an ethical stance that is good for society as a whole. They seek to identify not only what customers require, but also how the company and its products can be good for the wider society. Societal marketing seeks to balance customer satisfaction, the interests of other stakeholders and company profit.

A related approach is **cause-related marketing**. Here a company combines its advertising and promotional activity with a good cause: for example, donating a percentage of its revenue to a designated charity.

The benefits of societal marketing are the intrinsic worth of an ethical approach, and that the company is perceived to be doing the right things for society, which should enhance its brand reputation and sales. Disadvantages of societal marketing are that it may be regarded with suspicion and that it increases company costs.

Summary table

Marketing concept	Description and focus
Production	Producing low-cost/available products
Product	Producing better-quality products and products that improve over time
Selling	Selling activity (e.g. advertising and promotion) to support sales
Marketing	Seeking to identify customer requirements and then meet them
Societal marketing	Meeting wider needs of society using an ethical approach

KEY TERMS

Cause-related marketing: a joint funding and promotional strategy by a company and a charity or good cause, in which a percentage of sales revenue is donated to the charity.

Did you know?

One aspect of societal marketing is making sure that advertising and promotion are not misleading or unethical.

Summary questions

1 Why might a company that uses a production/product or selling approach find it more difficult to make sales than one using the marketing concept?

2 Why might smaller companies find it more difficult than larger companies to engage in societal marketing?

On completion of this section, you should be able to:

- assess the implications of the marketing concept.

The marketing concept: a company's approach

Marketing is a management process that identifies, anticipates and satisfies customer requirements profitably. The emphasis in the marketing concept is on findin1g out about customers and understanding their needs and requirements. Most companies that are successful focus on this marketing concept: if a company loses touch with the marketing concept, it may well lose customers – and sales.

The following extract sets out the marketing approach of an international pet-food manufacturer:

> Constantly striving to identify our customers' needs, we aim to go beyond satisfying pets and their owners. To achieve this we carry out thorough research of the multiple requirements of consumers. We understand that we need to convince consumers that our product is the best, and that to do this we must provide what they would truly like to see in our products. Our market research enables us to put their needs first and produce pet food that surpasses that of our competitors.

This statement tells us that the company engages in markct research to identify customer requirements in order to produce desirable products. The company is then able to provide products that appeal to consumers – in this instance, pets and their owners. The company is confident that it can provide products that are superior to those of its competitors.

The role of marketing

Businesses would not exist without customers. It is essential, therefore, to find out what customers want and need. A business then needs to satisfy these needs by providing what can be remembered as the four Ps:

- Product – the right goods and services
- Price – at the right price
- Place – where customers want them
- Promotion – by providing the right sort of encouragement.

The four Ps summarise the role of marketing and the marketing department in a company: anticipating and identifying consumer wants and needs, and then planning the means to meet these requirements.

Figure 2.3.2 provides an overview of the key elements of marketing. It shows that a company with a marketing orientation (focus on marketing) carries out a **marketing audit** to identify what it currently does well (or badly) and to identify new opportunities that are opening up. It carries out market research into what customers want, and uses this information to design a marketing mix to persuade customers to buy its products.

KEY TERMS

Marketing audit: a comprehensive, systematic evaluation by a company of its current marketing activities and markets.

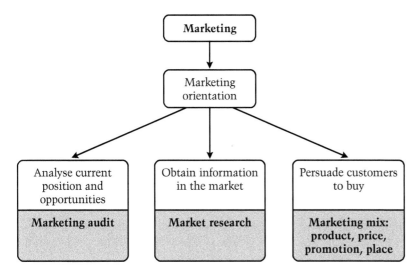

Figure 2.3.2 *The key elements of marketing*

Focus on customers

The following statements have been made by managers of companies.

Ethics lies at the heart of our marketing process. We seek to provide beauty products that people tell us they see as being good for them, for others with whom they interact and for the environment.

The key to our success lies in telling customers about our excellent luxury hotel facilities. We know that we are the best in Jamaica and seek through strong promotional messages to convince thousands of customers that this is the best place to stay for all their holiday needs.

We are the most efficient mass producer of canned drinks in the Caribbean. By producing large quantities of canned products we are able to benefit customers through the low prices that we charge to them.

Our unique selling point is the high quality of the wind turbines that we manufacture. The detailed specifications and attention to technology are what separate us from other manufacturers.

We are a successful company because we engage in painstaking market research. Through detailed research with our customers we are able to find out exactly what they want and then provide them with the benefits for which they are looking.

1 Identify what approach to marketing is being employed in each one – production, product, marketing, selling or societal marketing

2 Which of these approaches do you think are likely to be the most successful and why?

Summary table

What is the marketing concept?	A focus on anticipating, identifying and meeting customer requirements at a profit.
What is the implication of the marketing concept for consumers?	Suppliers in the exchange process focus on meeting their needs and requirements.
What is the implication of the marketing concept for suppliers?	To be successful they need to meet the needs and requirements of customers (e.g. by applying an appropriate marketing mix).

Summary questions

1 What advantages does the use of the marketing concept have for businesses operating in the Caribbean?

2 What businesses are you familiar with that appear to pay particularly close attention to your requirements? What marketing activities do they engage in to achieve this?

The macro- and micro-environment

Marketers and businesses interact with a macro- (wider) and micro- (closer) environment. The macro-environment consists of elements that are outside the control of the marketing department. In contrast, the department can influence the components of the micro-environment.

The micro-environment

The micro-environment consists of individuals and organisations that are close to the company. The activities of these organisations impact on the customer experience for customers of a specific firm.

Think about a fish restaurant: which organisations impact on the customer experience? First, what sorts of facilities does the organisation (sometimes referred to as the 'internal environment') have? How extensive a menu does it offer? What about the quality of its staff – are they helpful and polite when serving customers? The customers are also part of the micro-environment: the business interacts with them every day and good customer management is important.

Next, there are the suppliers of produce to the restaurant: for example, the suppliers of fresh fish and the accompaniments, or the laundry cleaning the tablecloths and napkins in the restaurant.

There are also organisations that carry out marketing activities for the restaurant: for example, market research companies identifying what customers want, or advertising agencies that help the restaurant to produce advertising material.

The media can also be seen as part of the micro-environment. The fish restaurant can try to win support from food critics who work for newspapers and report on the quality of different restaurants.

Finally, the organisation interacts with the wider public: this includes anyone else who interacts with the restaurant, such as householders and businesses nearby. For example, are they adversely affected by people parking outside the restaurant or making a noise at night?

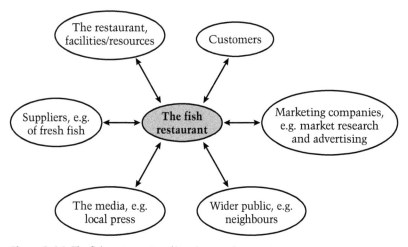

Figure 2.4.1 *The fish restaurant and its micro-environment*

Competitors

Some business writers believe that competitors should be included in the micro-environment. This is because by developing strategies to beat the competition, a company can be said to have some control over competition. The fish restaurant might show this control by offering fresher fish and a better service than its nearest rivals.

By analysing competitors and checking on what they are doing, it is possible to develop a competitive **marketing strategy** to beat the competition. In this way, a company develops a unique selling point (USP), which differentiates it from its rivals.

How the micro-environment impacts on marketing strategy

Every organisation has a set of goals that it wants to achieve. These might include becoming the best fish restaurant in Barbados, or the most popular fish restaurant in Grenada. An understanding of the micro-environment helps an organisation to devise a marketing strategy to achieve these goals. Remember that marketing is all about finding out what customers want and giving them the best possible customer experience.

Companies therefore need to focus on the key components of the micro-environment and consider how they can enhance the marketing mix. Table 2.4.1 shows an effective strategy for improving the customer experience at a fish restaurant: by engaging with stakeholders in the micro-environment, a company is best placed to improve the customer experience and hence the sales and profitability of the business.

Table 2.4.1 Strategy for improving customer experience at a fish restaurant

Customers	Find out what type of product experience they want (e.g. varieties of fish, side dishes and quality of service). Marketers can find this through market research.
Suppliers	Deal with the fishermen and other suppliers who supply the best-quality and freshest fish and vegetables, fruit and so on.
Restaurant facilities (internal environment)	Make sure that these match with market research findings. Build relationships with customers. Carry out regular reviews to identify customer feedback on the dining experience.
Marketers	Engage with professional market research companies to research the fish restaurant market. Use suitable advertising and promotions.
The media	Engage with food critics. Place advertisements in relevant periodicals that feature dining out.
Wider public	Talk to neighbours. Find out about their concerns.

Summary table

The difference between the micro- and macro-environment	The micro-environment involves people and organisations that the company deals with regularly in relation to the customer experience. Marketing can influence the micro-environment. The macro-environment involves factors over which the company has little control.
How the micro-environment impacts on marketing strategy	A company can build close relationships with organisations in the micro-environment to improve the customer experience. This will help to improve the marketing mix: for example, better-quality supplies (product) and superior advertising (promotion).

Summary questions

1   Identify a local business with which you are familiar. Who makes up the micro-environment for that business?

2   How does your chosen business seek to work with organisations in the micro-environment to influence the customer experience?

Specific objectives

On completion of this section, you should be able to:

- understand the forces in the macro-environment

- understand the effect of the macro-environment on the marketing strategy of the firm.

Figure 2.5.1 *External factors may have a significant impact on the choice of dish a fish restaurant chooses to sell*

KEY TERMS

Scanning the environment: the process of examining and researching the macro-environment in order to identify changes that are taking place and develop a strategic response.

The macro-environment

The macro-environment consists of influences, or factors, in the external environment of a business, over which it has little or no control. Table 2.5.1 summarises these factors, continuing the example of a fish restaurant introduced in 2.4.

Table 2.5.1 *Factors in the external environment of a business*

Political factors	These are government influences that impact on the market in which the business operates. The government may establish rules about which fish may be caught by fishermen in the Caribbean, and this in turn affects which products can be offered.
Economic factors	These relate to how quickly an economy is growing, which in turn impacts on living standards and spending patterns. When the economy is growing, consumers may be able to afford more expensive varieties of fish (affecting both price and product).
Social factors	A range of social/cultural and religious factors impact on what customers prefer to buy. Some types of fish preparation are seen as more healthy (for example, steamed compared to battered fish). Some people may be vegetarian and prefer not to eat fish (again impacting on the product and also influencing the promotion and advertising). Cultural and religious factors often determine which foods people will eat and some foods are forbidden.
Technological factors	Changes in technology impact on all businesses. The development of new ways of cooking fish impacts on costs and the time required to prepare, which in turn impact on price and product.
Legal factors	These overlap with political factors and relate to laws impacting on business.
Environmental (natural) factors	These are very important in the Caribbean (and elsewhere in the world). It is essential for food preparation businesses to show that they are using resources wisely (for example, respecting maintenance of fish stocks).
Demographic factors	These are part of changing social patterns. The most important demographic factor is changes in the age structure of the population. If there are more people, demand for all goods, including fish, increases. There may be demand for certain products (for example, some types of fish may be preferred by older people).

Scanning the environment

Through **scanning the environment** a company is able to identify opportunities and threats to its marketing activities. It may do this by various analyses, including SWOT, PESTLE (see Unit 1) and an analysis of its competitors.

SWOT analysis

The acronym SWOT refers to strengths, weaknesses, opportunities and threats. SWOT analysis can be used to examine how well the business fits into its environment and to build a strategy for dealing with external changes.

- **Strengths** are internal to an organisation and typically relate to its resources and competencies (the things it does well). One strength might be a strong marketing department that uses the marketing concept.
- **Weaknesses** are internal and relate to lack of experience, poor management and insufficient resources.
- **Opportunities** are external to the organisation (therefore relating to the macro-environment). Opportunities usually relate to the development of new products, new markets and new technologies.
- **Threats** are external and usually relate to competition and changes in any of the PESTLE factors.

Strategies for the macro-environment

Having conducted a SWOT analysis, a company needs to develop marketing strategies for the macro-environment. Typically, these strategies relate to adjusting the marketing mix to deal with opportunities and threats:

- **Product strategies:** develop new products, improve existing products, sell in new markets, use new technologies and adapt products to comply with new legislation.
- **Pricing strategies:** reduce prices below those of competitors, or increase them to emphasise the quality of the product.
- **Promotional strategies:** increase advertising and other promotional activities.
- **Place strategies:** change where the product is sold and how it is distributed.

Did you know?

The acronym PESTLE (or PESTLE analysis) describes the process of scanning the macro-environment to identify political, economic, social, technical, legal and environmental changes. It should be coupled with a competitor analysis.

Did you know?

A competitor analysis involves researching what the competition is doing and then using this to form a view of the strengths and weaknesses of competitors. This helps a business to improve its own competitive position.

☑ *Exam tip*

When conducting a SWOT analysis, remember that the strengths and weaknesses are internal to the business while the opportunities and threats relate to the external environment (including the actions of competitors).

Summary table

The **macro-environment** consists of factors that are external to the business.
A **PESTLE analysis**, coupled with a competitor analysis, can be used to scan the macro-environment.
A **SWOT analysis** helps an organisation to develop a strategy to cope with changes in the macro-environment.
Product, pricing, place and promotional strategies can be used to align marketing in a company with changes in the external environment.

Summary questions

1 The telecoms market, particularly the market for smartphones, is growing rapidly in the Caribbean. What challenges would a supplier of smartphones to this market face as a result of the macro-marketing environment?

2 What strategies could the supplier employ to manage these challenges?

KEY TERMS

Target market: a specific group of customers who are the focus of marketing efforts.

 Exam tip

A simpler definition of market research that is easy to remember is: 'keeping those who provide goods and services in touch with the requirements of those who buy them'.

Market research is the systematic gathering, recording and analysis of data to identify the best solution in marketing of goods and services. This definition can be broken down as follows:

- **Systematic:** research is carried out in a careful and organised way.
- **Gathering and recording of data:** data are collected and set down in writing or (more likely) recorded electronically on a computer.
- **Analysis of data:** data are analysed to identify patterns and trends.
- **Problems relating to marketing:** these include what price to charge, how best to advertise the goods and services, and where to sell them.

Why carry out market research?

Market research provides an organisation with information so that it can have a deeper understanding of its business environment, its customers and the nature and attitude of the markets in which it operates. While not eliminating the risks associated with being in business, it helps to reduce them by identifying the **target market**. As a management tool, it serves as an information centre for decision making, providing meaningful information for planning and control and helping to focus organisational activities upon the needs of the customer in the marketplace.

Developing a research plan

A company may carry out market research internally or use an external market research agency. Either approach involves developing a clear market research plan. The plan provides researchers with a clear brief, by outlining what they are required to research, objectives for carrying out the research and a clearly defined time period in which to conduct it. A clear plan enables market researchers to identify suitable methods for collecting and recording information. The plan should also establish the budget for the research.

The starting point is establishing a research brief. For example, it might begin with 'City Drinks believes that there is a market opportunity for a resealable plastic drinks container to replace cans. The company requires a thorough investigation before proceeding to production, pricing and promotion.' The brief would then set out some more details that would provide a focus for the market research. Table 2.6.1 outlines the various

Table 2.6.1 *Stages of planning market research*

1 Research brief	Present market researchers with brief
2 Define the issue	Define problem to be researched
3 Set objectives	Create set of objectives to be achieved
4 Write a research proposal/plan of work	Specify data to be collected, method of collection and timings
5 Collection of data	Gather data
6 Analysis and evaluation	Store data, retrieve, organise and interpret
7 Presentation of the findings	Present findings to a relevant audience (e.g. managers), with conclusions and recommendations
8 Re-evaluate market	What could have been done better? What was missed out?

stages involved in planning market research. These are examined in greater detail in 2.7.

A market research plan needs to be time-related: in other words, end dates need to be established for the stages (as in Table 2.6.2).

Table 2.6.2 Example of a market research plan

Date	By 8 August	By 15 August	By 22 August	By 29 August	By 5 September
Plan research (project manager)	✓				
Create survey for street interviews (market research team)		✓			
Plan focus group research (project manager)			✓		
Conduct street interviews and focus group sessions (interviewers and research team)				✓	
Analyse results of research (all team members)					✓
Present data to client					✓

Limitations of market research

A company should not rely on market research to find all the answers it seeks. Markets change constantly, so that by the time research findings are published, the relevant market might have moved forward. Table 2.6.3 shows the limitations of market research.

Table 2.6.3 Limitations of market research

Reliability	The data may not be reliable for a number of reasons, such as leading questions, interpretation of questions, unrepresentative samples and biased interviewers. Also what consumers say they will do often differs from what they actually do
Budgetary constraints	The more money available for research, the better the results. Less money usually results in less-effective sample sizes and less time to analyse results
Time limitations	Results are often required quickly and there may not be enough time to engage in sufficiently detailed research
Legal and ethical constraints	Some questions cannot be used, or consent may be required of participants to publish their views and opinions

Summary table

What is market research?	A systematic process designed to identify, analyse and record information about a product or market
What are the benefits of planning market research?	■ Provides clarity for the researchers ■ Sets out objectives and deadlines ■ Helps market researchers to identify appropriate methods for carrying out research

Summary questions

1 Set out the stages that you would use to research whether there is a market for a new mobile DJ service in your local area.

2 How is market research different from marketing?

3 What might happen if you failed to make a plan before carrying out market research?

Specific objective

On completion of this section, you should be able to:

- describe the stages of market research, with reference to problem identification, research objectives and sources of data (primary and secondary).

Key stages

There are six stages of market research, covered here and in 2.8–2.11. In outline, the stages are as follows:

1 problem identification by management
2 setting objectives
3 choosing which sources of data to access: primary and/or secondary
4 deciding how to select a sample, including probability and non-probability sampling
5 deciding which research techniques to use, for example focus groups, surveys, interviews and observations
6 analysis and presentation of results.

Problem identification by management

With any form of research, a business needs to begin by identifying what it is that it wants to research. For example, what types of new products or variants on existing products do customers require? How well will a new product, which is about to be launched, be accepted by the market? In establishing a marketing brief, the purpose of the research and what will be researched must be clearly established and set out.

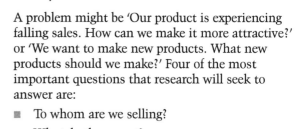

A problem might be 'Our product is experiencing falling sales. How can we make it more attractive?' or 'We want to make new products. What new products should we make?' Four of the most important questions that research will seek to answer are:

- To whom are we selling?
- What do they want?
- When and where do they want it?
- What price are they prepared to pay?

Continuing the example of the company that is considering replacing cans with plastic drinks containers (see 2.6), it is important for management to be clear about the extent of the required research project and what exactly they want to find out. For example, will the plastic drinks container replace all cans, or just cans for some types of drink?

An important aspect of defining the problem is to be clear about the target population at which the research is aimed. In researching the market for plastic drinks containers, will the target be consumers of all types of drinks (for example, iced tea, fizzy drinks and beer) or just specific groups of consumers (for example, a particular age range of fizzy-drink consumers)?

Figure 2.7.1 *Is there a market for plastic drinks containers to replace cans? It is important to define the problem and set clear marketing objectives.*

Setting objectives

Market research projects should have clear objectives, so that there is something to check against when the research has been done and the data have been collected. Having clear objectives also enables regular progress checks. Some objectives that might help the drinks company team are to:

- identify whether there is a market for plastic drinks containers
- identify the purposes for which plastic drinks containers are used
- identify who would make up the market for plastic drinks containers
- identify the percentage of the market that would switch to plastic drinks containers if these were available.

Like other forms of objectives, market research objectives should be SMART:

- Specific in setting out what needs to be researched
- Measurable in terms of what the results should look like
- Assignable to different members of the research team (or Agreed – they can be shared among the people in the team and be accepted by them)
- Realistic (or Relevant), given the budget available for marketing and the size of the company
- Time-related – that is, deliverable within a given time frame.

Choosing the sources of data

The researchers need to decide on the sources of the data to be collected. Data will be **primary** or **secondary data**. They are often a mix of the two.

- Primary data are collected by, for example, questionnaires, interviews or surveys. A time plan for each stage of the collection process should be set out.
- Secondary data are internal: that is, already available within the organisation from customer records or existing research reports.

KEY TERMS

Primary data: data that are collected for the first time by the researcher (e.g. through answers to a questionnaire).

Secondary data: data that are already published (e.g. in the form of existing market research reports).

Summary table

The first three stages of market research	
1	**Problem identification:** establish what the business wants to research and set this out in a market research brief. What key questions should the research seek to answer?
2	**Research objectives:** what does the business want to find out through the research? At the end of the research process, what should have been found out? The research objectives should be specific, measurable and time-related.
3	**Choosing the sources of data:** identifying the best sources (primary/secondary, internal/external) of data related to market characteristics and then using these data to make marketing decisions.

Summary questions

1 You have developed a new toothbrush for children, which plays a song when they clean their teeth. What problems would you want to resolve in designing market research around the new concept?

2 How could you make your objectives SMART for carrying out market research into the new toothbrush?

Specific objective

On completion of this section, you should be able to:

■ describe the stages of market research, with reference to sampling (probability and non-probability).

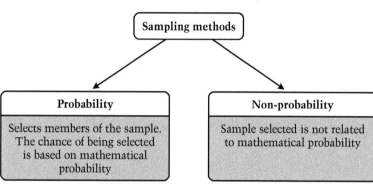

Figure 2.8.1 *Sampling methods*

Did you know?

Another sampling method is **cluster sampling**: the population can be split into clusters of individuals with behaviour or buying patterns similar to the total population. If clusters across the Caribbean have similar purchasing patterns for washing powder, it is reasonable to research a small number of clusters in different countries.

Deciding how to select a sample

Deciding how to select a sample is the fourth stage of market research (see 2.7). Market researchers need to decide how many people to question in their research. Asking everybody in a particular population takes a long time and is costly unless the population is very small. The preferred alternative is to research a representative selection of respondents (people taking part in the survey) from the target market. Figure 2.8.1 outlines two main ways of selecting the sample: probability and non-probability.

The more systematic the sample, the greater the time required to plan and carry out the research. In systematic sampling:

■ the **sampling units** are defined clearly: for example, people who eat red snapper, or members of a local cricket club

■ a **sampling frame** is compiled. This is a list of the sampling units. The sampling frame should be the same as the target population. For example, if the population is 'learning in a particular year in a college', the sampling frame will be the registers (or other lists) showing the names of these learners.

Probability sampling

In probability sampling, the chances of someone being part of the sample can be expressed as a mathematical probability. The main types of probability sampling are described below.

Random sampling

Random sampling includes the whole population in the sampling frame: for example, everyone who is male and over the age of 30. Everyone in this category has an equal chance of being picked out.

Systematic random sampling

This method requires a list of all of the members in a particular population: for example, women living in Kingston whose names are listed on the electoral register (those who have registered to vote). You would then select everyone at a set interval on this list: for example, every tenth female person listed.

Stratified sampling

Stratified sampling takes into account the proportions of different groups in the population. For example, about 50 per cent of the population is female, so a stratified sample would be made up of half women and half men. Other factors can be used, such as age ranges, or people living in rural or urban areas.

Multi-stage sampling

This develops a sample in different stages. For example, to sample radio listeners across the Caribbean, you would first take a sample of geographical locations, such as St Kitts and Nevis, Grenada or Trinidad. A sample of households in each area would then be taken. This should yield reasonably accurate results, but is time consuming and costly to set up.

Non-probability sampling

Probability sampling can be costly both in planning and in carrying out the research. Non-probability methods, which can save time and money, are outlined below.

Quota sampling

The population is divided into groups by, for example age, sex and income level. The interviewer is told how many people to interview in each group. This approach is widely used in street interviews in shopping areas. It is quick and uncomplicated, and any member of the sample can be replaced by another with similar characteristics. However, it is not random and there is a possibility of bias: for example, the interviewer may choose people who look likely to be cooperative.

Judgement sampling

Researchers choose respondents they think most likely to represent the views and choices of the target population. The success of this approach depends on the experience of the researcher.

Convenience sampling

The most convenient sample is chosen, regardless of their characteristics: for example, people walking through a shopping centre. This method is easy and cheap to use, but the results are not particularly reliable.

Observation

The researcher watches people to see, for example, what shoppers buy in a supermarket. The advantage is the focus on what people do rather than on what they *say* they do. It is expensive, however, and takes a lot of time.

Focus groups

A small group of consumers are brought together to focus on a particular issue, such as discussing a product or advertisement. This can be costly to set up and the group may not be representative because it is likely to consist of people with the most time to take part. Focus groups can, however, find out rich data about people's views and opinions.

> ☑ *Exam tip*
>
> Remember that in non-probability sampling the selection of data subjects (e.g. who to interview) is based on factors other than mathematical probability.

Summary table

Sampling: stage 4 of market research		
Ways of sampling	**Strengths**	**Weaknesses**
Probability sampling (random, systematic random, stratified, multi-stage)	Systematic sampling	Takes time to set up and run, and to analyse results
Non-probability sampling (quota, judgement, convenience, observation, focus groups)	Easy to set up and run	Results are less reliable than for probability sampling

Summary questions

You have been given a research brief by the marketing department of your educational institute to identify new courses that learners would like to see being offered at CAPE level.

1 How would you select an appropriate sample to carry out this research?

2 What are the benefits and drawbacks of the sampling method that you have chosen?

Deciding what research techniques to use

The fifth stage of market research is deciding which research techniques to use. This section will consider primary research techniques, while 2.10 will focus on secondary techniques.

Primary research techniques

Information that an organisation collects from its own research is called 'primary' research. There are several techniques for carrying this out.

Observation

The main advantage of observation is that the researcher can watch specific behaviour directly, such as customers shopping. The observer can identify how long customers spend in particular aisles of a supermarket and which products they look at. This can provide useful information about, for example, the best layout, the most tempting displays and what offers might be made.

Focus groups

In a focus group, actual or potential customers are brought together for a focused discussion on a particular product or consumer issue. This generates 'rich' information rather than standard responses. The group usually ranges from about five to 15 members. The structure depends on whether the market researchers want to explore specific themes or take a more open-ended approach that generates some new ideas.

One method is to use a set of cue cards containing topics or suggestions for discussion. Researchers watch the focus group interacting and note such things as language used when talking about a product, or views about the product.

Surveys

A **survey** is a detailed study on a market research topic, often involving a large number of respondents and usually including **questionnaires**. There are several different types:

- **Face to face:** this is probably the most effective form of survey, allowing two-way communication between the researcher and the respondents. Experienced researchers may find out more detailed and sensitive information, and can note gestures, facial and other expressions.

- **Postal:** postal surveys are cheap to administer, and can be used in a wide geographic area. Answers may, however, not be representative as **response rates** can be low (10 per cent or less) if the reader thinks the survey is too long or irrelevant, or the topic is uninteresting. Postal questionnaires should be brief, and sent only to those for whom they are directly relevant.

- **Telephone:** telephone surveys can be useful and cost-effective for businesses as a way of catching respondents who are otherwise unavailable. However, calling people unprepared in their homes can be intrusive and lead to negative views. Key benefits are geographical coverage and a relatively high response rate (compared with postal and face to face).

■ **Email and m-mail:** This involves delivering a survey to a computer or mobile phone email address. This can be effective when the questionnaire relates to an interest of the recipient. It may be easy to complete the survey on the keypad when the recipient has nothing else to do.

Among the drawbacks of this approach are not just the time and cost required to create a suitable questionnaire but the knowledge and skills required to construct a survey, administer it and correctly interpret the results to obtain valid information may be lacking. Also, surveys involving the general public, even under the best of conditions, may not provide valid information because of irrational behavior patterns (for example consumers can be influenced by a high pressure sales pitch).

Interviews

While a questionnaire is usually based on relatively closed answers, an interview allows for more flexibility and may be structured, semi-structured or unstructured.

■ A structured interview involves the use of pre-set questions. This makes it possible to compare the answers of different respondents.

■ A semi-structured interview includes a number of structured questions, but the interviewer or interviewee may deviate from the script to elaborate on questions or answers, revealing more insightful details and richer data.

■ An unstructured interview has no script and the interview develops depending on the answers given by the respondent and the direction in which the interviewer wants to take the interview.

While a question such as 'Which of the iowing supermarkets in Trinidad do you use for regular shopping (that is, once or more a week)?' might yield quantitative information, it would not reveal *why* customers prefer one supermarket over another. The personal and flexible nature of an interview can reveal this richer data. However, interviews are costly: they take time to organise and the data are more difficult to record and analyse. The analysis can also lead to a biased interpretation.

Did you know?

Many mobile phone and computer users are suffering from 'survey fatigue': they receive so many surveys that they are reluctant to spend time on them.

Did you know?

Leading questions should be avoided in questionnaires and interviews. A question such as 'Many people think that Brand A is the best brand – do you agree with this view?' suggests a particular answer.

Summary questions

1   Choose a local shop with which you are familiar and imagine that you need to find out customers' views of the service offered there. Identify the methods of carrying out primary research. Compare the benefits and drawbacks of each method.

2   In what situations is an interview likely to be more effective than a questionnaire? In what situations would a questionnaire be more effective than an interview?

Summary table

Research techniques: stage 5 of market research			
Primary techniques	Description	Benefits	Drawbacks
Observation	Watching how those being researched act or behave	Focuses on what they do rather than what they say they do	Open to interpretation about what was observed Time consuming
Focus groups	Bringing together a small group to focus on discussing an issue	Allows for in-depth discussion, providing rich information	Costly to set up Availability of participants may lead to a biased sample
Surveys	Detailed in-depth study, often using questionnaires	Possible to gather quantitative data from a large number of respondents	Takes a long time to set up with cost implications May have a relatively low response rate
Interviews	Personal discussion with respondent to find more detailed information	More in-depth and yields richer information than surveys	Typically involves only a relatively small number of respondents Subject to bias in questions and answers

Stages of market research 4: secondary research techniques

Specific objective

Specific objective

On completion of this section, you should be able to:

- describe the stages of market research, with reference to secondary research techniques.

KEY TERMS

Databases: stores of data gathered for particular purposes. Today they usually refer to computer programs designed for the storage of data.

Did you know?

A cookie is a small file that a web server places on a computer so that it can identify who has been browsing. The next time the site is visited, the web server will recognise that the computer is calling again.

Secondary research uses existing information rather than finding out new facts. There are two main sources:

- **internal sources:** information that already exists within a business
- **external sources:** information published by other organisations.

Internal sources

Businesses have a variety of information about their market available to them. This information is often collected for purposes other than market research.

Data records

Organisations maintain a range of information, such as sales records, in their **databases**. When the bar code is scanned at the electronic point-of-sale terminal, information is passed to a back-office computer which records what has been sold. These data can reveal:

- who the existing customers are
- where they live
- how much they spend
- how often they make purchases.

This information from its customers helps the company to analyse customer wants and needs, and respond to changing patterns of demand.

Website monitoring

It is essential for companies with an online presence to keep a record of users who have shown an interest in their website and the goods and services it offers. Most websites log visits, recording details about visitors such as the pages requested and how long the visitor browses for.

E-transactions

Electronic transactions provide much useful secondary information for businesses. The seller can see:

- who bought the items
- how much they spent
- how frequently they purchased.

Another aspect of online market research beneficial to businesses is that users voluntarily submit further details, which can be stored in a database referenced against the browser's 'cookie'. Website providers seek to gather information about the email addresses of customers, so that they can communicate directly with them.

Sales records and sales personnel

People who work in a company's sales department are very knowledgeable about customers' buying behaviour. A company's sales records provide invaluable customer information about who is buying, in what quantities and at what times.

External sources

Many businesses use existing published research. This can save a lot of time and effort, but can be expensive. Cheaper sources include the internet and government publications.

Internet

The internet is the most accessible source of information. Search engines usually rank results according to their relevance, validity or how frequently they are searched for. When you carry out a search, such as 'market trends in rice', you are likely to find very recent information that is valued by other researchers.

Government statistics

Governments regularly analyse business trends and changes taking place in the economy. The information is published in reference books and journals as well as online. Caribbean governments' statistics are networked through the Caribbean Community Regional Statistics Department.

Libraries and universities

A library is a good starting point to search for secondary data, with relevant books and journals located in the business section, as well as market research reports, telephone directories and newspapers.

Company reports

A company report typically includes an outline of current market trends in the area in which it operates. So a researcher looking at trends in the household goods market would find it helpful to study the most recent report of the US multinational Procter & Gamble.

Market research reports

Reports on markets and products by market research companies can give a good idea of trends. Several specialist market research agencies in the Caribbean provide high-quality information: Caribbean Market Research Ltd provides a range of industry and country reports, and the Caribbean Tourism Organization produces tourism-related research information.

Did you know?

Individual countries provide their own statistics, which are useful for anyone wanting to explore marketing potential. The St Lucia Government Statistics Department provides readily available statistics about, for example, size of population, growth of national income and inflation rates. The Barbados Statistical Service provides detailed figures in areas of interest to marketers, such as employment statistics and monthly tourist arrivals.

Summary table

Research techniques: stage 5 of market research			
Secondary techniques			
Internal sources		*External sources*	
Data records	Databases provide information about who customers are and what they are buying	Internet	An accessible source, with recent information
Website monitoring	Using cookies to log visits from viewers	Government statistics	Likely to be detailed and accurate, focusing on economic and other data
E-transactions	Show who is buying, how much they spend and when	Libraries and universities	Provide access to reference books and journals, usually up to date
Sales	Businesses record purchases made by customers, and sales staff know who the customers are and what influences their purchasing patterns	Company reports	An accessible source, with recent information
		Market research reports	Provides information on markets and products to give an idea of trends

Summary questions

1 A hotel chain in Barbados is considering expanding its existing scale of operations in the territory. What sources could the chain use to help it decide if this would be beneficial?

2 Which market research sources are best at identifying who customers are and how they are spending their money?

2.11 Stages of market research 5: presentation of results

Specific objective

On completion of this section, you should be able to:

■ describe the stages of market research, with reference to analysis and presentation of results.

KEY TERMS

Analysis: making a detailed examination of the results of research, in order to find patterns and structures.

Analysis

Once data have been collected, they need **analysis**: that is, they need to be organised to show meaningful patterns. For example, analysis of primary research among the potential users of plastic drinks containers might reveal the following pattern of results:

▤ the percentage of those who stated that they would purchase the new containers

▤ the use they would have for the containers

▤ how much would they be prepared to pay for them

▤ how often they would purchase them.

Presentation of findings

The data can be presented in charts, tables and graphs. They should be set out clearly to back up any recommendations made by the researchers.

CASE STUDY

Tourism spending in the Caribbean

The graph opposite, provided by the Caribbean Tourism Organization, indicates changes in the number of tourists arriving in the Caribbean and the amount that they spent in the years 2002–10 (compared with a base figure of 100 in 2000).

1 What are the main things that you notice from studying Figure 2.11.1?

2 What are the implications for companies in the Caribbean?

3 Why is a time-series line graph like the one shown here a suitable method for illustrating this information?

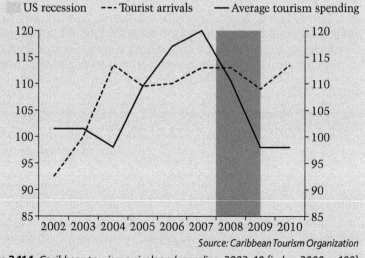

Source: Caribbean Tourism Organization

Figure 2.11.1 *Caribbean tourism arrivals and spending, 2002–10 (index: 2000 = 100)*

Did you know?

The following method can be used to convert the relevant proportion to degrees for a pie chart:

$$\text{number of degrees} = \frac{\text{proportion}}{\text{total}} \times 360$$

For example, if we know that Blue Mountain accounts for 50% of coffee sales in a particular area, we will record this as:

$$\frac{50}{100} \times 360 = 180 \text{ degrees}$$
(half of the pie)

Different techniques can be used to illustrate market research information.

Line graphs

Line graphs illustrate changing trends and patterns over time, such as rises and falls in consumer spending and sales. Time is shown along the horizontal axis; variables, such as spending, are on the vertical axis.

Pie charts

Pie charts illustrate percentages and segments of opinion. They might show the market share of a product or the percentage of people who answered 'yes' or 'no' to a dichotomous question (one that has two possible answers). Each 'slice' represents a component contribution to the total amount. The pie must total 360 degrees.

Bar charts

Bar charts can show, for example, sales values of several different items (for comparison), consumption of different types of product, awareness of an advert or growth over time. The bars representing the areas of comparison can be vertical or horizontal. The length of the bar gives a clear indication of the relative importance of the data.

Frequency curves

Frequency curves can be drawn by constructing a **histogram**, marking off the mid-point of the top of each rectangle and then joining the mid-points together. They can illustrate the **frequency** with which customers spend different sums of money in a shop, or the frequency of responses in particular ranges of answers.

Market research report

A market research report is produced for a target audience – usually the client who has commissioned the report. A typical format for presentation is:

1 Title page – setting out the title of the research and the name of client, as well as the name of the research organisation and the date presented.
2 Contents – a numbered guide to sections.
3 Research brief – an outline of the research requested.
4 Objectives – a summary of the market research objectives.
5 Summary of conclusions and recommendations.
6 Methods employed – the research techniques used.
7 Findings – key findings using charts and tables.
8 Conclusions/recommendations (more detailed than 5 above).
9 Appendices – supporting materials that are cross-referenced in the Findings section.

Limitations of market research

As you saw in 2.6 there are a number of limitations to market research. These should be taken into account when analysing and presenting the findings.

Summary table

Analysis and presentation of results: stage 6 of market research
■ Analyse results: organise the data collected in a structured way.
■ Present findings in visuals: using line graphs, bar charts, pie charts, etc.
■ Create a structured report: set out a market research report – from brief, down to findings and recommendations.

Summary questions

1 What methods would you use to present the following?
  a Tourism statistics showing tourist numbers to your territory
  b The proportions of respondents to a market research survey showing buying preferences for different types of car
  c The relative market size of different supermarket chains in a territory

Specific objectives

On completion of this section, you should be able to:

- assess the principles of market segmentation
- understand the importance of segmentation
- define target, niche and mass marketing.

KEY TERMS

Market segment: a large, identifiable group within a market, with similar wants, purchasing power, geographical location, buying attitudes or buying habits.

What is market segmentation?

Markets can be divided into **market segments**. Marketers use the analogy of an orange with separate segments that make up the total. Unlike an orange, however, the size and composition of market segments are different: each segment has its own distinct profile which is defined in terms of a number of criteria, referred to as bases or variables.

CASE STUDY

The car market

Many people want to buy cars. However, they have different ideas about the car they are looking for, so the market can be split into segments; for example:

- **Basic transportation:** these buyers are looking for a car that will get them from their starting point to their destination – they are quite happy to buy a cheap car with 'no frills attached'.
- **High-performance driving:** these buyers want high-specification models with all the latest features.
- **Family driving:** these buyers are conscious that they have a family that needs transporting together – to school, for outings, religious festivals, etc. Safety is a key consideration.
- **Luxury driving:** these buyers want to stand out from the crowd, having a car fitted out with luxurious features and extras, and which draws admiration.

1 Can you identify any other segments of the car market?

2 How does segmentation help car salespeople and companies marketing cars?

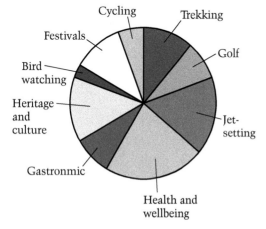

Figure 2.12.1 *All markets can be split up into segments, each containing buyers with common characteristics that are different from buyers in other segments. The diagram here shows how tourism might be divided into niche markets.*

Importance of segmentation

Segmentation facilitates the development of a marketing mix which satisfies the requirements of different groups of customers. It can be contrasted with market aggregation (also known as mass marketing (see p87) and undifferentiated marketing) where a single marketing mix is developed for an entire market. Segmentation helps an organisation to identify marketing opportunities such as market development, for example developing existing products in segments identified in new markets. Segmentation also enables an organisation to develop a better understanding of customer needs and requirements. An organisation can therefore make fine adjustments to the marketing mix of each segment, enabling it to respond more swiftly to any changes in the marketplace. Segmentation also allows resources to be used more efficiently. For instance, the efficiency of activities is likely to improve when they are focused on those sectors most likely to respond to such activities.

Limitations of segmentation may occur in trying to serve too many segments at a time which can be expensive, especially in terms of marketing. Also, when segments get smaller and smaller, this can lead to production and cost problems for the business.

Approaches to segmentation

Target markets

You read in 2.6 about the need for a business to aim its marketing efforts and its products at a target market. Target markets are made up of groups of individuals with similar characteristics. In 2.13 and 2.14 we examine some of the ways of identifying targeted segments based on the characteristics of the consumers in those segments.

Niche markets

A **niche market** is a distinct, targetable portion of an overall market. It may be chosen as a focus by a business seeking to address the needs of customer groups that are currently poorly met, or not met at all. Suppliers of niche markets might be vegetarian food producers, or suppliers of specialist activity holidays.

Niche markets enable smaller firms and specialists to develop, as there may be less competition and in some instances relatively high prices can be charged. The target customer is also clearly defined.

Disadvantages of niche markets include the smaller market scale and the fact that, where competition exists, profits may be low or non-existent. The niche marketer uses specialist marketing channels, such as specialist magazines and websites with links to products and services in which specific customers are interested. It can, however, be challenging to reach the target customer.

Mass markets

In a **mass market**, marketers ignore segmentation to try to appeal to the whole market with a single offer to all segments. Typically, mass marketers use marketing techniques that appeal to a wide audience: for example, advertisements on television or radio or in newspapers, or on websites with mass appeal. By communicating with a mass audience, a mass marketer is able to produce in bulk and typically sell at cheaper prices than products offered by niche markets.

The benefits of mass marketing are that:
- it is targeted at a wide audience
- risks are spread over a range of market segments
- mass marketing leads to higher sales and potentially higher profits
- the mass sales that result enable lower-cost production
- scale helps to reduce unit costs of market research and advertising.

Summary table

Niche marketing	Focuses marketing activity on one segment of the overall market	■ More focus on needs of customers ■ Product offering is easier for customers to understand ■ Gains loyal customers
Mass marketing	Focuses marketing activity on many segments of the overall market	■ Appeals to more customers ■ Enables mass marketing media to be employed ■ Spreads marketing and other costs over larger sales volumes

Did you know?

Mass marketers include some of the largest producers of household products such as Procter & Gamble, Coca-Cola, PepsiCo, Heinz and Nestlé.

Did you know?

Fast-food restaurants typically target a mass market, whereas health-food restaurants focus more on a niche market.

Summary questions

1 Can you identify markets in which there is a mix of mass marketers and niche marketers? What are the main differences in the marketers' approaches to these markets?

2 How is the targeting of customers different between mass marketers and niche marketers?

Specific objective

On completion of this section, you should be able to:

- assess the principles of market segmentation, comparing and contrasting demographic and geographic segmentation.

Demographic segmentation

Demographic segmentation separates the market according to information about consumers: for example, their gender, age, family size or income, where they live (rural or urban) or the type of work they do. These factors determine **consumer choices** in many product categories.

Demographic segmentation can be applied to discrete segments. These include age groups in the context of clothes retailing, gender groups for the sale of cosmetics, and family size for different-sized packages of breakfast cereals. Marketers may also segment using **ethnic group** classifications, say for food and music.

Figure 2.13.1 *Extreme sports holidays are targeted at males aged between 20 and 35 years old*

CASE STUDY

Targeting extreme sports enthusiasts

Extreme sports, such as bungee jumping, paragliding, kiteboarding, hang-gliding, caving, white-water rafting and coasteering, are popular on an international scale and there are many opportunities in the Caribbean. The targets are a specific demographic, 20–35-year-old males (although there is some interest from females and older participants). The 'extreme sports market' should be seen as a niche in the wider market of 'adventure sports'. There are some specialist holiday companies operating in this sector and they promote themselves through social networking sites, and niche magazines such as *Kitesurf*.

1 Why is demographic segmentation an appropriate way of identifying target customers in the case of extreme sports?

2 What other sports might require the targeting of a different demographic group?

3 What other examples of demographic segmentation can you identify in the Caribbean tourism industry?

Geographic segmentation

Geographical areas are affected by climate, physical features, population density, different levels of income, different levels of education and cultural differences. By using geographic segmentation it is possible to identify and cater for the customer needs in a specific region. For example, some of the Windward Islands are more exposed to hurricanes and high winds than Barbados, which will impact on the nature of buildings and the demand for building products and storm shelters. Trinidad, Barbados and Jamaica have larger populations than many smaller territories in the region, as well as a higher average income per head, making them more attractive to businesses seeking to sell to larger markets.

Geography also impacts on ethnic and religious differences. Around 25 per cent of the population of Trinidad is affiliated to the Hindu religion, which impacts on food-buying patterns to meet the needs of vegetarians. As with any form of segmentation, the marketer needs to ask, 'Does my product appeal broadly across the Caribbean (that is, is there a mass market?) or do we need to target specific niches in particular geographical locations in the Caribbean?' Even within a country, marketers may need to consider the effect of location, such as urban and rural areas, on their strategy.

A key consideration for marketers is the total population size in a country. On this basis, Cuba, Jamaica and Trinidad and Tobago are more attractive than, say, St Kitts and Nevis which has a relatively smaller market. Table 2.13.1 contrasts the size of population in some Caribbean states.

Did you know?

It is not always the biggest segments that represent the most substantial opportunity. It is important to identify how particular segments relate to the products offered. This helps you to identify whether customers in that segment will buy your product, how much they will be prepared to pay and how often they will make purchases.

Table 2.13.1 Population sizes in some Caribbean states

Country	Population from national statistics (2013)	Type of marketing population size enables
Cuba	11.1 million	Mass marketing and targeting of niche markets
Jamaica	2.7 million	Mass marketing and targeting of niche markets
Trinidad and Tobago	1.3 million	Mass marketing and targeting of niche markets
Bahamas	368,000	Targeting of niche, regional markets
Barbados	276,000	Targeting of niche, regional markets
St Lucia	170,000	Targeting of niche, regional markets
Grenada	103,000	Targeting of niche, regional markets
Antigua	88,000	Targeting of niche, regional markets
Dominica	71,000	Targeting of niche, regional markets
St Kitts and Nevis	55,000	Targeting of niche, regional markets

Summary table

Demographic segmentation	By population characteristic (e.g. sex, age)	Enables accurate targeting of specific groups in the population
Geographic segmentation	By country/region/area	Enables marketer to focus on significant regional populations with targeted marketing

Summary questions

1 Table 2.13.1 shows the relative size and hence market opportunities of Caribbean states. How might this information be useful to marketers using a demographic segmentation approach? What additional information might they require to improve the precision of their targeting?

2 A Caribbean manufacturer produces coffee in several locations. How might it use geographic and demographic segmentation to target its advertising campaigns?

Specific objective

On completion of this section, you should be able to:

- assess the principles of market segmentation, with reference to the purpose and operation of behavioural segmentation.

Did you know?

Some researchers into marketing make an additional distinction between psychographic and behavioural segmentation, although these are closely related. Psychographic segmentation is based on mapping the personal characteristics of potential consumers and grouping similar customers into segments based on lifestyle (active outdoor types, partygoers, etc.) and other characteristics such as social class. Behavioural segmentation focuses more on how consumers behave (e.g. the benefits they seek in purchasing a product, and when and how often they make purchases).

Behavioural segmentation

Segments can also be identified by behaviour patterns: for example, how often people buy a product and how loyal they are. Some people always buy the same brand of coffee, for example, while others compare price and taste before making a choice. People may be loyal to a particular newspaper, such as *The Gleaner*, because of the way it presents the news.

Figure 2.14.1 *There is a variety of newspapers available in the Caribbean but some people buy a particular newspaper every day because they like the way it presents the news.*

Lifestyle segmentation

There are a number of approaches to behavioural segmentation. One of the most widely used is lifestyle segmentation, determined by customer lifestyles. These change as people age: a young single person is likely to have a different lifestyle from a couple with the responsibility of a family.

CASE STUDY

Sagacity lifestyle model

The sagacity lifestyle model segments the market into groups of customers who fit into four main categories, in turn helping to define their purchasing behaviour. The groups are as follows:

1 **Dependent:** including children still living at home with their parents.

2 **Pre-family:** young people with their own household but no children.

3 **Family:** parents with at least one dependent child.

4 **Late:** parents with children who have left home, and older childless couples.

Sagacity lifestyle models differ from demographic segmentation by focusing on behavioural differences in the segments. For example, families purchase family entertainment and products related to children. A pre-family segment might concentrate on buying items for home improvement or for their personal satisfaction.

1 How might a sagacity lifestyle model enable marketers to target marketing communications (for example, advertising) at specific groups of consumers?

2 How would you expect the behaviour of the late group to differ from that of the family group?

3 How is the behaviour of the late group likely to impact on buying decisions?

Other forms of behavioural segmentation

There are several other approaches to behavioural segmentation.

Identifying loyal customers

Identifying the segment of customers who are loyal and make regular purchases helps marketers to focus marketing activity, such as by making promotional offers to this group. Identifying the media channels that appeal to this group is very important.

Identifying occasions

Identifying occasions when people buy products enables marketers to focus marketing activities at these times: for example, florists concentrate on birthdays, weddings, funerals and Christmas. Marketers may try to change customer perceptions about when to buy by promoting new occasions, such as Nurses' Day or Grandparents' Day.

Interests and hobbies

Marketers can reach people who are interested in, say, cricket by advertising in cricket magazines, in television slots, between breaks in cricket games and at the ground itself.

Usage

It is also possible to segment according to product usage: does a consumer use toothpaste three times a day, twice, once or not at all? Usage can be split into categories such as high, medium and low. The key benefit of behavioural segmentation is a focus on actual purchasing behaviour – what people actually do.

Segmentation by income and social class

A final approach to segmentation is by income bracket or social class. Annual income can be categorised: for example, up to $10,000, $10,001–$20,000 and above $20,000. Social class is usually determined by job: the professional class may consist of doctors, lawyers and senior managers, the manual class of plumbers, bricklayers, road diggers and so on.

The key benefit of this type of segmentation is the focus on a key determinant of purchasing behaviour – whether people have sufficient income to make particular types of purchase. Income is often a determinant of what people buy, how often, and how much they spend when the purchases are made.

Summary table

Base for segmentation	Features	Benefits
Behavioural segmentation	Recognises segments by aspects of behaviour	Segments are based on patterns of how consumers act – what they actually do.
Income/class segmentation	Focuses on income bands and social class	Segments are based on a key ingredient that impacts on purchasing – how much available income a consumer has.

Summary questions

1 Marketers are seeking to identify segments to target marketing activity for the following products:

   a perfume

   b sports magazines

   c hearing aids.

   Which of the different approaches to behavioural segmentation do you think would be the most helpful in each case?

2 For what type of product marketing do you think that social class/income segmentation will provide helpful analysis?

Specific objective

On completion of this section, you should be able to:

- assess the principles of market segmentation, with reference to consumer buying behaviour.

What makes people buy?

Finding out what drives consumer buying decisions makes a company well placed to meet consumer needs.

The seven-stage approach

The buying decision can be broken down into seven stages as shown in Table 2.15.1.

Table 2.15.1 *The seven stages of a buying decision*

1	Recognition	A consumer recognises that there is a problem: 'We're running out of breakfast cereal, so we will have to buy some more soon.' Or the consumer recognises an opportunity: 'It's time for the seasonal sales. If we look carefully, we may be able to buy some electrical goods at bargain prices.'
2	Researching	The consumer then searches for information that enables them to make a good buy. He or she may look in catalogues or on websites, or go round several shops comparing prices.
3	Refining and reflecting	The consumer then begins to weigh up the alternatives, refining their thinking and reflecting. He or she weighs up alternatives and rejects solutions that seem less effective. 'Cola costs 45 cents at the cricket stadium, 30 cents in a small shop and 25 cents in a supermarket.'
4	Reaching out	The consumer may 'reach out' and look for the views of other consumers. He or she may look at online forums, and talk to friends about making a purchase.
5	Resolution	The customer then decides whether to buy or not, and where to purchase the item.
6	Purchase	The consumer makes the purchase.
7	Review	The customer then reviews the purchase: 'I thought I was getting a bargain when I bought that television in the discount store. But there's no after-sales service. Next time I may buy from a more expensive shop that does offer this.'

Illustrating the purchasing process

Understanding the consumer purchasing process helps marketers design a suitable response, to win sales. Table 2.15.2 illustrates the model. The left-hand column shows the steps made by the purchaser, while the right-hand column shows actions that the seller can take to 'convince' the purchaser.

Table 2.15.2 *The purchasing process*

Steps		Marketing response
1	Recognition	Make the product visible and illustrate its strengths.
2	Researching	Focus on the benefits (i.e. how the product will provide solutions beyond those offered by alternatives).
3	Refining and reflecting	Emphasise the additional extras of the product (e.g. quality, customer service, guarantees, etc.).
4	Reaching out	Having strong brand recognition and a strong reputation will help to get those recommendations.
5	Resolution	Make it easy for the consumers to complete the purchase (e.g. easy online payment).
6	Purchase	Thank the consumer for making the purchase. Wish them a good day and say you are looking forward to seeing them again.
7	Review	Follow up with a courtesy call to check that the consumer is happy. Offer the customer a money-back guarantee if he or she is not happy.

The review stage should have a feedback loop to earlier stages in the process to indicate whether the satisfied (or dissatisfied) purchaser will make (or not make) repeat purchases, based on the customer's perception of whether or not he or she received value for money.

Stimulus–response approach

A stimulus encourages people to do things. There is a range of stimuli that a marketer can apply to encourage purchasing or to make purchasers change their buying habits. To do this the marketer must understand what takes place in the customer's decision-making process – sometimes called the consumer's 'black box' (because what goes on inside is invisible). In this process, buyers choose the brand or product, where to buy it (that is, which shop to go to), when to buy it, in what quantity and how often.

Marketers can go some way towards understanding what is in the black box by finding out consumer characteristics, as these influence the decision-making process. Characteristics may be:

- **personal:** for example, age, lifestyle, occupation, income and personality
- **social:** family, role in society and **reference groups**
- **cultural:** culture- and class-related factors
- **psychological:** for example, motivations and drives, beliefs and attitudes.

Figure 2.15.2 summarises the **stimulus–response** approach.

Figure 2.15.1 A consumer weighs up alternatives before making a purchasing decision

> **KEY TERMS**
>
> **Reference groups:** groups that consumers look to as role models or influencers when making purchasing decisions.
>
> **Stimulus–response:** in the context of marketing, where particular marketing actions lead to buyer responses. Understanding customer characteristics helps marketers to predict the likely responses.

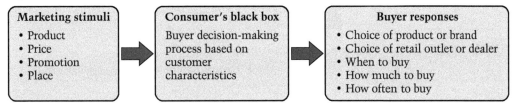

Marketing stimuli	Consumer's black box	Buyer responses
• Product • Price • Promotion • Place	Buyer decision-making process based on customer characteristics	• Choice of product or brand • Choice of retail outlet or dealer • When to buy • How much to buy • How often to buy

Figure 2.15.2 The stimulus–response approach

Summary table

Ways of analysing buyer behaviour	
Seven-stage approach	Recognition – researching – refining and reflecting – reaching out – resolution – purchase – review Understanding this model helps the marketer to identify marketing steps to take at each stage.
Stimulus–response approach	Marketing stimuli are interpreted in different ways depending on customer characteristics – resulting in different responses. Challenge to marketers to understand what lies inside potential buyers' black box.

Summary questions

1 A coffee shop wishes to increase demand for its products in a busy retailing area where there are already other coffee shops. Illustrate ways in which a marketer can respond at each of the seven steps in the purchasing process.

2 How might knowledge of what lies inside the customer's black box help a car showroom to sell more cars?

On completion of this section, you should be able to:

- explain the principles of product management, with reference to the concept of product: core, formal or actual and augmented.

The product

In an everyday sense, we know what a product is: a bar of soap, an umbrella, a car and so on. However, marketers think more deeply about the product to build on this crucial part of the marketing mix in a way that appeals to customers. They identify three aspects of the product:

- the core product
- the actual product
- the augmented product.

Figure 2.16.1 *What is a product?*

Did you know?

In general terms, a product is a good or service that provides value for customers. In terms of marketing theory and practice, however, it is helpful to differentiate between the core product, the actual product, and the augmented product. It is the 'actual product' that fits most closely with the everyday use of the term 'product'.

Figure 2.16.2 shows how these aspects can be seen as a series of circles leading out from the core product.

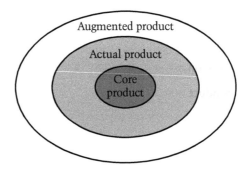

Figure 2.16.2 *The product concept*

The core product

The core product consists of the benefits that customers seek when making a purchase. For example, when a customer purchases a car, the benefits might need to include the following if there is to be a successful sale:

- the car offers a safe and comfortable ride
- the car looks good and stylish
- the car is economical to run.

The more benefits that the product can provide for customers (which are related to their requirements), the more likely it is that the product will be able to satisfy them. The marketer therefore focuses initially on what **product benefits** the customer wants:

- something to hang clothes on – a washing line
- a cheap and convenient method of personal transport – a bicycle or motor scooter
- something to shave with – a razor.

Armed with this knowledge about benefits, the marketer can provide solutions to the customer's needs, and also target advertising at what the customer is seeking.

'You want a close shave – buy our new four-blade razor!'

'You want instant refreshment after playing sport – buy our energy drink!'

The actual product

At the next level, the marketer is able to focus on the actual (or formal) product and its features. A family car needs to have safety air bags, childproof locks in the rear and plenty of space for luggage. Branding is also important at this level. Consumers are very aware of brand image, so branding is regarded as part of the actual product: for example, a Toyota car.

The augmented product

The 'augmented' or 'extended' product consists of additions such as after-sales service, warranties and delivery. A car dealer might offer extras such as an interest-free loan, free insurance on the car or free servicing for the first 20,000 miles.

The benefit of understanding the augmented product concept is that it enables marketers to focus on additional benefits for which customers are looking, particularly in terms of customer service. Customers often want more than the actual or formal product – they want the product (such as a car) to be serviced, and for there to be a helpline to solve any problems they have (for example for computers and electrical gadgets). A product that offers this will be more appealing to the customer.

☑ *Exam tip*

Make sure that you are clear that a marketer should focus their marketing activities not just on the details of the actual product, but just as importantly, on the benefits that the customer is seeking (core product) and the additional extras and service arrangements (augmented product).

Summary table

Product levels (based on example of a washing machine)		
Level 1: the core product	**Level 2: the actual or formal product**	**Level 3: the augmented or extended product**
The benefits that the consumer seeks: ■ the ability to wash, rinse and partially dry clothes automatically at different temperatures.	The type or model of washing machine: ■ a front-loading, family-sized washing machine.	Additional extras that are provided with the machine: ■ free servicing and parts for the first year ■ a guarantee to repair faults ■ fitting of the machine in the home.

Summary questions

1 Differentiate between the core product, the actual product and the augmented product for a consumer electrical item that you, your family or friends have recently purchased.

2 How can it help a marketer when selling products to focus on:
 a the core product
 b the augmented product
 c the actual product?

On completion of this section, you should be able to:

- explain the principles of product management, with reference to the dimensions of the product mix, product line and product extension.

Figure 2.17.1 *The Gillette Fusion Power razor, a product in the beauty and grooming line that makes up part of the Procter & Gamble product mix*

☑ *Exam tip*

Make sure that you can explain the difference, with examples, between product mix, product line and product, and between product width and product depth.

You should be able to explain the benefits of line extension.

The product mix

A company's product mix consists of all the products that it offers. Within the mix we can identify:

- product lines (a series of related products)
- individual products (each product that contributes to the line mix).

The US household goods company Procter & Gamble (P&G) produces many leading fast-moving consumer goods (FMCGs) that are distributed throughout the Caribbean and across the world. Its product mix includes Nice 'n Easy, Gillette, Olay, Puma, Align, Scope, Oral-B, Crest, Vicks, Ace, Charmin, Tide, Lenor and Fairy.

Its product lines fall into three main areas (Table 2.17.1). Within each product line there are separate products, such as the Gillette Fusion Power razor illustrated in Figure 2.17.1.

Table 2.17.1 *Procter & Gamble product lines*

Beauty and grooming	Health and wellbeing	Household care
e.g. Safeguard, Fusion, Nice 'n Easy, Gillette, Olay	Align, Always, Oral-B, Crest, Vicks, Scope	Ace, Charmin, Tide, Lenor, Fairy

Width and depth of product mixes

Product mixes are measured in terms of width (the number of products in the mix) and depth (the varieties of each product – colours, sizes or models offered).

Large multinational producers of FMCGs such as P&G have a wide product mix with many different product brands. Additionally, within each product line there is considerable product depth, so for example, you can buy shampoos for many different types of hair conditions and styles.

Product mix strategy

A company can have a concentrated product mix strategy, focusing on narrow width and depth, or a broad strategy with a wide and deep approach. Market research is needed: if most people want similar products, a focused strategy would be suitable, but if the market is fragmented, a wider and deeper strategy might be more appropriate. The strategy chosen will also depend on the business's marketing resources: a company with limited resources may have to focus its strategy, while a larger organisation such as Unilever or PepsiCo can differentiate its products more and adopt a broader approach.

Product mix strategy is particularly important in deciding whether to introduce new products, or reduce the number of existing products. An organisation may decide to expand its mix by increasing the depth of a line or increasing the number of lines. Gaps in the mix can be filled with new products or modified versions of existing ones. A company will wish to avoid introducing a new product that adversely affects sales of one of its existing products: this would 'cannibalise' the line, with one product eating into the sales of another. Marketing research should be able to assess this danger, allowing the business to forecast how much a new product would add to overall sales.

A product mix decision forms a key part of the overall marketing plan, affecting the combination of the company's product lines. Senior marketing managers have the responsibility for making decisions about the mix, which include:

- which product lines to concentrate on
- which new lines to add, and which existing or old lines to cut
- how much emphasis to place on existing lines and products, and how much on new
- how much emphasis to place on internal development of new lines, and how much on acquiring new lines and products from other companies.

Line extensions

Developing new products that appeal to an existing or new market segment is referred to as a 'line extension'. New products are added to an existing brand line, so for a particular brand of soap there might be a change in the fragrance, the shape or the pack size. Line extensions often involve ' stretching' the product line to reach new groups of customers. For a mid-market shampoo, aimed at middle-income consumers, a company could engage in:

- 'upmarket stretch', modifying the product, price and promotion to appeal to wealthier consumers
- 'downmarket stretch', modifying the product, price and promotion to appeal to less well-off consumers
- 'sideways stretch', modifying the product, price and promotion to appeal to additional consumers in the same market segment.

Line extension can reinvigorate an existing brand by appealing to new customers and helping to stimulate interest among existing customers. The extensions can also eat into competitors' sales.

The main disadvantage of line extension is that it can increase marketing costs because advertising has to be spread over more products. The new line may also cannibalise an existing line.

Did you know?

Multinational companies can offer a wider and deeper product mix because they can market product lines and products on a global scale. Smaller, national companies tend to be more focused.

Summary table

Components of the product mix	
The product mix	All the products a company produces or sells
Product lines	Groups of similar products that are the focus of marketing efforts
Products	Individual products that make up the product lines and the product mix
Line extensions	Introducing new products into product lines, and so the overall product mix

Summary questions

1 Choose a company with whose products you are familiar. Identify some of the main components of the product mix. What are the main product lines of this company? Has the company recently made any line extensions?

2 How might a Caribbean chain of holiday hotels engage in a process of line extension?

Specific objective

On completion of this section, you should be able to:

■ explain the principles of product management, with reference to the Boston Matrix.

The Boston Matrix

Companies with several product lines need to make decisions about how to allocate their marketing budgets. The greatest efforts may need to be placed on products likely to be the most profitable, either now or in the future. Fewer resources should be given to products that are already in decline or are likely to decline shortly.

The Boston Matrix, or Growth Share Matrix, was developed by The Boston Consulting Group (BCG) in the US. It was devised in 1970 to address investment strategy on a product. However, is still a useful way of grouping a company's products. The matrix enables a company to make marketing decisions by organising its products according to two criteria:

▩ how quickly the market for the product is growing

▩ the current market share of that product.

Identifying where a product sits on the chart helps to determine a marketing strategy for it. This is based on the key assumption that a larger market share will reduce unit costs, and so increase profit margins.

Quadrants of the Boston Matrix

Figure 2.18.1 *The Boston Matrix*

The Boston Matrix is divided into four quadrants, as shown in Figure 2.18.1. These are:

▩ **'Stars':** these are products that have a high market share in a high growth market. They have the ability to generate significant sales in the short and long term, but require promotional investment to maintain their high market position.

▩ **'Question marks':** these have a low market share in a market that is growing rapidly. Their low market share normally indicates that competition is strong. If the market looks like having long-term potential, the organisation needs to decide whether to invest heavily in building market share. If the market is unlikely to continue growing, or the investment requirement is too great, the organisation may consider abandoning these products.

▩ **'Cash cows':** these have a high market share in a market that shows little growth. The products are generally well established with plenty of loyal customers. Product development costs are low and the marketing campaign is well established. Cash cows normally make

✅ Exam tip

Remember that the Boston Matrix helps a business to identify:

■ which of its products are currently placed in high growth market sectors as well as those in low growth sectors

■ the relative market share for a specific product

■ which products to invest in and the ones for which investment should be reduced.

a substantial contribution to overall profitability. They finance the investment needed to maintain the high market share of 'stars' and to develop the 'question marks'.

- **'Dogs':** these are products with a low market share in a market experiencing little growth. Organisations must consider whether to 'harvest' the revenues from them in the short term by raising prices, or to remove them from the product range altogether.

Channelling of funds

We can superimpose on to the Boston Matrix the flow of funds that can take place between one line of products and another. For example, revenues can be channelled from cash cows to stars and question marks. This is illustrated in Figure 2.18.2. At the same time, we can delete the dogs to show that they no longer require funding.

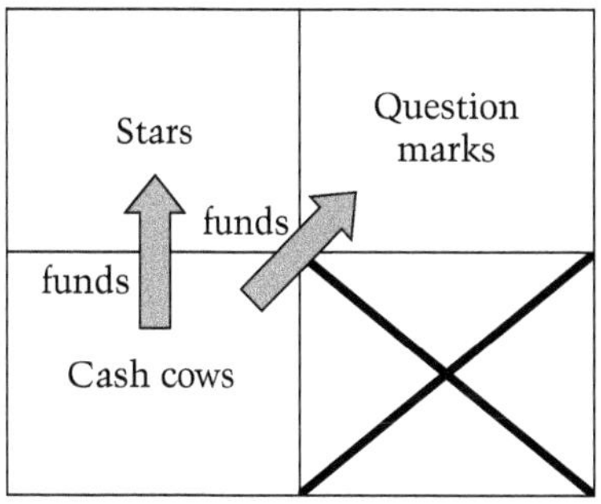

Figure 2.18.2 The Boston Matrix showing channelling of funds

CASE STUDY

Grace Foods

Grace Foods is one of the best-known Caribbean companies, providing a range of celebrated Caribbean foods. Key brands in its product mix are Encona (sauces), Dunn's River (seasoning, sauces and marinades), Tropical Rhythms (blended fruit and vegetables in glass bottles) and Nurishment (nutritionally enhanced milk).

1 From your own experience of these products, which of them do you consider to be stars, and which are cash cows?

2 Can you identify any products produced by a food-processing company in your area that might be considered 'dogs' or 'question marks'?

3 How does knowledge of where products fit within the Boston Matrix help a company with its marketing activities?

Did you know?

A widely used approach to selecting products is portfolio analysis. A company reviews its current and potential product portfolio to identify which products should be introduced, maintained, reduced or eliminated.

Summary table

Product type	Description	Investment strategy
Dogs	Market share small; market growth slow; no opportunities	Cut investment
Stars	Market leaders in fast-growing markets, generating large profits	Need investment to continue growth
Cash cows	Profitable with large market share in slow-growing markets	Channel some of the profits to the development of newer products
Question marks	Rapid growth but low profit margins	Need investment to defend market share

Summary questions

1 Choose a company that is familiar to you. Look at its product portfolio and identify some products in which you think the company should invest. Give reasons for your choices.

2 Which other products of that company might help to generate surplus funds for investment purposes?

Specific objective

On completion of this section, you should be able to:

- explain the principles of product management, with reference to the NPD (new product development) process.

Figure 2.19.1 *Commercialisation of a sunscreen based on aloe vera will take place only at the end of a detailed new product development process*

KEY TERMS

Screening: using predetermined criteria to eliminate options that are less likely to be effective.

Product development: all stages involved in the development of a new (or existing) product.

Test marketing: trying out a product in a smaller market that is representative of the main market, in order to trial marketing activities.

The new product development process

Marketers typically identify six stages in the new product development (NPD) process.

1 Idea generation

The development of a new product begins with an idea. This might be generated from the sales force, customers, research and development, retailers or wholesalers. It might relate to a completely new product or the modification of an existing one. For example, a Caribbean cosmetics company might identify the opportunity to develop a new sunscreen product from the aloe vera plant, based on its soothing and healing properties.

2 Initial screening

The company may begin with a range of product ideas, which are then reduced so that only one or a small number of products remain at the final commercialisation stage.

Ideas that have potential need to undergo **screening** tests: that is, separated from those that do not meet marketing and corporate objectives. Organisations may use a checklist for this, which might include factors such as product uniqueness and compatibility with the existing product range.

3 Business analysis

Product ideas that pass initial screening tests are then exposed to a rigorous business analysis. As with the initial screening, the aim is to eliminate options that are unacceptable and to focus on what works. A key consideration will be to ascertain whether there is a sufficiently large market for the product and whether the returns from the product will outweigh the costs of development, production and product support, such as advertising activity.

As we have already seen, it is important to find out information such as how consumers will use the product, when, how often and what they will use it for.

4 Product development

During **product development**, selected ideas that have the potential to generate profit move towards becoming physical products. Many parts of the organisation are involved. Product technologists may explore ways to blend aloe vera with other ingredients and bring samples to company meetings for discussion. The marketing team can provide consumer impressions of the product, its look and feel, scent and smell, pricing and packaging. Tests, revisions and refinements will take place that should increase the chances of the new product being successful.

5 Testing

Test marketing is the first stage of presenting the product in a real consumer market. The test market may be a specific location, perhaps part of a specific city that is considered typical of the final market for the product. Test marketing might involve a launch which it is hoped will be representative of the final wider launch and use the same marketing and media sources – television, magazine advertising and so on.

The benefits of test marketing include the opportunity to check whether a product will sell in a real setting, and to adjust the marketing mix in line with research results. However, some companies leave out the test marketing stage because it can be expensive, and because competitors may become aware of the product before it is fully launched.

6 Commercialisation

At the end of the development process, products that have successfully completed all previous stages proceed to full-scale marketing: the **commercialisation** stage. Marketing programmes have to be set up, outlays for production are agreed, and the sales force, marketing intermediaries and potential customers need to be made aware of the new product and when it is to become available.

As you can see in Figure 2.19.2, the series of screening processes involved in new product development helps to narrow down options to the 'best' or small number of 'best' options.

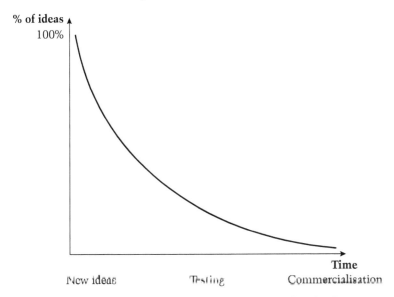

Figure 2.19.2 *Many ideas are discarded in the process of new product development*

Summary questions

1   Which are the most important steps in new product development?

2   Why are far fewer products commercialised than the number considered at the ideas stage?

Summary table

New product development		
Stages	**Description**	**Number of ideas**
1 Idea generation	Generating ideas for NPD	Many
2 Initial screening	Establishing which ideas meet given criteria	Some ideas have been screened out
3 Business analysis	Calculating demand/market size and financial analysis	Only ideas left are those for which a business case can be made
4 Product development	Production and marketing resources channelled into producing products for market testing	Small number of ideas being developed for market testing
5 Testing	Small number of prototypes tested in live markets	Very small number of options left
6 Commercialisation	Full-scale launch of products in real markets	One or a small number of products taken to the target market

Specific objective

On completion of this section, you should be able to:

- explain the principles of product management, with reference to the product life cycle.

Product life cycles

A product life cycle consists of the stages from the initial introduction of the product to market, to the decline and eventual termination of the product or its withdrawal from sale.

Stages in a typical product life cycle

Many products experience the classic life cycle illustrated in Figure 2.20.1. Note the two curves on the graph illustrating the sales and profits of the product in different stages of the cycle.

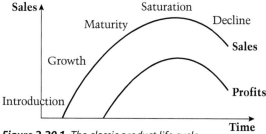

Figure 2.20.1 *The classic product life cycle*

Introduction

During the introductory phase, it is necessary to use marketing activity to stimulate demand. Growth and the volume of sales are low because of limited awareness of the product's existence. Here marketers will need to increase the awareness and appeal of the product, for example by using advertisting and introducing the product at a lower price.

Growth

Sales increase more quickly. It is during this phase that the profit per unit sold usually reaches a maximum. Towards the end of the phase, competitors enter the market, which reduces the rate of growth. Marketers will need to continue advertising and promoting the product.

Maturity

Most of the potential customers have been reached. However, there is still plenty of scope for repeat purchases. Competition from other sellers becomes stronger and new firms enter the market. Marketers may need to consider using rejuvenation strategies (see next page).

Decline

The product becomes 'old' and sales start to fall. Perhaps a new or improved product has entered the market. The firm will need to decide whether to rejuvenate the product or abandon the marketing.

Alternative life cycles

Figure 2.20.2 illustrates a number of alternative life cycles that are relevant today.

- **Straw on fire:** products that rise quickly in popularity and are 'burned out' in a very short period. This is the case with some children's toys that become a temporary craze.
- **Flop:** products that fail to capture the public attention (often because the NPD process has been weak).

- **Long cycle:** products, such as the Mars Bar, which continue to go from strength to strength for long periods of time.
- **Staircase:** products that are regularly revitalised with new advertising campaigns and promotional initiatives.
- **Fashion:** products that have booms and slumps in sales according to fashion or season, such as umbrellas and fireworks.
- **Leapfrog:** when companies compete with each other strongly, they may regularly leapfrog each other in product design and development. When they get the advantage by leapfrogging a rival, sales rise; when the rival leapfrogs them, sales fall.

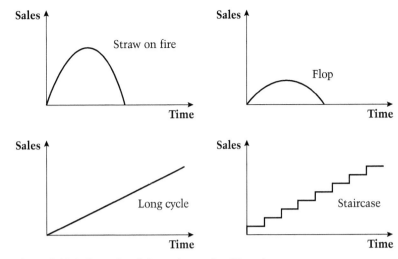

Figure 2.20.2 *Examples of alternative product life cycles*

Rejuvenation

Figure 2.20.3 shows how a company can rejuvenate its product life cycle through marketing activity to secure regular periods of growth (the 'staircase' life cycle described above). Injections of new life are made by altering the product, promotion or distributional methods, or by pricing to rejuvenate interest. Here are some examples of rejuvenation:

- altering the shape, flavour and taste of food products to add a bit of 'zing'
- engaging in a television advertising campaign to capture the public imagination
- distributing the product through more convenient locations
- lowering prices to undercut rivals.

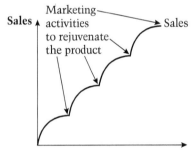

Figure 2.20.3 *Rejuvenation*

Summary table

Stage	Description	Marketing activities
Introduction	Product is launched and introduced to the market (e.g. television advertising campaign)	■ Try-one-at-low-price promotion, mass media launch
Growth	Sales of the product start to take off as awareness grows and more outlets stock it	■ Continued media activity, sale of product through more outlets
Maturity	Established sales, consumers familiar with product	■ Advertising designed to remind the market about the product ■ Product differentiation (e.g. line extensions) to differentiate product from competition ■ Promotions to reward loyalty (e.g. buy one, get one free)
Decline	Falling sales	■ Either seek to rejuvenate product or cut marketing

Summary questions

1 Identify products with which you are familiar that appear to have experienced the classic product life cycle. Where are they now in the life cycle? What marketing activities are taking place around the product?

2 Identify products that have experienced alternative product life cycles. What product-related marketing activities have taken place?

Specific objective

On completion of this section, you should be able to:

- explain the principles of product management, with reference to branding and packaging.

KEY TERMS

Brand: a brand consists of elements such as a brand name (e.g. Nike), a logo (the distinctive Nike symbol) and a slogan ('Just do it').

Branding: all the processes involved in creating a unique name and image of a product in consumers' minds.

Branding

A **brand** is a product or series of products with a unique, consistent and easily recognisable character. Figure 2.21.1 shows some of the Caribbean's best-known food brands from Grace Foods. On a global scale, perhaps the best-known brand name is Coca-Cola, instantly recognisable by its logo, the shape of its bottles, the colour of its cans and the taste of the product.

Figure 2.21.1 *A well-known food brand from Grace Foods*

The uniqueness of a brand comes from its physical characteristics: for Coca-Cola, its taste and unique ingredients, plus its image – the logo, the advertising. These are usually created by the manufacturer through advertising and packaging.

Branding helps to influence buyer behaviour. A strong brand sticks in potential customers' minds and helps to link products with particular producers or suppliers. Popular Caribbean tourist destinations use advertising slogans or 'straplines' to promote the holiday brand. For example, Aruba has adopted the slogan 'One happy island', Jamaica uses the strapline 'Once you go, you know!' and Barbados tourism promotes itself through 'It doesn't get better than Barbados'.

A strong brand adds value to the product. This can be seen with leading world brands such as Dolce & Gabbana, Calvin Klein and Christian Dior. The owners of these brands are now able to charge higher prices even for small items that people want because of the name that appears on them.

Building a brand

Companies invest in brand building. A starting point is to establish 'brand values': that is, the values that the brand represents, such as quality and enjoyment. For example, as a vehicle manufacturer Toyota stands for high-quality, driveable and safe vehicles. Brand values need to be conveyed to consumers by:

- adopting a consistent and clear style in all promotional material
- using specific visual images, fonts and wording to convey these messages
- training staff to portray the company's values when dealing with customers.

Did you know?

The term 'powerbrand' is sometimes used in business to describe the brands of a company which are particularly important because the reputation of the brand is high, as are the sales. For example, a powerbrand for the Unilever company is Magnum ice cream.

The product too must convey this consistent approach. Consumers should receive what they are promised in terms of quality, whether this is a car, a packet of coffee or a holiday with a well-known travel agency.

Brand extension

Once a brand is established, a business can reduce the risk associated with developing a new product by using brand extension. A well-developed image based on an existing recognised brand helps to market the new product. One of the best-known brands in the Caribbean is SM Jaleel's Chubby carbonated drinks. Targeted at four- to nine-year-olds, the drinks come in a range of flavours such as Action Apple, Megastar Mango, Sorrel Soda and Bubble Gum. When the company wanted to introduce a new carbonated drink, Martian Magic Green Crush, it was easy to extend the Chubby brand to include this new offering.

Figure 2.21.2 *The Chubby brand has been extended to include Martian Magic Green Crush*

Packaging

The basic function of packaging is containing and protecting the product. Packaging helps to keep products fresh, and to protect them during transportation. Packaging is also an important part of the marketing mix because it promotes the product. With the growth in branding, packaging is a particularly effective way of getting a product noticed.

Successful packaging has to be distinctive and recognisable, and fit in well with the brand image appropriate to the target market. It needs to give a clear message about the product and can differentiate a product from that of a competitor, particularly if the packaging is innovative.

Although both branding and packaging increase costs, they can substantially increase revenue through encouraging increased sales. Packaging can also reduce costs in terms of fewer damaged goods and keeping perishable products fresh.

Did you know?

Packaging and branding are often closely related. Packaging can be used to project the brand image either through its design or through the logos and imagery that appear on the packaging. Packaging can also be used to give information about how to use the product, as well as the ingredients and price of the product.

Summary table

Benefits of branding for a business	Makes the product recognisable, distinguishes it from rivals, helps to promote brand values, leads to increased sales, adds value to the product
Benefits of packaging for a business	Can be used to make a product stand out, to promote the product, to provide useful information about the product, to protect and preserve the product

Summary questions

1 Identify five well-known Caribbean brands. In each case, identify the benefits of branding the product. Are the benefits broadly similar for all of the products?

2 Identify a packaged product that is produced in your territory or the wider Caribbean. How is packaging used and what are the business benefits?

Specific objectives

On completion of this section, you should be able to:

- explain the principles of product management, with reference to the characteristic of services compared to goods

- show the similarities and differences in approaches to marketing goods and services.

☑ *Exam tip*

Make sure you understand an additional distinction between core and supplementary services:

- Core services are the primary purpose of a transaction (e.g. a personal manicure).

- Supplementary services are provided in addition to a good (e.g. home delivery (the service) of a pizza (the good)).

KEY TERMS

Homogeneous: of the same kind.

Did you know?

In the provision of services, personal service is particularly important because providing a service typically involves direct interaction with customers.

Goods and services

A good is a tangible object (that is, one you can touch), a product that a consumer will use, either once or over a period of time. A service is intangible: the consumer uses it, but it is not a physical product and you cannot touch it. Table 2.22.1 provides some examples.

Table 2.22.1 *Goods and services*

Examples of goods	Examples of services
▪ A bread roll (consumed once) ▪ A mango (consumed once) ▪ A dish of fish and rice (consumed once) ▪ A motor car (consumed over a period of time) ▪ A factory machine (we call this a 'producer good' because it enables a producer to manufacture over a period of time) ▪ A commercial aeroplane (another producer good, enabling a business to fly passengers over many journeys)	▪ Insurance (providing cover for a period of time) ▪ Hairdressing ▪ Waiter/waitress service at a restaurant ▪ Delivery of mail ▪ Safekeeping of money in a bank (providing security over a period of time) ▪ Transportation of goods on behalf of a business

Both goods and services can be placed into categories:

- personal consumer goods that are consumed immediately (the bread roll, mango, dish of fish and rice)

- personal consumer durable goods consumed over a period of time (motor car)

- capital goods used by business (factory machine, aeroplane)

- personal services providing immediate satisfaction to personal consumers (hairdressing, waiter service, delivery of mail)

- personal services over a period of time (insurance, safekeeping of bank deposits)

- services to business (transportation of goods).

Implications for marketing

Some of the differences between goods and services are relevant to marketing.

Goods are typically **homogeneous**. That is, they are identical or broadly similar: your tuna sandwich will be very similar to mine (if we buy them from the same provider). Services are likely to be much more differentiated: my haircut will be different from yours. As services vary far more in terms of quality, output and delivery, human interactions are a much more important element. You will probably never talk to the people who helped to manufacture a carbonated drink you bought last week, but you will usually have a conversation about the news and the political situation with the person who cuts your hair.

Another difference is that the production and consumption of goods usually take place at different times; services are usually consumed at the time they are produced.

The implications for marketing are as follows:

- Personal attention is much more important in the provision of services. Customer service and personal attention are key parts of marketing services.
- Differentiation is more significant in the provision of services. Individual customer needs can, and should, be attended to, whether the service is waiting on a table, dealing with a customer's financial requirements in a bank or polishing a customer's nails.
- Relationships are a key factor in marketing services. A key part of the decision to buy is whether the buyer trusts the seller. To maintain customer loyalty, the supplier of services must listen to the buyer and find out about his or her wants and needs.

Marketing services

In marketing services, it is important to consider the following, referred to earlier as the four Ps:

- **Product:** designing the service offering to meet the needs of customers without adding too much to costs through differentiation.
- **Pricing:** making sure that pricing takes into account intangible aspects of the service, such as the atmosphere in a restaurant or coffee shop.
- **Place:** choosing a place that is representative of the service – for example, siting a seafood restaurant next to the sea.
- **Promotion:** promoting your service in a way that sends clear messages about what it provides.

There are three other Ps that are relevant to service marketing:

- **People:** people help to attract customers, as in the interaction between staff in a hotel and the clientele.
- **Process:** having a clear service delivery process – for example, providing a high-quality service in a restaurant according to a preset standard.
- **Physical evidence:** for example, uniforms that staff wear, the physical layout of a surgery waiting area – tangible supports for the service being provided.

Figure 2.22.1 *The uniform that company employees wear acts as part of the physical evidence that supports the service being provided*

Summary table

How services are different from goods	Implications for marketing
Services are intangible.	Focus is required on the quality of the experience.
Services involve more human interaction.	The quality of staff and their interactions with customers is important.
Services are more differentiated.	Focus is required on the differentiation (particularly in comparison with rivals).

Summary questions

1 Choose one good and one service that you purchase regularly. Compare the marketing of the service with the marketing of the good: what are the main differences in the relationship between you (the consumer) and the suppliers in each case?

2 What actions might a doctor, dentist, lawyer or accountant take to attract more loyal customers?

Did you know?

Price is the only element of the marketing mix that does not involve a cost. It can be adjusted without incurring business costs (except the cost of changing your price lists).

Pricing

The price of a good or service is the sum of money that the seller asks for when supplying the market. There are several factors that affect pricing decisions. These are dealt with in the following sections, but the most obvious ones can be mentioned here:

■ pricing to cover the costs of supplying a good or service

■ pricing to make the purchase attractive compared to goods or services supplied by competitors.

Role of pricing in the marketing mix

For marketers, pricing is an important variable in the marketing mix. Prices need to attract sufficient numbers of targeted customers. Pricing also reflects other aspects of the marketing mix.

CASE STUDY

Positioning your product

'Positioning' of a product or service refers to marketing attempts to influence customers' perception of where a product stands in a market in relation to competing products. A key element of positioning is pricing. This is illustrated in the Figure 2.23.1.

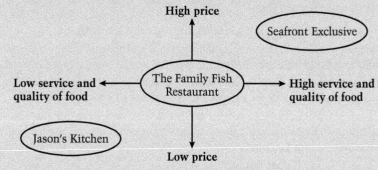

Figure 2.23.1 Positioning for three different restaurants

The diagram shows the market position of three restaurants in an imaginary Caribbean capital. Jason's Kitchen sells cheap food, without much service, and at low prices. The Family Fish Restaurant offers medium service and medium-quality food at mid-market prices. The Seafront Exclusive sells the most expensive seafood with premium service and premium prices.

1 What do you think the advantages would be of taking the positions shown by the three restaurants in the positioning map?

2 Why is it important for price to reflect other elements of the marketing mix?

KEY TERMS

Upmarket: expensive goods and services designed for more affluent consumers.

A key function of price is to tell customers about the business's market position. Think about an expensive **upmarket** item such as a BMW: customers who want to buy a car like this do so partly because they want the luxury and features in the car, but also because they want to feel different from drivers around them who are in merely standard models. The pricing of luxury goods like these sends out important signals about the positioning of the product.

Price is also one of the most significant components of the purchasing decision. People buy goods when they feel that the price is right, or that the good is a bargain. (Sometimes purchases have to be made reluctantly because they are essential, if expensive, such as household fuel or children's shoes.) Pricing of **downmarket** items can sometimes be set too low, however, and potential purchasers may assume that the quality is also low.

An important part of marketing research, therefore, is to ask potential customers how much they would be prepared to pay for a good (see Figure 2.23.2).

KEY TERMS

Downmarket: cheap and low-quality products designed for less well-off consumers.

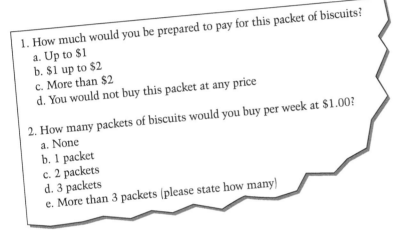

1. How much would you be prepared to pay for this packet of biscuits?
   a. Up to $1
   b. $1 up to $2
   c. More than $2
   d. You would not buy this packet at any price

2. How many packets of biscuits would you buy per week at $1.00?
   a. None
   b. 1 packet
   c. 2 packets
   d. 3 packets
   e. More than 3 packets (please state how many)

Figure 2.23.2 *Part of a market research questionnaire*

Summary table

Definition of price	The sum of money charged for a good or service by a producer or seller
Role of pricing	A key mix component that can be adjusted easily because it does not involve a cost, and which needs to be aligned with other elements of the marketing mix
Importance of pricing	Sends out important signals about the positioning of a product Is a significant part of the consumer's purchasing decision

Summary questions

1 Identify products in a particular product category that you use, some of which are downmarket and some upmarket. How does the pricing strategy used by the company differ for these different categories of products?

2 Explain how pricing can help a business with which you are familiar to position specific products in its product portfolio.

On completion of this section, you should be able to:

- outline key factors that influence price, including demand, income, elasticity of demand and consumer preference.

Table 2.24.1 *The effect of price on demand and supply*

High price	Low price
Demand relatively low	Demand relatively high
Supply relatively high	Supply relatively low

Table 2.24.2 *The price of bread*

Price ($)	Demand (quantity)	Supply (quantity)
80 cents	7,500	12,500
60 cents (original market price)	10,000	10,000
40 cents	12,500	7,500

Influences on market price

Goods and services are priced at the 'current market price'. This is determined by the interactions between buyers and sellers. 'Demand' identifies the quantity of a good that consumers will be prepared to buy at different prices. 'Supply' identifies the quantity that suppliers will be prepared to supply to the market at different prices.

- The higher the market price, the greater the quantity that suppliers will be willing to supply.
- The lower the market price, the greater the quantity that consumers will be willing and able to purchase (see Table 2.24.1).

Consumer preference

Consumers prefer some products more than others. They will demonstrate their preference in the form of their demand for a product. For example, many migrants may arrive in a country with a preference for particular types of food products. A popular product will have a high level of demand.

Demand for a product

Changes in demand for a product have an impact on price. Tables 2.24.2 and 2.24.3 show this, using the example of demand for and supply of bread.

Table 2.24.2 shows that the price of bread will initially be set at 60 cents, where the quantity that consumers want to purchase equals the quantity that bakers are willing to supply.

However, if bread becomes more popular, demand might rise so that consumers are willing to buy 12,500 loaves for a new market price of 80 cents (Table 2.24.3).

Table 2.24.3 *Effect of a price rise on supply and demand*

Price ($)	New quantity demanded when good becomes more popular	Supply (quantity)
80 cents (new market price)	12,500	12,500
60 cents	15,000	10,000
40 cents	17,500	7,500

Demand for a product can also increase when the price of a competing product goes up, and when the number of consumers increases.

Changes in income

Increases or falls in income across a country or area may also impact on price. Over time, average incomes tend to rise. When this happens, the demand for most products increases, encouraging suppliers to produce more goods. A rise in incomes in the short run may therefore lead to an increase in prices.

The opposite can happen, however, if incomes rise in the longer term. Prices could fall if producers are able to produce on a larger scale and cut costs.

Price elasticity of demand

In most cases, when the price of an item rises, people will buy fewer. For example, a rise in the price of bus travel will lead passengers to take fewer bus journeys or switch to other means of transport. When the price of an item falls, more will be bought. For example, when the price of computers fell, more households bought them.

It is clear, therefore, that when prices change, so will the quantities bought. However, businesses need to have a clear measure of *how much* the quantity bought will change as a result of a price change.

A useful measure of this relationship is called 'price elasticity of demand'. It can be shown by a simple formula:

$$\text{Price elasticity of demand} = \frac{\text{Percentage change in quantity}}{\text{Percentage change in the price of the good}}$$

For example, if the price of a coconut fell by 50 per cent (for example, from $1.00 to 50 cents) and the quantity demanded increased by 100 per cent (for example, from 1,000 to 2,000), the elasticity of demand is 2:

$$\frac{100\%}{50\%} = 2$$

If the price of a mango fell by 50 per cent (for example, from $1.00 to 50 cents) and the quantity demanded increased by 25 per cent (for example, from 1,000 to 1,250), the elasticity of demand is $\frac{1}{2}$ or 0.5.

$$\frac{25\%}{50\%} = \frac{1}{2}$$

In business we use the term 'elastic demand' to describe a position where the quantity demanded changes by a higher percentage than the initial price change. We use 'inelastic demand' where the change in demand is a smaller percentage than the original price change.

Producers or sellers need to know how much demand will change as a result of price changes, so that they can calculate the effect on sales and on the amount of money they receive from sales, their 'revenue'.

Table 2.24.4 *Effect of elasticity of demand on sales and revenue*

If producers know that demand for a product is **elastic** around the existing price:
- it may make sense to **lower the price** – to increase sales and revenues
- it would be unwise to raise the price – because sales and revenues will fall by a larger percentage than the price rise.

If producers know that demand for a product is **inelastic** around the existing price:
- it may make sense to **raise the price** – because revenues will increase
- it would be foolish to lower the price – because even though they are selling a few more items, they are losing revenues on all of the units they sell.

Summary table

Elastic demand	A change in price leads to a more than proportionate change in quantity demanded.	Producers are likely to respond by reducing their prices at least a little to increase their revenues.
Inelastic demand	A change in price leads to a less than proportionate change in quantity demanded.	Producers are likely to respond by raising their prices a little in order to increase their revenues.

Summary questions

1 A bus company is not making much money because its buses are only half full. What pricing decision might it make if it finds, through market research, that there is an elastic demand for bus travel? What decision might it make if the research finds that demand is inelastic?

2 What factors might increase the demand for hotel rooms in a Caribbean territory? How might the increase in demand impact on price?

On completion of this section, you should be able to:

■ evaluate various pricing strategies by explaining and illustrating competition and going rate pricing.

Figure 2.25.1 *Many budget airlines base their pricing strategy on competition pricing*

The nature of competition

Organisations need to be aware of their competition and its strategies. Competition occurs when two or more organisations act independently to sell their products to the same group of consumers. In some markets there may be a lot of competition, with an abundance of products and services, so that customers have a great deal of choice. These markets are characterised by promotional activities and price competition.

'Direct' competition exists where organisations produce similar products and appeal to the same group of consumers. A private bus company in Barbados is in direct competition with a rival private company, and with government buses.

Even when an organisation provides a unique end product with no direct competition, it still has to consider 'indirect' competition. The budget Barbados-based airline REDJet faced indirect competition from ferry services in the Caribbean as well as direct competition from other low-cost airlines. A car manufacturer might face indirect competition from a scooter company if a person decides to buy a scooter instead of a small car.

Did you know?

A good example of competitive pricing is in telecommunications. The competition to win customers between Digicel and Lime involves making competitive offers to attract mobile use away from the rival service provider.

KEY TERMS

Competitive price: price perceived to offer better value for money (when combined with other elements of the marketing mix) than prices offered by rival firms.

Competition pricing

Several pricing strategies can be followed in a competitive market.

Competitive pricing

A **competitive price** is one that gives an edge in the marketplace. It is not necessarily a lower price than those of rivals, however, because of other elements in the marketing mix. It is possible to argue that, say, Gillette razor blades are of better quality than rival brands, and because of this the company can charge a higher price that is still more competitive than the prices of other blades.

Competitive prices can be offered at different pricing levels:

■ Low prices can be set to attract customers away from competitors and increase sales.

■ Average prices mean that a company has to compete with rivals by other means, such as having better-quality products or better promotions.

- High or premium prices can be competitive if the price offered is coupled with other important aspects of the marketing mix, such as a superior product or superior service.

A competitive price is thus not necessarily a low price, or one that is lower than those of rivals, but one that is *perceived* to be competitive by potential and actual consumers. In reality, however, a competitive price is likely to be lower than the price of a similar rival product. Businesses can use a **competitive pricing strategy** as a way to win **market share** and sales.

Predatory or destroyer pricing

Predatory or destroyer pricing, as its name suggests, involves selling a product at a very low price to destroy new or existing competitors. A good or service is sold at or below the cost of manufacturing the good or providing the service.

KEY TERMS

Competitive pricing strategy: pricing plan designed to use pricing of goods as a means to attract and win customer purchases.

Market share: proportion or percentage of total sales in a particular market held by a specific firm.

CASE STUDY

Airline accused of predatory pricing

AirJet was a Trinidad-based low-cost airline running on a no-frills, low-cost basis. It began trading in 2010 and established routes to, amongst other destinations, Barbados and Jamaica. However, it faced opposition in Barbados, where there were concerns that the company was engaging in predatory pricing in order to win market share. The airline ceased trading in 2013.

1 How might a case be made that a budget airline is engaged in predatory pricing?

2 Why might businesses in Barbados with an interest in the airline industry make a case that a rival like AirJet is engaged in predatory pricing?

3 How might AirJet have argued that it was engaged in competitive and not predatory pricing?

Going rate pricing

In highly competitive markets, companies may base their pricing strategies on what their competitors are offering. Prices are likely to gravitate towards a 'going rate': a business examines competitors' prices and chooses a price broadly in line with them. In a competitive market, the 'going rate' is likely to mean that firms are able to make only limited profits.

Did you know?

Destroyer pricing is illegal. It is considered anti-competitive on the grounds that firms using it are seeking to eliminate competitors.

Summary table

Pricing strategy	What it involves	Benefits
Competitive pricing	Using price as a means to gain a competitive edge in the eyes of consumers	Leads to increased sales and potentially more profits
Destroyer pricing	Charging extremely low prices at or almost at a loss	Helps to eliminate existing rivals and potential new entrants to the industry
Going rate pricing	Charging the market price (i.e. that set by key competitors)	Means that you are able to focus on other aspects of competition to secure market share

---

Summary questions

1 To what extent is a competitive price the lowest price charged in the marketplace?

2 What is the difference between 'destroyer pricing' and 'competitive pricing'?

On completion of this section, you should be able to:

■ evaluate various pricing strategies by explaining and illustrating cost-plus pricing.

Did you know?

A small service business such as a boat sign writer will often calculate cost plus pricing in the following way. They will work out the typical cost per hour for the labour and materials they supply. As well as this they will charge an extra margin for profit enabling them to set an hourly charge to their customers.

Figure 2.26.1 *Cost-plus pricing involves calculating the cost of completing a job, in this instance painting a boat sign, and then adding a set margin on top for profit*

How cost-plus pricing works

In practice, cost is the most important influence on price. Many businesses base prices on simple cost-plus guidelines. Costs are calculated and then a profit margin is added in order to determine the price. For example, if a shop sign writer knows that it will take 10 hours to produce a shop sign at a cost of $10 per hour, she knows that her costs of producing the sign are $100:

$$10 \text{ hours} \times \$10 = \$100$$

If she sets herself a profit margin of 25 per cent, then the selling price will be:

$$\$100 + \$25 = \$125$$

Benefits and drawbacks of cost-plus pricing

The cost-plus approach leads to price stability. Prices change only to reflect cost changes. This approach provides an understandable, practical and popular solution to pricing issues.

Cost-plus pricing is very popular for small businesses because it is easy to calculate and make sure that a margin is added for profit.

Cost-plus pricing is also popular for large firms. For a large business, unit costs will fall rapidly at first as the overheads are spread over a larger output. Unit costs then become relatively stable over a considerable range of output (Figure 2.26.2, right-hand part of the curve). It is therefore a relatively simple calculation to add a fixed margin (for example, 20 per cent) to the unit cost. The firm is able to select an output to produce (Q) and to set a price that will be 20 per cent higher than the unit cost of production (Figure 2.26.2).

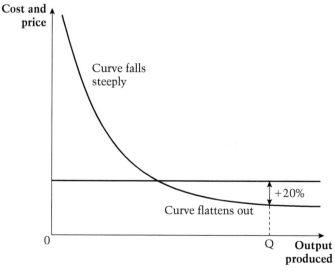

Figure 2.26.2 *Cost-plus pricing*

Table 2.26.1 shows the benefits and drawbacks of cost-plus pricing.

Table 2.26.1 Benefits and drawbacks of cost-plus pricing

Benefits of cost-plus pricing	Drawbacks of cost-plus pricing
■ Calculations of price are simple ■ Quick calculations enable rapid quotation ■ Profit margins are predictable	■ If price is set too high, sales may fall short of expectations. If set too low, potential revenue is sacrificed ■ Focus is product- or producer-led rather than based on customer requirements ■ Ignores competitors and their actions, so may be uncompetitive ■ Inflexible: it does not consider changing market conditions ■ Ignores the impact of price elasticity of demand

Mark-up

The concept of 'mark-up' is associated with cost-plus pricing, particularly in the context of trading companies – that is, companies that buy products in order to sell them.

Mark-up is the difference between the cost of a good or service and the price at which it is sold. For example, retail mark-up is calculated as the difference between the price at which the purchaser buys a good from the supplier and the retail price.

There are two main approaches to marking up a product as part of cost-plus pricing.

1 **Charging a fixed mark-up.** For example, a retailer may purchase dresses from the manufacturer at $50 each and then add an extra $60 on in order to secure a profit:

   Cost price = $50

   Fixed retail margin = $60

   Selling price = $110

2 **Charging a percentage mark-up.** It is not uncommon for clothing retailers to mark their goods up by 100 per cent, 200 per cent or even 300 per cent for luxury items. A luxury designer dress bought by a retailer for $500 and with a mark-up of 300 per cent would be sold for $2,000, that is, cost price $500 + (3 × $500).

You can calculate the percentage mark-up on an item if you know the sale price and the cost price:

$$\text{Mark-up} = \frac{(\text{Sale price} - \text{Cost})}{\text{Cost}} \times 100$$

So for our luxury dress, mark-up is:

$$\frac{(\$2,000 - \$500)}{\$500} \times 100 = 300\%$$

Summary table

Pricing strategy	What it involves	Key benefits
Cost-plus pricing	Charging a price by adding a margin to costs	■ Easy method to calculate ■ Ensures costs are covered

Summary questions

1 To what extent are cost-plus pricing and competitive pricing incompatible?

2 A manufacturer of soft drinks in the Caribbean employs a cost-based pricing strategy.

   a What is likely to be the impact on the pricing of different soft drinks in its product range?

   b What difficulties might it encounter in employing the cost-plus pricing approach?

Did you know?

Psychological pricing emphasises the emotional element of customer perceptions: for example, odd-pricing at $99.99 assumes that consumers will be more prepared to pay that price than $100.

Perceived value pricing

Most surveys show that customers choosing where to shop prioritise prices and value for money as the main ingredients in their choice. If prices are too high, they may think that they are not getting value. If prices are too low, however, they may question the quality of a product.

CASE STUDY

Customer perception of price

Figure 2.27.1 shows the alternatives faced by a seller when making a pricing decision.

High prices E Maximum price that consumers will pay

$\left.\begin{matrix} D \\ C \end{matrix}\right\}$ Price band of competing products

   B Minimum price that customers would see as appropriate

Low prices A Cost of production

Figure 2.27.1 Possible prices

Assume that a product cost A to produce. The business cannot sell the product for less than B without its quality being questioned ('How can it be sold for such a low price? Is there something wrong with it?').

Competing products are selling for prices between C and D, and the maximum chargeable price would be E. If the product is 'nothing special' in terms of customer perception, the price should be pitched between B and D. However, if the product is really exciting and captures the imagination of consumers, it can be pitched anywhere between C and E.

1 Why would you not charge the maximum price (E) for a 'nothing special' product?

2 Why would you not charge the minimum appropriate price (B) for a special product?

Price skimming

At the launch of a new product, there is likely to be little competition in the market: demand for the product may be somewhat inelastic. Consumers will have little knowledge of the product. **Skimming** (named after the process of taking cream off the top of milk) involves setting a reasonably high initial price in order to yield high initial returns from those consumers willing to buy the new product (Figure 2.27.2).

Once the first group of customers has been satisfied, the seller can lower the price in order to make sales to new groups of customers. This process can be continued until the business is confident that it has catered for a larger section of the total market. In this way, the business removes the risk of under-pricing the product. A possible disadvantage of skimming is that consumers who buy the product when it is expensive might feel that they have been

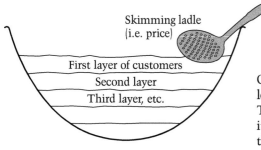

Skimming ladle (i.e. price)

First layer of customers

Second layer

Third layer, etc.

Figure 2.27.2 Skimming pricing

cheated when the price falls, and so may be reluctant to buy the product again or to make purchases from that supplier again.

Penetration pricing

Skimming may be an appropriate strategy when a seller is unsure of the elasticity of demand for the product (see 2.24). **Penetration pricing**, on the other hand, is appropriate when the seller knows that demand is likely to be elastic. It is normally associated with the launch of a new product (Figure 2.27.3) when a low price is required to attract customers to the product. As the price is low, the product may make a loss until consumer awareness is increased.

A typical example is a new breakfast cereal or a product being launched in a new overseas market. Along with a relatively low price, it would be launched with **discounts** and special offers. As the product rapidly penetrates the market, sales and profitability increase. Prices can then rise slowly.

- New products
- High fixed costs associated with set-up
- Need for large volume of sales

Figure 2.27.3 *Penetration pricing*

Penetration pricing is particularly appropriate for products where economies of scale can be employed to produce large volumes at lower unit costs. Products that are produced on a large scale are initially burdened by high fixed costs for research, development and purchases of plant and equipment. It is important to spread these fixed costs quickly over a large volume of output. Penetration pricing is also common when there is a strong possibility of competition from rival products.

Did you know?

A disadvantage of penetration pricing is that consumers become used to the low price. As a result, when the price is increased they may feel that the good is not worth the higher price. Demand may therefore fall when prices are raised.

Summary table

Pricing strategy	Description	Main benefit
Perceived value	Based on charging a price that consumers see as relevant/appropriate	Focuses on consumer requirements (a market-led approach)
Skimming	Initially charging a high price and then progressively lowering the price in line with elasticity	Enables marketer to capture a range of buyers with different intensities of demand for the product
Penetration	Charging a low initial price in order to enter a market	Makes it possible to capture attention and build up market share quickly

Summary questions

1 Compare and contrast skimming and penetration pricing as strategies for entering a new market.

2 Can you identify situations where a company has recently engaged in penetration pricing in your territory? What was the response of rival companies?

3 What are the dangers of charging prices that are higher than the perceived value?

> **KEY TERMS**
>
> **Intermediaries:** firms or individuals such as wholesalers, retailers and agents who help to move a product from the producer to the consumer or business user.

Did you know?

For many goods the cost of distribution may be the highest single cost of the product, particularly when goods have to be transported for long distances and stored in temperature-controlled conditions.

> **KEY TERMS**
>
> **Distribution channel:** a set of independent organisations that help to make a product available for use by consumers or business units.

Distribution

The component 'place' in the four Ps (see 2.3) refers to where a product is purchased from and how it is distributed. Most consumers of bottled or canned drinks buy them from a retail store – a supermarket or corner store. The manufacturer has to distribute the bottles and cans through a number of **intermediaries** to get them to the consumer. The role of distribution is to get goods from the producer to the user in the most efficient way possible.

Elements of efficient distribution are:

■ being cost-effective in distributing costs – that is, keeping transport, packaging, mailing and storage costs as low as possible (relative to the type of good being transported)

■ distributing in such a way as to protect the goods in the process of distribution (that is, without breakages or damage)

■ getting goods to the consumer on time – speed of delivery may be essential, particularly with perishable goods like fresh food

■ getting the goods to places that are convenient to the customer – this might mean delivering them to a convenient location, or the customer's door.

The importance of place in the marketing mix is that it enables the supplier to provide goods where and when the consumer wants them.

Distribution channels

To get the goods to the end consumer, the producer may supply 'direct' to consumers, or use intermediaries as part of the **distribution channel** – the means by which the goods are delivered.

Figure 2.28.1 illustrates alternative channels of distribution. The diagram uses the example of a large international soft-drinks company (the 'manufacturer'). The 'consumer' is people who drink the products.

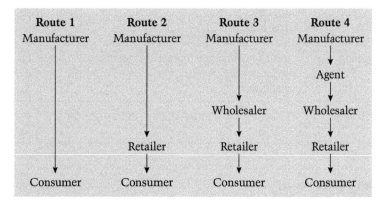

Figure 2.28.1 *Channels of distribution*

Direct selling

In direct selling, the producer of the goods sells direct to the consumer. Small-scale farmers may sell produce such as eggs, tomatoes, sweet potatoes direct at the roadside. On a larger scale, there are a number of types of direct selling:

- direct mail – promotional material posted to targeted customers
- mail-order catalogues sent on request, or unsolicited
- direct response advertising, often using magazines and newspaper advertisements, to arouse consumer interest and stimulate orders
- telemarketing – using the telephone to win customer sales
- internet marketing – using information on websites and links to generate online sales.

Indirect selling

Short channel

The short channel runs from manufacturer to retailer to consumer. This is the most popular method, and large supermarkets typically work on this basis. For example, a supermarket in Trinidad buys direct from local food suppliers and household manufacturing companies and from international suppliers (in this case, from the US and South America), and sells to consumers.

Long channels

There are two main types of long channel:

- Manufacturer to wholesaler to retailer to consumer. A wholesaler is a large storage firm that buys in bulk from manufacturers, stores the goods as necessary and distributes to smaller retail outlets. The wholesaler may also be involved in packaging and labelling. Wholesalers in the Caribbean may act as import agents, storing goods for large international companies. A 'cash and carry' is a type of wholesaler where small retailers can go to make bulk purchases.
- Manufacturer to agent to wholesaler to retailer to consumer. This channel is used in international trade. An exporter who wants to sell in an overseas market may hire an agent to operate on its behalf. The agent then works through a number of intermediaries in the host country.

The longer the distribution channel, the more separate intermediaries that will be taking a share of the profits, and the more complex the distribution arrangements. With the development of online communication, many manufacturers have sought to cut out intermediaries so as to sell more directly to consumers. Even online purchases need distribution, however, and internet companies use transport and delivery companies. Mail delivery companies have become an important part of the modern distribution system.

Did you know?

'Resellers' describes organisations that make products more easily available to their users. They include wholesalers, retailers, agents and other distribution companies. 'Physical distribution intermediaries' refers to warehouse companies and transport firms involved in moving goods from manufacturers to their destinations.

Summary questions

1 An exporter of Caribbean foods to other Caribbean territories is based in Trinidad. What would you recommend as the most effective distribution channels to use in the following scenarios?

   a The exporter has little knowledge of markets in other countries.

   b The exporter is seeking to share as little of the profit from selling as possible.

2 What are the benefits and drawbacks of direct distribution, for the following?

   a An online book retailer

   b A Caribbean music label

Summary table

Route	Benefits to producer	Drawbacks to producer
Direct selling	Controls distribution, does not share profits	Has to organise own distribution
Indirect selling: short channel	Only deals with retailer Retailer organises selling	Has to share profits with retailer
Indirect selling: long channels	Benefits from specialist knowledge of intermediaries and additional services provided by intermediaries	Complicated distribution routes which may lead to loss of quality along the distribution route

Figure 2.29.1 *Fresh tomatoes are perishable, so they need to be sold through a short channel; standardised bulk-manufactured tinned tomatoes can be sold through a long channel*

Choice of distribution channel

How a company distributes its products depends on the nature of the product. The distribution channel will accordingly be long or short, as outlined in 2.28. There are three main sets of factors that influence the choice of channel: product, market and company factors.

Product factors

Product factors result from the nature of the product being distributed. They include:

■ **Unit value of the product:** products sold at low prices – for example, snack foods such as potato chips (crisps) – are usually sold through a long channel because the producer wants to reach as wide a market as possible. High-value items such as industrial goods (for example, machinery) and designer clothing will be sold through a shorter channel, giving the producer more control of the distribution.

■ **Perishability of the product:** goods such as fresh tomatoes and fruit need to reach the consumer quickly and are most likely to be sold through a short channel. Non-perishable items such as canned food and furniture are more likely to be distributed through longer channels.

■ **Bulk and weight:** heavy and bulky items, such as steel girders, are likely to be distributed through shorter channels to keep down distribution costs. Lighter and smaller items, such as jewellery, can be distributed through longer channels: although it may be high in value, it is light in weight and so is less costly to distribute.

■ **Standardised/non-standardised:** mass-produced items, such as multi-pack razor blades and some cosmetics, are likely to go through longer channels. Products that are more differentiated and non-standardised, such as designer handbags, may go through shorter channels. In this way, producers have more control over the relationship that they build with the consumer.

■ **Technical/non-technical:** technical products that require detailed explanation, customer support and service, such as complex electronic gadgets, may go through shorter channels. This may also apply to new products that require more promotion and explanation. Less technical and older, established products can be sold through longer channels.

■ **Product lines:** if a good is one of a large product line, the producer may manage distribution directly because it can spread marketing efforts over a wide range of its own products. If the good is a company's only product, the producer may leave distribution to the intermediary.

Market factors

The type of market is also a factor in choosing distribution channels. Some examples of market factors are:

■ **Industrial or consumer market:** in industrial markets (such as that for agricultural machinery) the producer may prefer to deal directly with business customers; in mass consumer markets (say for household goods) longer channels may be used.

- **Number and location of buyers:** if there are just a small number of consumers located in a small area, a shorter channel may be used. Longer channels may be used for many consumers who are widely dispersed – tea and coffee drinkers for example.
- **Size and frequency of orders:** the producer may deal with customers directly for purchases that are infrequent; for large regular orders, the producer may be content to work through intermediaries.
- **Buying patterns:** the type of distribution channel will be affected by factors such as whether the customer spends a short or long time making a purchasing decision, whether he or she is happy to use self-service, and whether he or she is looking for credit arrangements.

Company factors

Finally, company factors may affect the choice of distribution channel:

- **The nature, size and objectives of the company:** a company that prides itself on its brand and reputation may prefer to deal directly with customers. A company should also consider how much control, as producer, it wants over the distribution process.
- **Financial resources available:** the resources available in the budget for distribution affect distribution decisions, as channels vary in their costs and revenues.
- **Management competence:** small, new companies with little experience may prefer to work through established distributors. Established companies may have distribution channels with which they are happy.

Summary table

Factors influencing choice of channel		
	Characteristics of short channels	**Characteristics of long channels**
Product factors	■ Perishable ■ Complex ■ Expensive	■ Durable ■ Standardised ■ Inexpensive
Market factors	■ Industrial/business users ■ Geographically concentrated ■ Technical products ■ Large orders for products	■ Consumers ■ Geographically dispersed ■ Low-tech products ■ Smaller orders for products
Producer factors	■ Producer has extensive resources ■ Product lines consist of many items ■ Control of the channel is important	■ Producer has fewer resources ■ Limited product lines ■ Control of the channel less important

Summary questions

1 Consider two manufacturers: one producing large quantities of low-value items across the Caribbean, the other selling small quantities of high-value items in targeted areas of a few territories. How might the distribution decisions be different for each manufacturer?

2 In what situations is a producer most likely to choose to distribute using direct selling rather than long-channel selling?

What is a logistics strategy?

A logistics strategy is a plan for the distribution of goods. It involves the choice of distribution channel, transportation and methods of delivery. A logistics strategy focuses on the **distribution intensity**: this may be intensive, selective or exclusive.

Intensive distribution

The aim of an intensive distribution strategy is to distribute goods and services through all the available channels in a geographical area. This is an appropriate strategy for items that appeal across broad groups of consumers, such as convenience goods.

CASE STUDY

SM Jaleel soft drinks

Busta soft drinks are one of the Caribbean's most celebrated soft drinks. They are produced by SM Jaleel in Trinidad and St Lucia and distributed throughout the Caribbean and across the world.

SM Jaleel drinks are distributed through many channels and intermediaries: for example, direct to bars, restaurants and cafés across the Caribbean. The company also supplies large and small retail outlets as well as vending machines, airport terminals, hotels and test-match cricket venues.

1　Why is an intensive distribution strategy suitable for SM Jaleel?

2　What are the product and market characteristics that make the company's products suitable for intensive distribution?

3　What other Caribbean manufactured products can you identify for which intensive distribution is suitable?

Selective distribution

Selective distribution involves making a product available through a limited number of channels. There are a number of reasons for this:

■ By working with selected retail outlets, the producer has much greater control of marketing activity and the way that the product is presented to the market.

■ The producer is able to build up much stronger relationships and develop more control over the distribution of the product. The distribution strategy might establish a set of rules and guidelines for distribution, such as the advertising, promotion, display and selling of the product.

■ The producer is better able to provide focused training on aspects of distributing the product.

■ The overall cost of marketing activity can be kept down because of the focus on narrower channels.

■ The producer can choose to work only with wholesalers and retailers who have a good credit rating, pay for supplies quickly and enable the producer to reach a large number of customers. So a manufacturer of confectionery or household goods, for example, might choose to focus on distributing primarily through larger supermarkets.

Selective distribution is common for consumer goods such as clothing, furniture, household goods and computers, where shoppers take time to visit a range of stores to compare prices and goods being offered. By working closely with retailers, producers can make sure that their goods are competitive and well presented.

Wholesalers and retailers favour selective distribution because it enables them to make higher profit margins. With non-selective distribution there is more competition between intermediaries.

Exclusive distribution

This extreme form of selective distribution is commonly used in the distribution of cars, where a manufacturer sells cars through exclusive dealerships. The producer deals with one distributor.

Exclusive distribution is very important when the emphasis is on quality and 'exclusivity' of the product. It is most likely to be used for high-specification, expensive products, such as top-of-the-range perfumes, handbags and designer labels. Advantages of an exclusive strategy include:

- low marketing costs, as there is only one outlet
- considerable understanding in the channel about marketing objectives, advertising, promotional techniques and pricing strategy
- close customer focus, through service arrangements with the exclusive seller.

Exclusive distribution strategies are beneficial when the market consists of a relatively small number of buyers in a particular geographical area, when buyers are wealthy or when they have specialist tastes – for fine wines, for example.

Figure 20.30.1 shows the different distribution strategies in terms of the number of intermediaries.

Intensive	Selective	Exclusive
**********		
**********	**********	*
**********		
(lots of intermediaries)	(small number)	(one)

Figure 2.30.1 *Distribution strategies*

Summary questions

1 What products have you bought recently that are distributed through the following distribution arrangements?

   a Intensive

   b Selective

   c Exclusive

In each case explain why a particular distribution strategy is likely to have been chosen.

2 Why might a company that currently focuses on an exclusive distribution strategy change to a selective strategy? What might be the disadvantages of changing the strategy in this way?

Summary table

Main distribution channels or methods			
Type	Features	Benefits	Examples
Intensive	Many intermediaries	Reaches a wider market	Common household goods (e.g. rice, sugar, detergents)
Selective	Small number of intermediaries	Enables producer to build relationship with intermediaries	Clothing, furniture, jewellery
Exclusive	One intermediary	Exclusive image and control of branding and presentation of product	Luxury goods (e.g. expensive watches and perfume, cars)

Specific objective

On completion of this section, you should be able to:

■ examine the major tools of promotion and their implications, with reference to the objectives of promotion.

Promotion

Promotion consists of the different methods of communicating with a business's target audience.

Promotional objectives

A business has four main promotional objectives:

■ **To increase demand for a product:** for example, to increase the sales of a product at different periods in the product life cycle. A simple two-for-one promotional campaign might have this impact.

■ **To inform the market about a particular product and its features:** for example, an advertising campaign that shows the product and how it works. The objective is to increase product knowledge.

■ **To differentiate the product from rivals:** for example, offering passers-by in the street a free sample of a new product so that they can get the feel of what makes it particularly special. This might be a small cup of a new coffee blend, or a new low-fat spread.

■ **To increase brand awareness:** to increase customer awareness not only of a specific product, say the Toyota Lexus, but of the whole Toyota brand and its emphasis on quality car products.

The promotional mix

The promotional mix comprises all the marketing and promotional communication methods used to achieve promotional objectives. They fall into two key areas.

Non-controllable communications

These consist of marketing messages that occur as a result of word of mouth, personal recommendation or a consumer's overall perception of a particular product or service. For example, consumers' opinions are influenced by a number of factors, such as whether the family has used the product regularly.

Controllable communications

These are marketing messages that a company directs and include:

■ **Advertisements**: messages sent via the media that are intended to inform or influence the people who receive them.

■ **Direct mail**: personally addressed advertising sent through the post or by email or other forms of electronic communication, such as pop-ups.

■ **Public relations**: non-personal communication using the media. Unlike advertising, the success of public relations is not measured by the product's popularity. It is used to develop favourable relationships between the organisation and its public.

■ **Sales promotions**: techniques designed to increase sales, such as money-off coupons, free samples and competitions.

■ **Sponsorship**: the financing or partial funding of an event, personality, activity or programme in order to gain consumer awareness or media coverage.

■ **Product presentation**: improving a brand's visibility through packaging, the use of labels, merchandising and branding.

- **Direct selling**: making sales with an emphasis on the importance of salesmanship.

Advertising, sales promotions and direct selling are the most significant elements because they usually account for the majority of a business's promotional expenditure. Advertising is discussed in 2.32 and the other promotional tools in 2.33.

The AIDA model

AIDA is a four-stage model that stands for attention, interest, desire and action. The model can be applied to communicating with a business's target market through promotional activity in order to achieve promotional objectives. The promotion should inform, persuade and influence a customer to purchase a product or service. The process is set out in Figure 2.31.1.

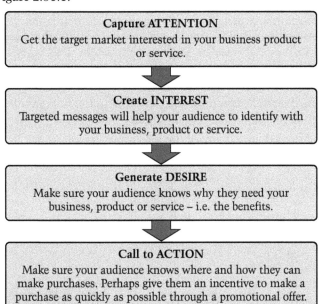

Figure 2.31.1 *The AIDA process*

Summary table

Promotional objective	How objective might be applied
Increase demand/sales	Special offers such as buy one, get one free
Inform the market	Advertising campaign to tell customers about a product
Differentiation (from competitors)	Trial offers so consumers get to know the distinctive features
Raise brand awareness	Prominent use of the brand name in promotional activity

Summary questions

1 How can the AIDA model be applied to each of the four main promotional objectives? Give examples to illustrate your answer.

2 The product life cycle goes through a number of stages: introduction, growth, maturity and decline. What promotional activities might be used by a company at each of these stages? Relate your answer to the four marketing objectives.

Specific objective

On completion of this section, you should be able to:

■ examine the major tools of promotion and their implications, with reference to the relative advantages of advertising.

> **KEY TERMS**
>
> **Advertising**: the promotion of a product using paid-for media (e.g. television).

Did you know?

A distinction is often made between informative advertising, which gives out information (e.g. government health advice), and persuasive advertising. Private businesses tend to focus on persuasive advertising, to persuade customers to buy their products.

Figure 2.32.1 *One way of promoting a product is through a brand ambassador. For example, SM Jaleel, the makers of Busta and other soft drinks, use the reggae artist I-Octane as their brand champion to help promote the brand across the Caribbean.*

The purpose of advertising

Advertising means promoting a product using paid-for media such as television. Advertising should 'speak to' its target audience and draw attention to the characteristics of the product that will appeal to the needs or wants of the potential consumer.

The initial purpose of advertising is to create awareness of a product, provide information and introduce an element of persuasion by pointing out the superior features of the advertised product compared with competing ones. If the product does not have a distinguishing feature – a unique selling point or USP – uniqueness can be promoted by brand image.

The ultimate purpose of advertising is to improve potential buyers' reactions to products by focusing their desires and giving them reasons for preferring a product over those of its competitors. This purpose can be expressed in advertising objectives such as:

■ increasing sales and acquiring a greater market share
■ showing the product features that outperform the competition
■ explaining the number of potential uses of the product
■ conveying the brand image of the product or organisation
■ introducing short-term promotional offers.

Choosing appropriate media

An important advertising decision is the choice of appropriate media. There are a number of criteria to consider.

Budget available

Here the key factors are cost and coverage. The higher the cost of advertising, the greater the market coverage. Booking prime-time 20-second advertising slots will be beyond the budget of most small companies.

Promotional campaign objectives

The choice of media must be in line with the company's marketing objectives. For example, if you want over 50 per cent of the population of Barbados to be aware of a new product, you will not advertise in a specialist magazine that has only a limited readership. Choice of media will be based on:

■ **coverage**: the percentage of the target audience who might see or hear the promotional message
■ **frequency**: the number of times the message will be seen or heard in a given time period
■ **media impact**: the extent to which the messages impact on the target audience and encourage them to respond (that is, buy) as required.

Appeal to target audience

Advertising messages must be relevant to the **target audience**. So a campaign to sell sports-related products might focus on a famous sports personality.

Timing

Advertising needs to coincide with when the company wants to generate interest in the product. This might be at the time of the launch, or when it wants to remind consumers about the product, perhaps to boost sales if the product has been available for some time.

Circulation and viewing figures

Information about, for example, how many people watch television at given times, and how many people read particular magazines, journals and newspapers, can be useful for marketers planning an advertising campaign.

KEY TERMS

Target audience: the specific group of viewers, listeners or readers who are the focus of appeal of advertisements.

Benefits and drawbacks of advertising media

Table 2.32.1 summarises the various media available to advertisers, with their advantages and disadvantages.

Table 2.32.1 Benefits and drawbacks of advertising media

Media	Benefits	Drawbacks
Newspapers	▪ High coverage (many readers) particularly for regional papers ▪ Eye-catching advertising	▪ Short life – thrown away ▪ Relatively expensive for short life
Consumer magazines	▪ Can be targeted carefully at readership ▪ Magazines may be kept for a long period (e.g. in health clinic waiting areas)	▪ Quite high cost relative to coverage
Television	▪ Mass market coverage ▪ Moving pictures help to display products and features ▪ Can be targeted at specific programmes	▪ Expensive ▪ Audience may be passive ▪ Some programmes have low viewing figures
Radio	▪ Can be targeted at specific groups of listeners ▪ Relatively low cost	▪ People may not pay attention ▪ Listening figures may be low
Cinema	▪ Concentrated viewing can be visual and impactful	▪ May have low coverage ▪ Viewers may forget advert once film starts
Billboard and transport advertising	▪ Low cost of advertising ▪ High audience coverage in urban areas	▪ Only a limited number of prime sites available ▪ Limited amount of information
Direct mail	▪ Targets specific households ▪ Personal communication	▪ No sound or movement ▪ May be thrown away without being read
Internet	▪ Can reach a wide audience ▪ Cheap to set up ▪ Can be targeted	▪ Not everyone has internet access ▪ Users may ignore online adverts

Summary table

Promotional method	Description	Examples
Advertising	Promoting a product using paid-for media	Television, internet, newspapers, radio

Summary questions

1 Recommend and justify an appropriate form of advertising for:

a a soft-drinks manufacturer introducing a new flavoured drink

b a car manufacturer launching a new model

c a business selling cricket equipment to cricket clubs.

2 In what situations might a company choose to promote its products using television advertising?

Specific objective

On completion of this section, you should be able to:

- examine the major tools of promotion and their implications, with reference to the relative advantages of personal selling, sales promotion and publicity.

Did you know?

One popular sales promotion approach is 'BOGOF' (buy one, get one free). This can be used to reward existing loyal customers.

Figure 2.33.1 *As part of a significant public relations exercise, the international telecommunications company Digicel is the main sponsor of the Caribbean Premier League*

KEY TERMS

Publicity: information about an individual, group, company, event or product that is spread through the media in order to attract public attention.

Advertising is the main promotional tool available to business, but there are three other main promotional tools: personal selling, sales promotion and publicity.

Personal selling

A company employs sales staff in the promotional process so that personal relationships can be built with the customer, whether this is to encourage a new or a repeat order.

Salespeople should be trained in the approaches and techniques of personal selling and know how to appeal to customers by focusing on the benefits that the customer is looking for, and demonstrating how the product outperforms rivals. They may be able to offer incentives such as discounts to clinch a deal. Typically, personal selling is used for more expensive goods such as cars, washing machines and electrical equipment, where the profit margin is high.

Sales promotion

Businesses often invest large sums of money in sales promotions. Sales promotions include money-off promotions, giving coupons to make new purchases, competitions and additional free content (for example, a 16 oz bottle of pepper sauce for the usual price of 11 oz). A common sales promotion is an introductory offer: for example, the first three months at half price for a new subscriber to a satellite television channel.

The marketing department of a company needs to calculate the cost of the sales promotion and evaluate it against the revenues that are likely to result.

In the market for some products, customers have come to expect sales promotions as part of the offer. For example, in buying a multi-pack of toilet rolls, you would expect to get two or three free. But sales promotions can lead to a perception that the product is of low quality. Sales promotion therefore tends to be used much less with exclusive items.

Publicity and public relations

Company **publicity** is information that a company produces to gain attention for the company or its products.

'Good' publicity is favourable media coverage. **Public relations** involves a deliberate attempt to generate this and build good relations with the public. A company seeks to manage and manipulate publicity through its public relations (PR) department.

'Bad' publicity occurs when information appears in the media and impacts badly on the company's reputation and brand, and the perception of its products. This might result from recall of a faulty product.

Large companies have specialist public relations departments that organise PR activities. These include organising and sponsoring events such as cricket matches, concerts, competitions and award ceremonies. The PR department produces a carefully worded communication (press release) that is circulated to newspapers and radio and television stations in a press conference or by email.

The advantage of good publicity and public relations for companies is that in most instances they can control the messages sent out. A press release can be carefully prepared and timed to accompany the launch of a new product or event, focusing on positive aspects that the company hopes will interest the media.

CASE STUDY

Digicel and the CPL

The press release below was produced by the PR department of Digicel when it became the prime sponsor of the Caribbean Premier League (CPL).

Digicel has been the main sponsor of West Indies Cricket since 2004. Since that time the company has proven its worth as a marketing leader in the region – something that CPL appreciates will bring great value to the tournament.

'The Digicel brand is a strong one – one that has captivated the Caribbean, and we are sure it will help us to do the same with the CPL brand,' concluded [CPL founder, Ajmal] Khan. 'Digicel has built a rock-solid reputation globally, and its positioning in the region and commitment to cricket can only serve to enhance the CPL product further.'

The sponsorship will be a multi-year deal and represents a significant investment from Digicel.

'The CPL is a perfect fit for Digicel. We're huge fans of West Indies cricket and this is a great opportunity for us to invest not only in what will be an amazing event, but also in the young cricketers who will benefit from around the region,' stated Digicel Group Marketing Director Kieran Foley. 'Having seen all the plans for the inaugural tournament, we know the CPL will be a spectacle like nothing else seen in the region and we are looking forward to being front and centre of the action.'

1 What do you see as being the main benefits to Digicel from sponsoring the CPL?

2 How does the press release enable Digicel to control public relations surrounding the process?

Summary table

Promotional method	Description	Advantages	Disadvantages
Personal selling	Use of sales staff to promote a company and its products	■ Enables relationship building ■ Enables communication of clear personal and targeted messages	■ Depends a lot on the qualities of the salesperson ■ Could be seen as too forceful
Sales promotion	Methods used to encourage the purchase of products	■ Act as incentives to encourage purchases ■ Add excitement to the purchase of products	■ Can give the impression that the product is low quality
Publicity	Information that can show a product in a good light	■ Messages can be controlled through public relations ■ Increases the reputation and attractiveness of products	■ Possibility of negative publicity

Summary questions

1 Identify situations where you personally responded favourably to personal selling, sales promotion or publicity. In each case, describe the promotional tool used and how this impacted on your actions.

2 Compared with advertising, what are the main drawbacks of the following?

   a Personal selling   c Sales promotion

   b Publicity

2.34 Internet marketing 1: development

Specific objectives

On completion of this section, you should be able to:

- describe the development of internet marketing
- discuss the importance of internet marketing decisions, including the importance of e-commerce to business organisations.

KEY TERMS

Bricks and mortar: describes businesses that do not trade online (e.g. your local bakery).

Clicks and mortar: describes businesses that cut their costs by using the internet as a shop window. Customers can browse for products and services from the comfort of their own home.

E-commerce: buying and selling goods online.

B2C: where a business sells goods to consumers using the internet.

B2B: where a business sells industrial or other products to other businesses using the internet.

E-marketing: finding out about customers' needs and wants online in order to meet their requirements.

Did you know?

Online purchasing reduces the influence of traditional personal selling and cuts out a number of intermediaries in the distribution process, so reducing costs for the business and the price for the shopper.

Development of internet marketing

Traditional businesses are based on a physical presence (**bricks and mortar**) and take the form of factories and shops, for example. In contrast, modern businesses usually also include an internet presence or website, providing **clicks and mortar**.

Buying and selling on the internet, also known as **e-commerce**, provides smaller companies with many of the advantages previously available only to large companies, particularly in market research. In the Caribbean it gives businesses in both **B2C** and **B2B** markets the chance to reach new customers on a global scale.

Web technology enables a business to display products and services in detail, make promotional offers and supply supporting information. A well-organised website plays a key role in **e-marketing**, capturing customer data such as names, addresses, phone numbers and email addresses. The business can use its customer database to send out further product details or news about the business (although some people find the many emails they receive quite intrusive).

Purpose of an online presence

Developing a high-quality company website is one of the objectives of a global company: it enables businesses to meet many of their marketing objectives. The website should encourage visitors and make them want to return repeatedly. The three main factors in a good website are content, community and commerce (Figure 2.34.1). Other key ingredients are ease of navigation (finding your way around the site), ease of making purchases and security of transactions.

Content	**Community**	**Commerce**
Content drives users to a website – content includes news, interviews and product information.	Visitors to a site need to feel that they are part of a group, and that they are valued by the site provider and the brand it represents	It is a way of generating income through shopping, advertising, sponsorship, etc.

Figure 2.34.1 The three Cs of a good website

Home shopping

Home shopping has been one of the most rapidly growing retailing sectors. It enables companies, in the Caribbean and elsewhere, to promote their goods to customers anywhere in the world who have internet access. Likewise, Caribbean shoppers can make purchases from online retailers across the globe. Shoppers can visit different sites to make comparisons before making a choice. They can even consult a 'buying guide' to check options and ratings from other consumers.

Following up website visitors

A key aspect of market research is to understand customers. An internet company keeps a record of people who have shown an interest in its website and the goods and services offered. A well-designed website permits follow-up communication from 'cookies' (2.10), which provide analysts with information such as the pages requested and how long the visitor stayed on the site. This information is stored using the computer's internet protocol (IP) address. However, because internet users are given a different IP address each time they log on, it is far more useful for analysts to log visits against a cookie ID, to recognise repeat visitors.

Even more desirable for the website provider is for users to submit further details (such as their email addresses) voluntarily, as these can be stored in a database referenced against the browser's cookie. The website provider can then make navigation to the site much easier. Users do not have to register information every time they log on and communication between the website provider and users is improved.

Booming e-commerce

E-commerce is booming in the Caribbean for a number of reasons:

- the increase in the number of e-tailers (online sellers)
- increased ease of making payments online (including improvements in security)
- the growth of social media and the sharing of information about good sites to visit
- the attractiveness of discounted online prices
- the spread of banking services including debit and credit cards.

E-commerce helps a business organisation to:

- lower costs through their entire supply chain
- improve customer relationships
- redefine business relationships
- increase the speed of nearly every stage of doing business
- keep all interested parties fully informed of market needs and opportunities.

It is predicted that e-commerce will grow faster than any other form of legitimate business dealing and business organisations are advised to have an e-commerce strategy to survive and grow in today's business world.

Summary table

Factors leading to the growth of online marketing and e-commerce	
Online marketing	**E-commerce**
■ Cookies enable the logging of visits. ■ Data can be stored in databases, giving details of customers and purchases. ■ Data can then be turned into marketing information, enabling e-marketers to know what customers want, when, and how much they are prepared to pay.	■ Development of e-tailers and their websites communicating directly with customers online. ■ Easier methods of making payment have fuelled the growth of companies selling through 'clicks' rather than 'bricks and mortar' customer interactions.

Summary questions

1 Identify the site of a Caribbean based e-tailer, perhaps one that you use regularly.

   a How is this e-tailer able to collect marketing information about you?

   b What sort of promotional activities does the e-tailer employ to entice you to purchase its goods?

   c To what extent does the company make its website particularly relevant to you as an individual consumer?

2 What do you feel are the principal benefits to the Caribbean from the growth of e-commerce?

On completion of this section, you should be able to:

- discuss the importance of internet marketing decisions, with reference to the opportunities created and challenges posed by internet marketing.

You can create a simple website by finding a free web-hosting service on the internet. This gives you instructions on how to build the site: for example, by filling in a set of templates, or dragging and dropping items into the site.

A product-related website can:

- educate consumers about new or existing products and their use

- provide information – for example, about new product developments, different product specifications and what to do if a product goes wrong

- provide recreational activities such as games and competitions

- offer commercial benefits, such as enabling consumers to buy on the internet, and sellers to sell their products and services.

The most obvious form of internet display advertising is banner ads – small rectangular adverts that appear on websites. If you click on them, your web browser takes you to the advertiser's website.

Creating an online site

The first challenge for online marketing is to create a commercial website. For a major business this may have thousands of pages, cost at least $100,000 and take six months to set up. It will then need full-time staff to look after it. However, a small business can employ a web designer to create a site of between five and 50 interactive screens much more quickly.

When a business has developed a website, it needs to find a server to host the work. 'Hosting' means storing, delivering to users and maintaining files for websites. Each website has its own domain name and set of email addresses. A business domain name should be simple, such as www.icerecords.com or www.go-jamaica.com.

A domain name that ends in .com in the US and the Caribbean shows that the website is owned by a commercial organisation. Domain names must be registered with a domain registry, which only allows unique names. The domain name is the web address of a business and gives a browser access to the webpages created for that business.

Opportunities of internet marketing

The internet enables a business to provide 24-hour access to the products and services that it sells online. A key benefit is that it is the customer who initiates the contact. For a short while at least, the seller has the undivided attention of the buyer. It is therefore important for website information to be easy to access, clear and interesting. It should also be easy to make payments and there should be well-organised delivery channels, usually based on a speedy delivery system.

Internet trading also provides increased flexibility of location for both consumer and providers. For example, you might see an advert for car insurance on TV while you are exercising in the gym. The advert is likely to give a phone number or website address. When you get home you can request a free quote by filling in an online application form, or by communicating details over the phone.

Benefits to the provider of an internet product or service include:

- low ongoing costs once the site has been established
- the provider does not need an expensive outlet in the town or elsewhere
- the provider can set out far more information about products or services on an easy-to-navigate site
- the provider can access a wide market from a remote location
- the provider can use online advertising to promote its product either on someone else's website or on its own.

Benefits to consumers include:

- lower prices resulting from providers' low costs
- they can browse the site in the comfort of their own homes or other convenient location
- they can spend time navigating the website, finding out information before making a choice
- they do not need to be near the provider.

Challenges of internet marketing

There are a number of key issues associated with internet marketing.

- **Channel conflict:** when an existing business develops an online presence, this disrupts its existing distribution channels. Existing channel partners, such as a retailer, may not be happy and may seek to develop relationships with other suppliers.

- **Payment security:** consumers are often concerned about 'identity theft' by people who hack into their account, and may be reluctant to give their credit or debit card details. A business trading online needs to develop a secure payment system, often by working with a specialist online payments company.

- **Meeting customer expectations:** online shoppers expect a quick and reliable service and the opportunity to return goods if they are not satisfied. An online business needs to build a rapid and efficient delivery service and have a clear policy for 'returns'.

- **Overload of market feedback:** using online databases, a company can find out a lot of information about its customers, such as when they purchase, what they purchase and how often. The company needs to build effective systems for analysing and using this information.

- **Quality of server:** a business needs its server to be reliable and efficient. The company that provides the server must be focused on the needs of its client and provide constant site availability.

- **Registering with a search engine:** internet users carry out most of their searches for sites through search engines such as Google. If a business has not registered with the widely used search engines, it is unlikely to be found, unless it has an extremely well-known brand name. Businesses can pay a search engine to place their company at the top of their listings.

- **Cultural issues:** Caribbean online businesses trade across the globe. It is important to consider how an overseas user will use your website. Oriental scripts are read vertically, and Arabic is read from right to left. This impacts on how webpages should be designed to appeal to overseas markets.

Summary table

Internet marketing: opportunities and challenges	
Opportunities	**Challenges**
■ Access to larger markets ■ Opportunity for international sales ■ Flexibility of location ■ Customer seeks buyer ■ Opportunity to find out about customers and store information in databases ■ Online advertising ■ Reduction of costs through simpler distribution channels	■ Creating website, high initial cost ■ Registration of domain name, arranging hosting and payment systems ■ Threats from internet fraud, customer reluctance to give details ■ Channel conflict ■ Complexity of online data ■ Cultural issues associated with international use of site

Summary questions

1 Carry out some online research on a Caribbean website designed for international commerce.

  a How recognisable is the domain name?

  b Are there any issues with loss of 24-hour, 7-days-a-week service?

  c How easy is it to make payment using the site?

  d What market research information does the site collect from users?

  e Does the site use banner advertisements, or can it be accessed from other sites using banner advertisements?

2 A small coffee-growing cooperative in the Caribbean, which produces premium coffee, is considering developing a website to market its coffee internationally. Evaluate the benefits against the costs of developing and using the site.

Answers to all exam-style questions can be found on the accompanying CD.

Section 1: Multiple-choice questions

1 Over which of the following does the marketing department of a company have most control?

 A Social trends that lead to changes in consumer buying patterns

 B The micro-marketing environment

 C The marketing of new products by competitors

 D Government actions to control advertising by companies

2 A company has developed an exciting new product based on detailed market research to identify customer needs and expectations. This approach most closely represents:

 A the selling concept

 B the marketing concept

 C the production concept

 D the societal marketing concept.

3 Which component of a SWOT analysis focuses on factors outside the organisation that are likely to have a negative impact on the sales of the company?

 A Strengths   C Opportunities

 B Weaknesses   D Threats

4 Which of the following provides the best definition of the 'target market'?

 A The section of the market that is currently dominated by competitors

 B A component of the market that is currently showing growth in sales

 C A specific group of customers on whom marketing efforts are focused

 D A distinct section of the market identified in the market research process

5 Which of the following would be an example of secondary market research data?

 A Interviews carried out by the market research department of a company

 B Focus groups held in the marketing department with potential customers

 C The use of government statistics to identify economic and demographic trends

 D The development of a questionnaire to test customer perceptions of a product

6 In carrying out market research it is decided to include a 50 per cent representation of females and 25 per cent of people aged over 60 in the sample. What type of sampling technique is being applied?

 A Random sampling

 B Judgement sampling

 C Stratified sampling

 D Convenience sampling

7 A travel company has segmented potential customers for its marketing activities in terms of their lifestyle patterns: for example, the frequency with which they take holidays, and how much they like to spend. This approach to segmentation is referred to as:

 A geographical segmentation

 B behavioural segmentation

 C demographic segmentation

 D ethnic segmentation.

8 Johanna wants to buy a lightweight racing bicycle to compete in competitions. She also wants the bicycle to look stylish. When the salesperson focused on her desire for a stylish product, he was therefore focusing on:

 A the core product   D the product life cycle.

 B the actual product

 C the augmented product

9 A company that manufactures mobile phones has developed a new multifunctional phone with a lot of exciting applications (apps). The product has already developed a high market share in this important growth market. In terms of the Boston Matrix the phone would be classified as:

 A a star   C a cash cow

 B a question mark   D a dog.

10 A trading company knows from market research that price is elastic at the current market price. A logical way to increase revenue would be to:

 A keep prices at the current market rate

 B raise price to get consumers to pay more for goods

 C lower prices to get consumers to increase demand

 D wait to see whether competitors change their prices.

Section 2: Structured questions

11 a State the FOUR components of the marketing mix, giving an example of each of the components in relation to a luxury car. [4]

b Outline THREE alternative pricing strategies that a sports goods manufacturer could employ when introducing a new variety of training shoe into a competitive market. [6]

c A sports goods retailer currently employs a sales focus. However, a marketing adviser has suggested that it should change to a marketing focus. Outline TWO benefits of a sales focus and TWO benefits of a marketing focus. [12]

d Outline THREE benefits that the sports goods retailer could gain from e-marketing. [3]

12 a A Caribbean-based pharmaceuticals company has developed some new sunscreen lotions using aloe vera. Why should it engage in market research before deciding whether to go ahead with a full launch of these products? [6]

b i Outline THREE benefits of carrying out primary research in order to find out consumer opinions about these lotions. [6]

ii Outline TWO benefits of carrying out secondary research into the market for sunscreen products. [4]

iii Outline ONE drawback associated with carrying out secondary research. [2]

c What is probability sampling? Give one example of this approach. [3]

d Describe TWO types of non-probability sampling that could be used to research the market for sunscreen lotions. [4]

13 a What is the product life cycle? Illustrate your answer by drawing a diagram to show what the typical product life cycle looks like. [6]

b Identify FOUR marketing actions that a marketer can take to rejuvenate the product life cycle when sales start to decrease. Each of the actions that you describe should relate to a different component of the marketing mix. [12]

c What is the likely impact of injecting new marketing activity into the product life cycle? [3]

d How might knowledge of price elasticity help a marketer to take pricing decisions associated with a decline in sales of a product? [4]

14 Bradley is a music graduate. On completing his studies he invested in a sound system for playing at live events, such as wedding parties, birthdays and other celebrations. With his knowledge of different types of music he is able to play a wide variety of different music, including jazz, calypso, hip-hop, funk and street. He wants to make a good living from his business. A friend has suggested that Bradley engages in a segmentation strategy.

a What is a segmentation strategy? [3]

b Identify THREE different types of approach to segmentation that Bradley could use for his music business. [3]

c For each approach, identify how Bradley might employ the strategy and what TWO benefits he might derive from doing so. [9]

d His friend has also suggested that Bradley positions his business carefully in the marketplace. What do you understand by the term 'positioning'? Relate your answer to the live music business. [4]

e Explain TWO methods that Bradley could use to promote his business. [6]

15 Trinidad Dry Cleaning Services Incorporated offers a new service for suits, dresses and a range of other garments. It was recently set up in Port of Spain and is seeking to carry out some marketing activities in order to win more loyal custom.

a One dimension of marketing that the company is exploring is building the augmented product.

i What do you understand by the term 'augmented product'? [2]

ii Describe THREE ways in which Trinidad Dry Cleaning Services might develop its augmented product offering. [6]

b Trinidad Dry Cleaning Services is considering extending the width and depth of its product offering. Explain how it might increase:

i the width of its product offering [2]

ii the depth of its product offering. [3]

c Trinidad Dry Cleaning Services would also like to explore the idea of new product development (NPD). It would like to come up with some new ideas to develop the business so that it provides additional dry cleaning services beyond those provided by its rivals. Outline the SIX stages of new product development that would be involved in developing an idea for a new product. [12]

> Further exam questions and examples can be found on the accompanying CD.

General objectives

On completion of this module, you should be able to:

- appreciate the nature of entrepreneurship
- have an awareness of the characteristics of small business management.

Module 3 is designed to provide you with an understanding of what it means to be 'entrepreneurial' and to help you to identify some of the knowledge and skills required to set up a small business unit of your own.

The Caribbean is full of young entrepreneurs – people with imagination who have good ideas that they can turn into a successful business.

In *The Making of a Caribbeanpreneur* (2009), Nerissa Golden set out her belief that successful entrepreneurs have a desire to 'spend their lives doing the things they love'. Entrepreneurs have an internal drive to make a success from championing ideas and products in which they believe.

Levi Roots is a good example of a British-Jamaican entrepreneur, whose ideas have led him to success

Models of enterprise include private enterprises, where owners seek to make a profit for themselves, and social enterprises, which are set up to achieve socially desirable products and outcomes.

You will meet some terms associated with enterprise that may be unfamiliar. An **intrapreneur**, a play on the more established 'entrepreneur', means an employee within (*intra-*) a large enterprise who shows creativity and drive. An **e-preneur** is a person who develops an enterprise online, selling through a custom-built website. These are both recently devised terms.

Business and economic systems

Enterprise needs to be understood within the context of the **economic system** in which an individual enterprise exists. The Caribbean is characterised by different systems in different countries, ranging from more state-controlled systems (for example, in Cuba where only certain types of enterprise are encouraged) to more entrepreneurial systems (for example, in Barbados, where different business enterprises are encouraged to develop – in fishing, agriculture, fashion, music, IT, private transport and many other areas).

KEY TERMS

Intrapreneur: an employee within a large enterprise who shows creativity and drive.

E-preneur: a person who develops an enterprise online and sells goods through a website.

Economic system: the overall pattern of decision making within a society, which is based on who makes decisions related to areas such as buying, selling, production and price setting.

Size and growth of businesses

One of the most famous businesses in the Caribbean, SM Jaleel (SMJ), was set up in 1924 by Sheik Mohammed Jaleel as a soft-drinks and juices manufacturer. It originally employed 25 people and delivered the product by horse and cart direct to people's houses. Today, SMJ products are sold through half a million retailers and wholesalers worldwide. SMJ is now a large global business; in 1924 it was a relatively small enterprise.

There are a number of ways of measuring the size of a business, including the size of its output and the number of people it employs. A company like SMJ benefits from the scale on which it operates: it can use similar advertising techniques and packaging across the five continents in which it manufactures and sells. However, there are also advantages of being a small-scale producer, for example entrepreneurs are in close personal contact with their employees and customers.

Did you know?

The classification of a business as 'small' is made with reference to output, number of employees, share of the overall market and amount of capital employed: all are small relative to larger businesses.

Major challenges and opportunities faced by small businesses

There are many challenges facing a new start-up small business. These range from 'How do I know my product will be a success?' to 'What sources of finance can I access?' and 'Where should I set up?'

Opportunities arise from the existence of an attractive market, perhaps for a new type of product. For example, Gregory Richardson, the entrepreneur behind St Maarten-based Secure Tech International, identified the opportunity to protect information technology systems against cyber attacks and online pirates. He set up the first, and most successful, IT security business in the northern Caribbean.

Assistance available to small firms

Main areas where assistance is provided include financial and technical support, and education and training. A number of specialist agencies exist to help small businesses, including government (and non-government) agencies and financial institutions (including banks and credit unions).

Preparation of a business plan for a small business

The second half of this module provides the opportunity for you to create a business plan for a small business of your choice. To help you do this, sections 3.13–3.21 focus on an imaginary business in Trinidad, Rohit's Rotis. This extended case study outlines the stages involved in setting out a plan.

A business plan is a relatively short document setting out details of how a new business will be organised, how it will market and sell its products, and how it will raise finance and organise production. It also sets out the skills and qualities of the company's management. The financial part of the plan sets out projected values of sales and costs, and hence estimated profits.

A business plan helps small business owners to think systematically about their enterprise and anticipate whether the business will be profitable. Moreover, it can be presented to investors and financial institutions in order to raise finance. Many small businesses borrow money from banks and the bank will want to check that the entrepreneur has a viable business plan in place.

On completion of this section, you should be able to:

■ explain the nature and characteristics of entrepreneurship.

Figure 3.1.2 *Chubby is representative of the imaginative and entrepreneurial approach of Sheik Mohammed Jaleel and SM Jaleel*

What is an entrepreneur?

An **entrepreneur** is somebody who sets up an enterprise. He or she takes a risk that the business may not be successful and that the time and effort and money put in may be lost.

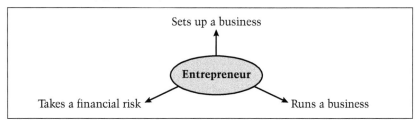

Figure 3.1.1 *Setting up a business*

Sheik Mohammed Jaleel provides an excellent example of an entrepreneur. In the 1930s he was manufacturing and distributing soft drinks and juices from his own home in Trinidad. Today everyone in the Caribbean knows SMJ's flagship product – Chubby Soft Drinks. The company founder had a good idea, spotted a real business opportunity, had good organisational skills and was prepared to risk his own capital to make the business a success.

To most people, an enterprise is a small business, usually a service or creative business. Every big company began as a small company, often with one enterprising individual as its head. Enterprise also means the act of setting up and running a business, being creative and taking a financial risk.

No business can begin without enterprise, and however big it becomes, it cannot continue without it. SMJ has continued to be successful through developing new and exciting products: in 1993 the company launched Chubby Soft Drinks, and in 1997 Busta Soft Drinks. Today the company has the largest blow-moulding facility in the Caribbean, where it manufactures its own plastic bottles. SMJ also has the **franchise** for distributing Cadbury Schweppes and Pepsi products in the Caribbean.

The business idea

Once you have a good business idea, the challenge is to sustain it, but of course the idea has to come first. Table 3.1.1 shows typical sources of ideas, and examples. Try to think of an additional example for each.

Table 3.1.1 *Business ideas*

Source of idea	Example
Developing a hobby	Making jewellery
Using your skills	Desktop publishing
A chance idea	A musical toothbrush
Spotting a gap in the market	A home hairdresser
Improving a product or service	A better hairdresser
Combining two existing ideas	Books and stationery shop
Solving problems for people	Financial adviser
Listening to what people want	Teenagers want a mobile disco

Types of enterprise

A starting point for the entrepreneur is to decide what type of enterprise to form. There are a number of options.

Sole trader

In a sole trader enterprise, the business is owned by just one person. The entrepreneur provides all of the capital and becomes the sole risk-taker in the business. The success of the business will be determined by how hard the entrepreneur works, and how good the business idea is. The benefit of this form of enterprise is that the owner takes all of the profits and can make his or her own decisions. The disadvantages are lack of funds, lack of a partner with whom to share ideas and the long hours required to turn a good idea into a sound business prospect.

Partnership

A partnership involves groups of entrepreneurs setting up a partnership, which they usually register in law as a partnership. The agreement sets out the terms of the partnership, such as how the work and profits will be divided up. Advantages of partnerships are that work can be shared and partners can benefit from each other's expertise and commitment. They also combine their capital. Weaknesses are that the partners may disagree, they have to share out the profits and, compared with companies, they have access to only limited capital.

Company

A company is different in law from the sole trader and partnership. It has to be officially registered with a registrar of companies in a particular territory. Before it is allowed to trade as a company it needs to lodge various documents setting out how it will be organised and run, and the rights of its owners – the shareholders. A small company is therefore more expensive to set up and requires more paperwork than other forms of enterprise. The advantages include access to finance from shareholders and a form of legal protection referred to as 'limited liability'. This limits the amount of money for which shareholders are liable if the company runs up debts that it cannot pay back – the maximum that they can lose is the value of their shares. This protection encourages shareholders to invest in a company.

Did you know?

Most of the large companies operating in the Caribbean began as small sole traders or partnerships owned by a small number of entrepreneurs, sometimes just one or two.

Summary questions

1 Identify a small local Caribbean enterprise with which you are familiar, such as a small business near you.
   a Who is the entrepreneur?
   b How is he or she taking a risk?
   c What form does the enterprise take?
   d What is the owner doing to sustain the enterprise?

2 Identify a larger Caribbean enterprise that was set up in a different part of the Caribbean from where you live. What imaginative and enterprising ideas do you associate with this enterprise?

Summary table

Enterprise involves:	Example:
Setting up an enterprise	SM Jaleel (SMJ)
Taking a risk	Sheik Mohammed Jaleel put his own capital into the start-up
Sustaining enterprise	SMJ has grown for 90 years
Choosing a form of enterprise	Sole trader or partnership or company

Specific objective

On completion of this section, you should be able to:

■ explain the nature and characteristics of entrepreneurship, with reference to corporate entrepreneurship (intrapreneurship).

KEY TERMS

Innovation: the introduction of new ideas or methods.

Think 'outside the box': come up with new and original ideas rather than tried-and-trusted approaches.

Did you know?

Lateral thinking is associated with thinking 'outside the box', but means coming to new ideas from an unexpected direction: for example, combining two existing, apparently unrelated ideas into a single unifying concept.

Intrapreneurship

Enterprise is also important in established businesses. Once a new business has settled down and become established, it is important that the people who make up that organisation continue to be enterprising. The term 'intrapreneurship' can be used to describe the qualities of someone working for an organisation who shows flexibility and imagination, and has a willingness to take risks and to be **innovative**. Caribbean businesses have a large number of people who are able to **think 'outside the box'** and come up with fresh ideas and solutions. Intrapreneurs often go on to develop their own business ideas and pursue a career working for themselves.

So if you are enterprising, there is also a place for you in existing companies because your ability to create new ideas will be valued.

How a company can use intrapreneurship

Companies are full of people with talent and good ideas. The challenge to an entrepreneurial company is to make use of its *intra*preneurial talent. There are a number of ways that a company can do this:

■ Encourage entrepreneurially minded people to innovate and provide them with the resources to back up their new ideas. This will involve providing intrapreneurs with the technical, financial and physical resources required to make projects a success.

■ Allow intrapreneurs to try out new things and take risks.

■ Identify intrapreneurs in the organisation and place them in positions where they can engage in innovative activity rather than restricting them to more mundane tasks (tasks that are nevertheless still important for the business).

■ Communicate clearly within the organisation that 'intrapreneurship' is valued – this should be reinforced by messages from people at the top, in company newsletters, training programmes and appraisal processes.

■ Make sure that managers listen to good ideas being generated from within their teams.

■ Reduce the 'red tape' involved when people come up with a new idea. Creative people can become frustrated by too many restrictions on their activities. They may even leave an organisation.

■ Reward good ideas, providing financial incentives and other rewards to encourage innovation in the workplace. A key part of rewarding intrapreneurs is to credit them for their good ideas: for example, publicising the ideas in a company newsletter.

■ Create systems through which intrapreneurial individuals can suggest new ideas, such as meetings to generate new ideas or a suggestion box. Traditionally, a suggestion box was an actual box into which slips of paper would be put with suggestions; today, a suggestion box could be an electronic database.

■ Accept that some good ideas may not succeed, but still encourage them.

Introducing intrapreneurship at GraceKennedy

In May 2012 young entrepreneur Yaneek Page introduced an intrapreneurial workshop at Jamaica Stock Exchange-listed company GraceKennedy. GraceKennedy prides itself on being an innovative company, so it was only natural for them to hold the workshop.

The training course was not like standard training courses with formulaic slideshow presentations, long training papers, booklets and handouts. Rather the focus of the course was on encouraging participants to come up with new and refreshing ideas.

1 Why might an intrapreneurship workshop be suitable for an innovative company?

2 Why does an intrapreneurship training course need to be different from a traditional course?

3 What sorts of activity would you expect to do in an intrapreneurship training course?

Figure 3.2.1 In 2012 young entrepreneur Yaneek Page introduced ideas about intrapreneurship to the Jamaican company GraceKennedy

Summary table

Nature of intrapreneurship	Enterprise from within an existing organisation applied by enterprising people
Characteristics of intrapreneurship	▪ Coming up with innovative ideas and solutions ▪ Thinking outside the box ▪ Exercise of imagination ▪ Willingness to take risks
How can intrapreneurship be encouraged?	▪ Allowing people to develop new ideas ▪ Giving them the resources to do so ▪ Listening to their ideas whilst acknowledging that some ideas might fail

Did you know?

Large organisations that encourage intrapreneurship are able to benefit from having lots of enterprising people who feel that they can make significant contributions to smaller units within the larger organisation. It is similar to having lots of small businesses inside a larger business.

Summary questions

1 Distinguish between *entre*preneurship and *intra*preneurship.

2 What are the similarities between intrapreneurship and entrepreneurship?

3 How might the way a company is organised and structured discourage intrapreneurship?

Specific objective

On completion of this section, you should be able to:

- explain the nature and characteristics of entrepreneurship, with reference to social entrepreneurship.

Did you know?

The profit of a private enterprise can be used for the personal use and benefit of the entrepreneur. The surplus of a social enterprise must be put back into the organisation to help its growth and improvement.

What is a social enterprise?

Both entrepreneurs and social entrepreneurs seek to use resources efficiently. However, a social enterprise is set up to achieve objectives that relate to meeting the needs of society or the environment. Social enterprises are sometimes referred to as 'not for profit' organisations. As a social enterprise, an organisation seeks to make a 'surplus' rather than a profit. Any surplus is used to further the purpose of the enterprise. Table 3.3.1 illustrates how a social entrepreneur is different from an entrepreneur.

Table 3.3.1 *Entrepreneurs and social entrepreneurs*

Entrepreneur	Social entrepreneur
Seeks to develop imaginative business ideas primarily for his or her own interest	Seeks to develop imaginative ideas for the good of society and the environment
Makes a profit (or loss)	Makes a surplus (or deficit)
Raises revenues from sales	Raises revenue from donations and some commercial activities (e.g. selling items)

CASE STUDY

Missionaries of the Poor

Missionaries of the Poor is a social enterprise first established by Father Richard Ho Lung in Jamaica in 1981. Father Richard's parents emigrated to Jamaica from China. Father Richard became a priest in Kingston and went on to found a social enterprise, Brothers of the Poor. Originally there were only four members of the enterprise and their work was to try and build family and community in poor areas.

The organisation later changed its name to Missionaries of the Poor. All the money earned by the organisation comes from donations. Money is given to poor people in need and funds are also used to build orphanages, for example in Haiti, and in Kampala in Uganda. Missionaries of the Poor now has 500 brothers who are social entrepreneurs working for the organisation across the world.

Figure 3.3.1 *Father Richard working with children*

CASE STUDY

Caribbean Harvest Foundation

The Caribbean Harvest Foundation is a social enterprise set up by Dr Valentin Abe in Haiti. It owns and operates fish farms and manages village development. In Haiti fish stocks have become depleted through overfishing. As a result Haitians consume only about half as much fish per year as people in other parts of the Caribbean.

The Caribbean Harvest Foundation has built fish hatcheries and fish farms that operate under the Caribbean Harvest banner, creating jobs and much-needed fresh fish stocks. In some of the villages where the project has been established, fishing lakes are split up into fishing cages and each family is given two cages. These contain fish stocks that enable them to generate income through selling, and use the surplus for their own consumption.

1 How do the two case studies outlined exemplify social enterprise?

2 Who were the social entrepreneurs and how are their objectives different from those of other entrepreneurs?

The goals of a social enterprise

The objectives of a social enterprise are essentially grounded in doing good for society and the environment. Guyana-based Help and Shelter was set up in 1994. It is a social enterprise focusing on the protection of women, children, the disabled, the elderly and others against domestic violence. Help and Shelter have counselled over 8,000 victims (85 per cent of whom are women). The enterprise has a board of directors and its staff are a mixture of paid employees and volunteers.

Help and Shelter has five goals, summarised as:

▨ to work to build respect for the right of women, children, youth and men to live free of violence and the threat of violence, by actively fostering a high level of awareness about the prevalence, causes and costs of violence

▨ to assist those suffering from violence to develop alternative ways of handling power and resolving conflict through counselling for victims and perpetrators of violence

▨ to widen options for victims by providing temporary shelter for abused women, and to provide training and skills to enable greater self-sufficiency

▨ to lobby for the strengthening of laws against violence

▨ to establish a resource base to enable the sustainable growth of Help and Shelter and to implement a clear fund-raising plan.

These objectives help us to understand how a social enterprise works. The first few objectives relate to exactly what the social enterprise seeks to achieve so as to change society. The final objective establishes more business-focused principles: to ensure financial solidity based on sound resourcing and well-organised fund-raising. Just as entrepreneurs seek to raise revenue, social entrepreneurs seek funds that enable them to run their enterprise and meet their other social objectives.

Did you know?

For private enterprises, profit is the major objective. This is easier to measure than social enterprise objectives, which tend to focus on benefits to the community and environment.

Summary questions

1 Identify a social enterprise in your locality. When was it set up and by whom? What are the goals of the social enterprise?

2 Some social enterprises focus on the environment. Give some examples of the types of objective such a social enterprise might have. How might it be able to measure its achievement?

Summary table

What is a social enterprise?	An organisation whose objectives relate to social and environmental purposes
How is it funded?	By donations/gifts and some commercial sales
What are its objectives?	Social and environmental goals as well as to raise funds to carry out its work
Who owns and runs it?	Social entrepreneurs

Specific objective

On completion of this section, you should be able to:

- explain the nature and characteristics of entrepreneurship, with reference to characteristics of successful entrepreneurs.

Starting an enterprise

People start their own enterprise for a variety of reasons. Some have a bright idea that they think will make them rich. Others find themselves unemployed and start their own business to survive. Some can only be themselves when they are their own boss. Others want to give something to the community and do this by setting up on their own.

However, setting up an enterprise is not for everyone. It requires a lot of hard work and long hours to make an enterprise a success. It also requires considerable attention to detail, not just the creation of exciting ideas. Often someone who has the important entrepreneurial qualities of being creative and imaginative will need a business partner with opposite, but equally important qualities, for example paying attention to detail and setting firm commercial foundations in place.

Characteristics of successful entrepreneurs

The characteristics of entrepreneurs depend very much on their line of enterprise. Someone who sets up a social enterprise will have a social conscience, whereas a more commercially minded entrepreneur might be more profit driven. A straightforward business idea, such as one person and a delivery van, may suit one person's ambition, while a complicated technical operation requires well-qualified people with specific knowledge. There are enterprises that suit brash, self-confident types and there are ones more suited to those who are more reserved.

It is possible, however, to identify a number of broad characteristics of entrepreneurs. Consider whether each of the characteristics in Table 3.4.1 apply to you and whether you can provide examples of your own experience as evidence for each one. These are characteristics that you would need to set up your own enterprise.

Table 3.4.1 Characteristics of an entrepreneur

Characteristics
Logical, perceptive, organised, realistic, responsible – good at getting things done
Outgoing, confident
Good communicator, able to make a point clearly
Sociable, good leader – can win people over instead of irritating them
Single-minded, decisive, independent
Open-minded, able to take advice
Flexible, adaptable
Opportunist, risk-taker, ambitious
Hard working, committed, determined, 'get up and go' type
Tough enough to deal with failure
Individual – not afraid to stand out from a crowd, or of what others think

☑ *Exam tip*

If asked to outline the characteristics of a successful entrepreneur, you should first identify each characteristic and follow with a brief explanation of each characteristic identified. Two marks are usually allocated to each characteristic outlined. You would receive one mark for correctly identifying the characteristic and another for briefly explaining the characteristic. One sentence would be adequate for the explanation.

Eddy Grant – Ice Records

Eddy Grant of Ice Records personifies many of the characteristics of a successful entrepreneur.

He was born in Plaisance, Guyana before moving to London in the 1960s, where he became a founder member of the chart-topping group, The Equals. As a solo artist, Grant wrote and produced a number of international hits including 'I Don't Wanna Dance' and 'Electric Avenue'.

He is a notoriously hard worker with a meticulous eye for detail, singing every vocal part and playing every instrument on some of his albums, which he also produced. At 23, however, he had a minor heart attack and that led him to rethink his approach to work.

In 1981 Grant relocated to Barbados where he set up a branch of his label, Ice Records. He has since acquired many master recording catalogues, considered to be the largest collection of early Classic Calypso, Ringbang and Soca Music. He is an excellent communicator with an easy manner and a flexible and adaptable approach.

Figure 3.4.1 *Eddy Grant of Ice Records, a successful Caribbean entrepreneur*

His career as a performer, songwriter, producer and entrepreneur has been characterised by being at the leading edge of innovative ideas and spotting opportunities before others. He has been true to his convictions.

As a musician Grant has a full appreciation of the rich cultural history of Caribbean music. Some of the Calypso greats on the Ice Records roster are Atilla the Hun, Roaring Lion, Lord Kitchener, King Fighter, Mighty Sparrow and Mighty Terror. Home to the most extensive catalogue of Steelband recordings, Ice Records is preparing to release these recordings in due course.

1 Match the profile of Eddy Grant with the characteristics of a successful entrepreneur listed in Table 3.4.1.

2 In what ways is Eddy Grant a 'serial entrepreneur': that is, someone who keeps coming up with good ideas?

Summary table

Key characteristics of successful entrepreneurs include:
■ willingness to work long hours and work hard
■ ability to take tough decisions and not to be put off by failure
■ ability to spot new opportunities
■ good communication skills and the ability to get on with people.

Summary questions

1 Identify a celebrated local entrepreneur in your country. To what extent do they have the characteristics that have been outlined in this section?

2 How could you go about developing the characteristics required to be a successful entrepreneur?

3 What enterprising ideas do you have? What would you need in order to turn these ideas into a successful enterprise?

Specific objectives

On completion of this section, you should be able to:

- explain the relationship between business organisations and the economic systems in which they operate
- differentiate between the main types of economic system
- explain the impact of the economic system on business decision making.

Figure 3.5.2 *While Barbados leans towards the market economy, the government is still involved in some sectors: e.g. there is competition between yellow private bus companies and blue government-run buses*

Did you know?

In Cuba many industries are government owned and controlled: officials working for the government decide what is produced, the methods of production and the prices charged. In recent times, the government has begun to allow entrepreneurs to set up small businesses such as taxi firms and hairdressers.

In Barbados and the Bahamas, the government plays only a minor role. It encourages new business start-ups and establishes the laws and regulations which ensure that contracts are upheld and that business is conducted fairly and ethically.

Economic systems

There are three main types of economic system: state-controlled or planned economies; market economies; and mixed economies. Figure 3.5.1 illustrates the extent to which governments are involved in business decisions.

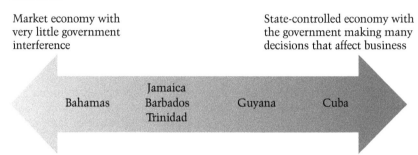

Market economy with very little government interference

State-controlled economy with the government making many decisions that affect business

Bahamas | Jamaica Barbados Trinidad | Guyana | Cuba

Figure 3.5.1 *Economic systems*

The advantage of a **planned economy** is that government control can ensure that most citizens have a job, working for the government, that they are paid fairly and are able to benefit from government-provided welfare services such as education and health care.

In a **market (or free) economy**, goods and services are freely exchanged and prices are determined by individual suppliers. Buying and selling decisions are made by buyers and sellers. Prices act as a guide.

- If prices are high enough, suppliers will be willing to supply to the market. High prices create profit and increased supply.
- If buyers think the prices give good value for money, they will buy goods. The lower the price, the more customers will buy.

Supporters of the market system argue that it is decentralised and automatic. The allocation of resources is determined by the wishes of individual consumers and suppliers.

In a **mixed economy**, decisions are made by a combination of the government and the market. Barbados (see Figure 3.5.2), Guyana and Trinidad are examples of Caribbean mixed economies.

Impact of the economic system on business

Business decision making in a country is affected by the country's economic system.

In a planned economy:

- there are few areas where private citizens can set up businesses
- there are more rules and paperwork associated with running a business
- business taxes are usually high
- private companies are unlikely to be able to compete with state-run companies
- prices that entrepreneurs charge are likely to be fixed, or limited by government rules

- there are likely to be laws relating to the wage that must be paid to employees
- there are more rules about what can be produced and how goods can be produced.

In a market or free economy:

- people can set up and run a business, providing they comply with legal rules relating to fair trading and honest dealing
- entrepreneurs are able to choose the prices they charge, what and where they sell, how they distribute their products, and how they promote them
- business taxes are relatively low
- businesses are able to make a profit and plough profits back into the expansion of the business
- business people are free to compete and purchase other businesses
- entrepreneurs are able to set their own wages (provided they comply with the minimum wage requirement), and choose whom they employ.

In a mixed economy:

- the decisions that a business owner can make lie somewhere between the two sets of factors outlined above. Where an economy leans more towards a planned economy there are more restrictions on business activity. Where an economy leans more towards a market economy, as in Jamaica, there are fewer government restrictions.

> **KEY TERMS**
>
> **Planned economy:** an economy in which the government runs many industries and establishes planning targets – how many goods will be produced, what type, where they will be sold and what prices will be charged for them.
>
> **Market (or free) economy:** economic system where prices act as signals to sellers about which goods it is profitable to produce, and to consumers about which goods provide value for money. Buyers and sellers consider prices when making buying and selling decisions.
>
> **Mixed economy:** an economy in which decisions are made by a combination of government decision making and the market.

Summary table

Type of economy	Key features	Impact on decisions
Planned	■ Government interference ■ Planning by government officials ■ Many state-run enterprises	■ Little scope for individual enterprise or individual decision making ■ Little choice about setting up an enterprise, pricing or what to produce
Market (free)	■ Enterprises run by entrepreneurs who are able to make their own decisions about how to run their business	■ Entrepreneurs make their own decisions about price, product, place and promotion ■ They can choose how to compete with rivals
Mixed	■ Combination of mixed and market systems	■ Some decisions can be made freely by entrepreneurs, but the government also has a say

Summary questions

1 In your territory, there will be a mixed economy. To what extent is it characterised by a market system and to what extent does government planning play a role?

2 Is there too much government interference or too little government interference in the way that businesses are run in your economy?

3 In what type of business activities would you like to see the government take more control? In which activities should it interfere less?

Did you know?

Some business activity can be offensive to communities. If the activity creates pollution or relates to drug dealing or other antisocial activities, there might be a case for government intervention.

3.6 The size of a business

Specific objective

On completion of this section, you should be able to:

■ assess the criteria for measuring size and growth of a business, with reference to output, labour force, market share and capital structure.

Figure 3.6.1 *Independent owners of taxis in Guyana are usually classified as small-business owners*

KEY TERMS

Criteria (singular criterion): the means by which a distinction or categorisation of an object, or group of objects, is made.

Capital employed: the total value of the funds put into the business internally (by shareholders and other owners) and externally (by lenders and other external sources of funds).

Measuring the size of businesses

You will often come across the terms *small*, *medium* and *large businesses*. Size, however, is measured in different ways in different industries. Definitions also vary from country to country. Table 3.6.1 shows how the size of a business is measured using different **criteria**.

Table 3.6.1 *Measuring the size of a business*

Method (criteria)	How is it done?
Output (a firm grows when it is able to produce more goods)	Output can be calculated in two ways: ■ volume of output (how many units of production are made and sold by the company ■ value of output (the value of company sales in a given period). Sales revenue is often used as a measure of output in money terms.
Labour force (a firm grows when it employs more people)	The number of employees: a 'small' firm might employ fewer than 50 people.
Market share (a firm grows when it controls a larger proportion of the market)	Market share is the percentage of sales in a particular market made by a specific business. Growing a firm would increase its market share.
Capital structure (a firm grows when it is able to acquire more capital, e.g. by becoming a company that is able to sell shares)	Firms can grow by changing the way they are structured in order to have access to larger pools of capital. The most obvious way of doing this is to become a company and to issue shares. **Capital employed** refers to the total amount of financial capital that a business is able to access from all sources, including owner's capital and shares.

Micro, small, medium and large enterprises

In different countries, definitions vary as to what constitutes a micro, small, medium or large enterprise. It is important, however, to have a clear understanding about what a small business is. Small businesses are seen as providing an engine for growth in many countries because of their importance in generating new ideas. Government and various international agencies therefore provide financial assistance and help with training entrepreneurs in small enterprises. A clear definition of what constitutes a small enterprise is important because this determines whether it will qualify for government assistance.

Small business in Guyana: a definition

In 2004, the government of Guyana passed the Small Business Act to give recognition to and provide support for small business. It created support agencies including the Small Business Council, the Small Business Bureau and the Small Business Development Fund (to provide funds for small businesses).

The Act defined a small business in Guyana as having the following characteristics:

- It can be a partnership, a private company, a cooperative, a holding company, an incorporated company or one registered by a business name.
- It must satisfy at least two of the following conditions:
  - it employs not more than 25 people
  - it has gross annual revenue of not more than $60 million
  - it has total business assets of not more than $20 million.

Typical areas in which small businesses exist in Guyana include retailing, photocopying, craft (furniture and leather), computer training, auto sales, farming, taxi services, and fruit and vegetable processing.

1 Why is it helpful to differentiate between small and medium-sized enterprises in Guyana?

2 Should a business in Guyana be considered a small business if it employs 25 people and has gross annual sales of $100 million?

3 Why do you think that more than one criterion is used to define a small business?

World Bank definitions

Table 3.6.2 illustrates the World Bank definition of micro, small and medium-sized enterprises.

Table 3.6.2 World Bank definitions of micro, small and medium-sized enterprises

Size of enterprise	Number of employees	Sales/turnover (US$)	Total assets (US$)
Micro	≤ 10	≤ 100,000	≤ 100,000
Small	≤ 50	≤ 3 million	≤ 3 million
Medium	≤ 300	≤ 15 million	≤ 15 million

Different approaches are used in the US, the European Union, Australia, Japan, South Africa and elsewhere. The challenge is to find definitions that are appropriate to a specific country. Not surprisingly, given the diverse nature of its territories and people, different definitions are used in different parts of the Caribbean.

Did you know?

In Japan, definitions of size vary across sectors of the economy: in manufacturing, construction and transportation the upper limit for a MSME (micro, small and medium-sized enterprise) is 300 people and ¥300m, but in retail it is only 50 people and ¥50m.

Summary table

Key ways to measure size	Output, size of labour force, market share, capital structure
Key sizes of enterprise	Micro, small, medium, large
World Bank measures	Number of employees, sales/turnover, total assets

Summary questions

1 Find out how enterprises are classified into different sizes in your own country. Usually the best source of information is the National Statistical Office or a government agency that supports small-business development.

2 Why is it important to be able to classify businesses according to whether they are micro, small or medium size?

3 Why are MSMEs so important to a country?

Specific objective

On completion of this section, you should be able to:

■ assess the criteria for measuring size and growth of a business, with reference to limitations of the various methods.

Figure 3.7.1 *Street sellers provide a good example of micro enterprises*

Weaknesses in size measurement

The criteria used to identify the relative size of a business can often be contradictory. For example, an IT consultancy might employ a very small number of people but achieve very high levels of sales. On the other hand, an organisation with a large number of employees might have very low sales. A large automated manufacturing plant using large numbers of factory robots and other automatic equipment might employ relatively few people compared with its revenue.

In 3.6 we saw that Japan has different definitions of size depending on the sector. A manufacturing enterprise with 299 employees and generating ¥299m of revenue would still be considered an MSME. But a retailer employing 51 people would be considered a large enterprise.

You might also find different definitions of size within a country, depending on who is collecting the data and the purposes for which they are being collected. The key groups interested in business size are summarised in Table 3.7.1.

Table 3.7.1 *Groups interested in business size*

Interested party	Reason
Businesses themselves	Size classification determines whether they qualify for tax breaks and incentives.
Government	Size determines which enterprises will receive assistance and support.
Development and specialist agencies	Size determines which enterprises will receive assistance and support.

CASE STUDY

Redefining MSMEs in Jamaica

Before 2012 there were several definitions of micro, small and medium-sized enterprises (MSMEs) in Jamaica. In 2012 the Ministry of Industry, Investment and Commerce held a one-day workshop with the Mona School of Business to come up with a suitable definition of MSMEs. This led to Jamaica's most recent definition:

Firm size	Number of employees	Total sales/turnover (J$)
Micro	⩽ 5	⩽ 10 million
Small	6–20	> 10 million ⩽ 50 million
Medium-sized	21–50	> 50 million ⩽ 150 million

Before 2012 the most widely used definitions had been from three sources. The Private Sector

Organisation of Jamaica used total sales as the criterion, the Planning Institute of Jamaica used total sales and total assets, and the Ministry of Industry, Investment and Commerce used number of employees and total sales.

It is beneficial to a country's businesses to establish an agreed definition, so that there can be a shared approach to supporting the development of small businesses. A key additional benefit is having the criteria set out in the local currency so it is not subject to international exchange rate fluctuations, and is based on local circumstances rather than the wider international picture.

1 What do you consider the principal benefit of creating an agreed definition of the size of MSMEs, as Jamaica has done?

2 What problems do you associate with establishing a single national set of definitions of MSMEs?

Another difficulty with classification is the cut-off points. This can involve differences of $1 or one employee. The case study on p150 shows that a micro enterprise in Jamaica can have up to five employees. With six it becomes a small enterprise. If grants and loans are available to micro enterprises but not to small enterprises, an entrepreneur might be reluctant to take on a sixth employee.

Small firms in Jamaica

In 2004 an analysis of MSMEs in Jamaica was carried out by the Group of Analysis for Development. This revealed the following characteristics:

- Of 1,226 firms, 37 per cent were micro enterprises (2–4 workers) and 11 per cent were small scale (5–20 workers).
- The average income of micro entrepreneurs was J$57,000. For small-scale firms it was J$900,000.
- Most of these enterprises were located in large metropolitan areas of Jamaica.
- Almost 80 per cent of small enterprises were run by males, with an average age of 46.
- Forty per cent of enterprises were in wholesaling and retailing, and 26 per cent in education, social work and other personal services.
- Other key areas were manufacturing (9 per cent), hotels and restaurants (9 per cent) and accounting (7 per cent).
- Small firms typically sold their goods and services to individual customers (rather than to businesses). Their main competitors were other small enterprises.

Summary table

Issues associated with defining size of enterprise	
Different definitions	May be a number of different ways of defining size within a country. Definitions also have different relevance to different users (e.g. to the business or providers of finance to a small enterprise).
Relevance to sectors	Definitions vary between sectors (e.g. between manufacturing and retail).
Need to define currency	Definitions not based on local currency may not be relevant to local needs, and may be subject to currency fluctuations.
Arbitrary choice of boundaries	One extra employee or $1 of extra revenue might change the classification of a business.

Summary questions

1 The Barbados Small Business Development Act defines a small business as any enterprise that meets two of the following criteria:
   - It is incorporated under the Companies Act of Barbados.
   - It does not have more than $1 million as stated or paid-up capital.
   - It does not have more than $2 million in annual sales.
   - It does not employ more than 25 people.

   Contrast this with the definition of a small business in Jamaica, outlined above.

2 Why is accurate classification of business size important? How might this classification affect a young entrepreneur deciding to set up a small business of his or her own?

Specific objective

On completion of this section, you should be able to:

- assess the criteria for measuring size and growth of a business, with reference to the advantages and disadvantages of large versus small firms.

Size and financial requirements

In 3.6 you saw that a large firm usually employs more people, has a higher sales turnover and employs more **capital** than a smaller firm. Here we consider some of the advantages and disadvantages of different business sizes.

As a firm grows it will require more finance for:

- investment in plant and equipment
- **working capital** for running its growing operations and sales.

A small firm has access only to limited sources of capital: the owner's capital and borrowing from banks and other financial institutions. A larger business can usually access more finance: for example, raising funds from shareholders.

Economies of scale

Economies of scale are advantages of producing on a larger scale. A larger firm can spread its fixed costs over a larger volume of sales. Table 3.8.1 compares 'Large Firm' with 'Small Firm': Large Firm mass-produces soft drinks using expensive automatic equipment. Small Firm produces soft drinks using non-automated machinery. Large Firm has higher fixed costs, but much higher sales, so that its unit costs are lower.

Table 3.8.1 'Large Firm' and 'Small Firm'

	Small Firm	Large Firm
Annual fixed costs	$100,000	$500,000
Sales	50,000	1,000,000
Unit fixed costs	$2	50 cents
Where sales achieved	In one territory only	Throughout the Caribbean

Larger firms benefit from a range of economies of scale. These include:

- **Manufacturing and technical economies:** these result from manufacturing on a large scale, using specialist manufacturing equipment unaffordable for a smaller firm. Nestlé has an automated factory plant in Jamaica mass-producing its milk-based drink Supligen at a low unit cost for the Caribbean market.

- **Marketing and selling economies:** these result from marketing and selling on a large scale. One advertisement broadcast across the Caribbean enables marketing costs to be spread over a large geographical area.

- **Financial economies:** larger enterprises can borrow from banks at lower interest rates because they are regarded as a lower risk.

- **Buying economies:** these involve securing bulk discounts from suppliers, and reduced delivery costs because supplies can be delivered in large consignments.

- **Risk-spreading economies:** a large company spreads the risk of business or product failure over a range of products, rather than one or a few.

Other advantages and disadvantages

Table 3.8.2 outlines other advantages and disadvantages of large and small companies.

Table 3.8.2 *Advantages and disadvantages of large and small companies*

Aspect of business	Large company	Small company
Management and control	■ Can employ specialist managers to manage specific aspects of the business, rather than having a general manager who has to carry out a range of different tasks.	■ Managers and owners more closely linked – owner may be the manager, enabling control over the business.
Record keeping	■ Required to keep more records (e.g. registering as a company, providing more detailed accounting records). ■ Can employ specialist administrators and use modern IT-based packages for keeping records in an easy-to-use and economical way.	■ Required to keep fewer records, which helps to reduce administration costs. ■ However, the person who keeps records may also be required to carry out many other business functions, so records may be neglected.
Access to working capital	■ Likely to access more finance for working capital, and by achieving higher sales can generate more cash to purchase stocks. ■ May have more power in getting people who have bought goods on credit to pay up sooner.	■ Likely to generate far less working capital to buy new stock. ■ However, they will not need so much working capital because of the relatively small size of stock required.
Regulation and legislation	■ May be faced by more regulation and control on their activities. ■ Listed companies have to comply with Stock Exchange listing rules. ■ However, meeting minimum standards helps increase the reputation of the business.	■ Fewer rules and laws with which to comply. ■ Simpler procedures to set up and report on the business's affairs each year. ■ Less stringent tax regime.
Closeness to customers and employees	■ May become distant from customers and employees.	■ May be closer to customers and employees and build close relationships over long periods.

Summary table

Benefits of being a large company	Benefits of being a small company
■ Economies of scale ■ Access to larger pools of capital and a wider range of finance (e.g. through shares) ■ Access to more working capital ■ Can employ specialist managers	■ Being close to customers and employees ■ Do not need to raise as much finance ■ Fewer records need to be maintained ■ Fewer rules and regulations and easier to set up

Summary questions

1 Hovill currently owns a small food-processing company operating in St Kitts and Nevis. However, she has ambitions to expand the business into other parts of the Caribbean by becoming a larger company. What would be the advantages of becoming a larger company, provided that she can access sufficient capital?

2 Why might it be beneficial for Hovill to scale down her ambitions and to continue to run the business as a small company, just focusing on customers in St Kitts and Nevis?

Specific objective

On completion of this section, you should be able to:

- assess the criteria for measuring size and growth of a business, with reference to strategies for growth.

Did you know?

In Unit 1 you learned that the capital employed in a business can be measured by fixed assets + current assets − current liabilities. Finance for capital expansion can be acquired from either additional owner capital or long-term borrowing.

The proportion of capital that is raised from borrowing is called the *gearing ratio*. It is risky for a firm to grow by increasing its gearing because borrowed funds involve regular interest repayments and increase the company's liabilities to people outside the business.

Business growth

Businesses can gain advantages over competitors by growing. They may be able to cut costs and win a greater share of the market, develop new products or sell to new markets.

Business growth can be measured in terms of:

- **growth of sales volume or value.** Growth from 1,000 to 1,500 sales per year is by volume. An increase from $100,000 to $150,000 is by value
- **growth of capital employed.** By acquiring more capital, the business is able to expand its production and sales capability
- **growth in the number of employees.** As a firm grows, it usually needs to recruit more employees.

Growth can be internal (from within the business) or external (joining with other businesses).

Internal growth is often called 'organic' growth. Many small businesses grow organically in their early years, financing expansion by ploughing back profits, putting in more capital themselves or borrowing from a financial institution such as a bank. Internal growth can then take place by investing in new products or selling more of existing products. However, this is quite a slow way of growing a business.

External growth usually involves a **merger** with another business. When a merger takes place, two or more enterprises cease to be distinct. This can occur in two ways:

- they are brought under common ownership and control
- there is an agreement between the enterprises that one of them ceases to trade. For example, Company X may agree with Company Y that the latter will close down any operations that compete with those of X.

A **takeover** is a form of merger. It occurs when one company buys a majority shareholding in another. **Acquisition** refers to the process where one business gains control of part of another. For example, a business may be prepared to sell off one of its divisions that it no longer wishes to keep.

It is possible to distinguish at a general level between full legal mergers and mergers involving only changes in the ownership of the companies concerned. A legal merger transfers the assets and liabilities of two or

KEY TERMS

Merger: when two firms voluntarily join together to become a single entity.

Takeover: when one firm gains control of another by purchasing a minimum of 51 per cent of the shares of the other company.

Acquisition: the process of acquiring (i.e. gaining an interest in) another business.

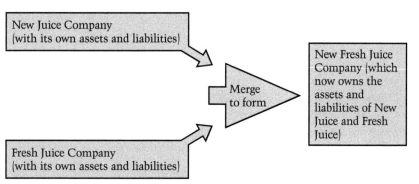

Figure 3.9.1 *A legal merger to form the New Fresh Juice Company*

more companies to a single new or existing company. Companies whose assets are merged may disappear into a new company, as in Figure 3.9.1, or one of the companies involved may absorb the other.

Strategies for external growth

There are a number of strategies for external growth that are based on integration: that is, joining enterprises together.

Horizontal integration

Here, two firms at the same stage of production, such as two businesses that process and bottle juices, join together. Advantages are opportunities for economies of scale (including marketing economies such as spreading the cost of advertising over a larger market), gaining a larger share of the market, reducing duplication of products and services, focusing on the best-selling lines, and removing duplication in management roles.

Vertical integration

In vertical integration, two firms at different stages of production join together. In *backward vertical integration*, one business takes over another in an earlier stage of the production chain: for example, a juice processor takes over a farm producing fruit. *Forward vertical integration* involves taking over a firm in a later stage of production, such as the juice bottler taking over retail outlets selling juice.

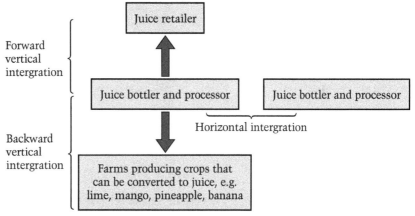

Figure 3.9.2 *Different types of integration resulting from takeover*

Lateral integration

This involves taking over a related but different type of firm, as when two firms producing consumer goods combine so that they can sell their products through the same retail outlets, cutting down distribution and marketing costs.

Conglomerate integration

This involves taking over a firm producing an unrelated product. The new product line might be growing and dynamic, and might benefit from the management and marketing experience of the firm taking it over. This integration also enables a business to spread risks.

Summary table

Internal growth strategies	■ Firm acquires more capital from profits. ■ Firm raises more capital from shareholders. ■ Firm borrows more from lenders.
External growth strategies	Firm merges with or takes over another business, involving: ■ horizontal integration (same stage) ■ vertical integration (backward or forward stage) ■ lateral integration (related product) ■ conglomerate integration (unrelated product).

Did you know?

Vertical integration enables a business to manage more stages of the production process, to improve quality, standards, delivery times and presentation. The vertically integrated firm also takes a bigger share of the profits.

Summary questions

1. What would be a suitable method of growth for a business whose owners want to do the following?
   a. Grow slowly
   b. Eliminate competition
   c. Reduce distribution costs
   d. Increase market share
   e. Spread its risks

2. What examples of takeovers have recently taken place in your country? What reasons were put forward to support the takeover?

On completion of this section, you should be able to:

- assess the challenges and opportunities faced by small businesses, with reference to identifying successful business opportunities, sourcing capital (finance) and selection of business type.

Table 3.10.1 *Criteria for assessing a business idea*

Market: Is there a big enough market to make sufficient sales?
Competition: How many competitors are out there? Can we compete with them?
Start-up cost: Do we have sufficient resources to start up the business?
Management expertise: Do we have enough management and enterprise skills to make a success of the business?
Legal barriers: Are there legal and regulatory barriers that will prevent the business idea from being developed, or make it too costly?
Return: Will the return (profit) from the business be sufficient to make the investment in the idea worthwhile?

Did you know?

A popular way for a small business to finance its purchases is using a credit card.

KEY TERMS

Collateral: property or goods belonging to a borrower which a lender can require to be sold in order to pay back a loan.

Starting with the right idea

Setting up and running a business needs people who are energetic and enthusiastic, who like hard work and enjoy challenges, and who can adapt to change and are not deterred by failure. The new entrepreneur needs to have a good, realistic idea that can be turned into an effective business proposition. Initial ideas can be brainstormed around a number of key themes (see Figure 3.10.1). Internet research can help determine whether similar ideas already exist.

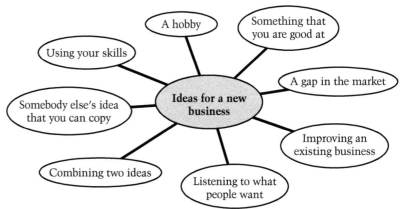

Figure 3.10.1 *The start of a business idea*

Having generated several possible ideas, ones less likely to work need to be eliminated through a screening process (see p100). Table 3.10.1 lists some simple criteria that can be used.

Sourcing capital

The availability of finance (capital) is a key challenge for small businesses and will determine whether a business idea gets off the ground. The principal sources of finance for a small business are:

- **Owner's own funds, usually in the form of savings:** for a small company this will be shareholders' funds. Once the business is up and running, profits can be ploughed back into the business. The challenge is whether the funds are sufficient.

- **Bank finance:** banks provide a number of different types of finance, including long-term finance in the form of a bank loan, and mortgages for the purchase of buildings and land. Short-term finance comes as short-term loans and overdrafts. The challenge is to convince the bank that repayments are feasible and will be made.

- **Venture capital:** venture capitalists are investors who provide funds for a business in return for a share of the equity. They need to be convinced that the business proposition is viable and will yield a sufficient return.

- **Other lenders:** bond holders are prepared to invest in a company in return for the receipt of company bonds. These entitle the owner to a fixed rate of return and are redeemable in the future. The lenders need to believe that these returns will materialise.

- **Hire purchase and leasing:** business owners can hire and lease out equipment in return for a deposit and regular repayments (at quite high rates of interest). The company providing the credit needs an initial downpayment and proof that the lender can make the repayments.
- **Trade credit:** a business can buy supplies on credit if it can convince a supplier that it will be able to make payments when they fall due.
- **Government funding:** the government provides a range of loans, training and other types of support for small business owners.

Selecting a business type

Another challenge facing the owner of a small business is to select a suitable business type. Table 3.10.2 summarises the range of different opportunities and challenges associated with each type.

Did you know?

To borrow finance an enterprise needs to be able to put down **collateral** against the loan. A small business with limited collateral is seen as a greater risk by lenders. They are likely to try to cover their risk by charging higher interest rates. Someone who wants to set up a small business may not have collateral in the form of real estate and motor vehicles. This is a particular problem for micro enterprises.

Table 3.10.2 Business types, challenges and opportunities

Type	Challenges	Opportunities
Sole trader	- Limited resources - Responsibility with just one person	- Opportunity to run something for yourself and take all the profit
Partnership	- Having to share profits with partner - Resources still likely to be limited	- Opportunity to share work and build on the skills of a partner - Profits shared with only small number of partners
Small company	- Profits need to be split among shareholders	- Spread of ownership - Access to more capital - Ability to bring more specialists into the business
Franchise	- Controls by the franchisor on running the business - Having to share the profits with the franchisor	- Opportunity to use someone else's established idea that is known to work - Brand recognition
Cooperative	- Having to cooperate with others and distribute rewards among them	- Sense of working together for the common good

Summary table

Key challenges and opportunities for small businesses	
Ideas	Generating a suitable idea that also passes through a screening process
Generating funds to set up and sustain a business	Accessing sufficient funds from own funds, bank borrowing and other sources. Lack of collateral to put up against loans
Choosing the type of organisation	Deciding whether to run your own business or run it with others, what your attitude is to sharing profit and the amount of work involved in running the business

Summary questions

1 Think of five ideas for setting up a new business. Screen these down to two, using the screening process outlined in Table 3.10.1. For each of your final two ideas, identify a suitable business type and where the necessary funds could be accessed.

2 Can you identify other screening tests or questions that you would want to add to the list set out in this section?

3.11 Small businesses: challenges and opportunities 2

Specific objective

On completion of this section, you should be able to:

■ assess the challenges and opportunities faced by small businesses, with reference to determining a location, globalisation and trade liberalisation, e-commerce and intellectual property.

Did you know?

The Ease of Doing Business Index was created by the World Bank. It takes into account 10 factors associated with doing business in a specific country: starting a business, dealing with construction permits, getting electricity, registering property, getting credit, protecting investors, paying taxes, trading across borders, enforcing contracts and resolving insolvency. Higher figures indicate simpler registration of companies and stronger protection for property rights.

Among 180 countries listed in 2012, St Lucia is 53rd and Antigua and Barbuda 63rd.

Did you know?

In 2010 a US court rejected a claim made by the Marley family that Universal Music had withheld royalties (including royalties from ringtones) which should have been paid to them for five of Bob Marley's most famous albums (*Catch A Fire, Burnin, Natty Dread, Rastafarian Vibrations and Exodus*). The judge decided that these were 'works made for hire', giving the copyright to the record label.

Location

Deciding on a location is an important business decision. In the Caribbean this might involve a choice of territory. Key considerations are the cost of setting up, levels of taxation and subsidy for small enterprises, size of the market, cost of distribution, availability of skilled (or unskilled labour) and ease of borrowing money.

A key opportunity comes from being close to market, or being able to distribute at low cost. This is particularly relevant for bulky products. Many companies in the Caribbean benefit from being close to transport links. Some businesses locate in an urban area, close to their customers, while others prefer the low rates and rents in rural areas or in business parks constructed by the government or private companies.

Globalisation

Globalisation provides a real opportunity for small businesses (see Ice Records in 3.4) to distribute worldwide. Cultural and creative industries (such as publishing, printing, multimedia, audio-visual, phonographic and cinematographic productions in Jamaica) have benefited particularly from liberalisation of trade. Many small businesses in these industries are operating in the fastest-growing sectors of the world economy. Jamaica's copyright industries, producing discs and books, account for almost 5 per cent of the country's GDP. A recent report published in Jamaica, *Vision 2030*, showed that the export market is far more important than the domestic market for creative industries. In order to sell across the globe however, they will have to incur costs to distribute their products globally.

Of course, globalisation also enables foreign companies to access domestic Caribbean markets: large multinationals can export into the Caribbean, using economies of scale to sell at relatively low cost. This can result in strong competition for smaller businesses who may not be able to produce goods at as low a cost.

E-commerce

While the Caribbean may be geographically far from huge markets in China, India, the US and Europe, e-commerce links enable thousands of Caribbean enterprises to reach global markets 24 hours a day. Billions of potential customers who are connected to the internet can be reached, particularly where the product is light and compact, such as DVDs. E-preneurs can sell goods from their own home, or from a convenient manufacturing or storage area in a low-cost location.

The challenges lie in the cost of both setting up and maintaining an effective and reliable website – one that is always available anywhere in the world. A secure, effective and trusted online payment system is essential. An online enterprise usually pays a commission to an online payments provider to maintain the system.

Intellectual property rights

Intellectual property is the output from creative endeavour: for example, when an author creates a book, or a software designer creates an online game. Intellectual property rights (IPRs) can be secured by registering a patent for a product design; copyright for a book, film or recorded music; registered design for the design of a product; or a trade mark for a brand or image.

When a firm has acquired a patent or copyright, others are not allowed to copy the idea. This only applies once the patent has been officially registered. Many small businesses, however, do not know how to apply for IPRs, or have insufficient resources to pay to register a patent.

Different countries have their own official departments for registering IPRs. The Barbados Corporate Affairs and Intellectual Property Office supervises the registration of intellectual property rights in Barbados. However, this only provides IPRs in a limited area. To gain worldwide protection a company must register IPRs through the World Intellectual Property Office. This gives exclusive rights to the IPR of the product – locally, regionally or globally. It is, however, a costly process and difficult to maintain on a global scale.

Infringing someone else's IPRs can result in large fines and legal costs.

Figure 3.11.1 *A key issue for small Caribbean enterprises is to retain intellectual property rights. The rights to a number of Bob Marley's recordings have been secured by large overseas corporations, enabling them to make huge profits.*

Summary table

Challenges and opportunities for small businesses		
	Opportunity	**Challenge**
Location	■ Being close to market and customers ■ Being able to reach customers ■ Being able to choose low cost area	■ Costs associated with bringing goods to the market: distribution costs
Globalisation	■ Accessing a world market	■ Cost of reaching other countries from the Caribbean base ■ Competition from multinationals with economies of scale
E-commerce	■ Low-cost way of reaching out to millions of consumers, 24 hours a day	■ Cost of setting up website, having the website hosted, payment issues ■ Maintaining the site
IPRs	■ Possibility of having exclusive rights to sell products and ideas	■ High cost of registering IPRs ■ Risk of someone else copying the ideas if owner does not have IPRs

Summary questions

1 Access the Ease of Doing Business Index for your territory online. In which dimensions is it easy to do business in your country? Where are the main weaknesses? Compare your territory with one other in the Caribbean.

2 Identify products that are produced by a local, fairly small Caribbean company. Do these products appear to have copyright labels or registered trade marks?

Did you know?

In Trinidad the government has a National Entrepreneurship Development Company (NEDCO) to support micro and small enterprises. It helps to develop new concepts into workable ideas, advises on the creation of an effective business plan, provides micro-finance (small-scale loans) at low rates of interest, offers training in business enterprise skills and gives marketing support.

What assistance is needed?

Table 3.12.1 summarises the assistance, or support, needed by small enterprises in the Caribbean and elsewhere.

Table 3.12.1 *Supporting small enterprises*

Advice on how to set up	How to business plan	How to raise finance including grants and loans
Ongoing advice on running the business	Advice on managing and marketing the business	Advice on compliance with regulations and technical support

Agencies offering support

There are three main agencies offering support for small enterprise development: government agencies, non-government agencies and financial institutions.

Government agencies

Government can play a significant part in helping new enterprises to set up and grow. This is particularly important in the Caribbean where most businesses are small, but provide extensive employment opportunities. In Barbados, the government offers a number of incentives:

■ reduction in corporation (business) tax from 25 per cent to 15 per cent

■ exemption from import duties on raw material, plant and equipment imports

■ exemption from stamp duty on business documents

■ a Holding Hands Mentorship programme to bring experienced business people together with new entrepreneurs

■ the Incubator Programme to provide advice and support for start-up businesses

■ a Small Business Development Centre, which is part of the Barbados Investment and Development Corporation. This offers advice and assistance for Barbadians involved in the development, intellectual property rights protection and commercialisation of new product ideas.

There is an inter-governmental initiative in the form of the Caribbean Development Bank (CDB), which lends to local development banks. In 2010 the CDB lent to the St Lucia development bank so that, among other activities, it could make loans to small start-up enterprises in St Lucia. The CDB also provides technical assistance and advice to small businesses.

Non-government agencies

The objectives of non-government agencies include supporting small enterprises. Examples of these agencies include the following:

■ The Caribbean Small Business Development Centres project is a US government funded initiative that currently operates in St Lucia, Dominica, Belize, Jamaica and Barbados to provide loans to small businesses, as well as some technical advice. Its aims include the encouragement of enterprise in the area, and it works closely with Small Business Associations.

- Small Business Associations such as the Small Business Association of Jamaica exist to provide help and advice to entrepreneurs in a specific area. They are typically funded by government and businesses, mainly to carry out specifically targeted projects.

Financial institutions

Financial institutions such as banks and credit unions provide advice, support and loans to small businesses as a part of their lending activities. Small businesses are important customers for banks. The bank looks after their money, helps to provide payment systems for employees and lends money for working capital and the purchase of fixed capital. When the small business sector does well, banks also do well.

CASE STUDY

Assistance from a bank in Jamaica

A bank in Jamaica provides a range of services and support for small businesses. These include business accounts, different types of insurance, internet banking, mortgages on property and buildings, credit cards and debit cards, as well as a range of loans and methods for making payments.

In addition the bank provides advice and support on a range of important topics, including how to

engage in international trade, how to set up a small business and how to budget.

1 Investigate a major bank in your area to find out the range of support it provides to the small business sector.

2 How are some of the services provided by this Jamaican bank likely to do the following?

   a Help a new company to get started

   b Help an existing company to run its operations more effectively

Government agencies, non-government agencies and financial institutions also provide small and medium-sized enterprises with advice on how to create a business plan. Having an effective business plan is an essential requirement for setting up a **sustainable enterprise**.

KEY TERMS

Sustainable enterprise: a business that continues to flourish and grow over a long period.

Summary table

Who provides the support?	Government agencies	Non-government agencies	Caribbean Development Bank	Financial institutions
What does the support include?	■ Low taxes ■ Loans ■ Advice and support ■ Training in enterprise	■ Some small-scale funding ■ Advice and support	■ Loans through local development banks ■ Technical support	■ Loans and other financial banking services, e.g. insurance, mortgages, business accounts ■ Advice and support

Summary questions

1 What are the best sources of advice on how to set up a new enterprise?

2 How can a small business acquire funds to start up, apart from those supplied by the owner?

3 Why are financial institutions and governments keen to provide advice to new businesses about business planning?

On completion of this section, you should be able to:

- develop a business plan, with a focus on defining a plan.

Figure 3.13.1 *Rohit's rotis*

A business plan

A business plan is a complete description of a business and its plans for the next 1–3 years. It explains what the business does (or will do, if it is a new business); it suggests who will buy the product or service and why; it provides financial forecasts demonstrating overall viability; and it indicates the finance available and explains financial requirements.

Who uses the plan?

The plan is meant for two main parties:

- **The business owner and his or her advisers:** it shows that they have a clear understanding of their business and how it is going to generate profit for the owners. In the next few sections we examine a business plan for a roti delivery business in Trinidad, owned by Rohit (Figure 3.13.1).
- **Lenders:** any suppliers of funds to the business will want to know that it is sound and well structured.

Template of a business plan

It is important for a business owner to be able to construct a business plan. The template outlined in Table 3.13.1 can be used as a model on which to construct a plan. A basic business plan includes six components:

1 Introductory (executive) summary
2 Outline of the environment in which the business is operating
3 Analysis of competitors and the market environment
4 Marketing plan
5 Operations plan
6 Financial plan.

Table 3.13.1 explains these components in more detail.

Table 3.13.1 *Components of a business plan*

Heading	Suggested content
1.1 Executive summary	An at-a-glance summary of the main points, including the objectives of the business.
1.2 The business and the business idea	Give the name of the business and the address, before going on to describe your product or service. Explain how long you have been developing the business and the steps taken so far. Give an overview of the start-up plans.
1.3 The legal status of the business.	Is it a sole trader, partnership or company?
2 The nature of the business environment	Here you need to set out: ■ the target market ■ customer needs ■ the location of the business.
3 An analysis of competitors and the market environment	Outline the industry background. How big is the market and who are the main competitors? Provide broad details about your customers (e.g. age, gender and income). Briefly outline key findings of the market research.

Table 3.13.1 Components of a business plan – continued

Heading	Suggested content
4.1 The marketing plan – promotional strategies	Explain how you are going to make customers aware of your product (e.g. through advertising).
4.2 Other marketing aspects	These could include details of pricing and where the product will be sold or made available.
4.3 Sales targets	How much of your product or service do you expect to be able to sell? What is the basis of making these claims?
5.1 Operations plan – resources required	Set out the physical resources required (e.g. equipment and supplies). Set out the human resources required (i.e. people and their skills).
5.2 Operations plan – managerial summary	Who will manage your business? What skills do they possess?
6.1 Financial plan – sources of finance	What are the main types of finance required and who will provide them?
6.2 Financial plan – cash flow and break even	Expected cash flow in the first year of running the business and a calculation of sales needed to break even.
6.3 Financial plan – profit and loss account	What will the profit and loss account look like at the end of the first year?
6.4 Assumptions around which the financial plan is built and suitable financial ratios	In constructing a business plan, assumptions are made about the figures that are set out. It is important to state these assumptions. It is also helpful to set out some illustrative financial ratios (e.g. to illustrate profit performance).

The template shows the basis of a well-structured business plan that will be taken seriously. The plan should be simple and clear so that it does not confuse the reader with too much detail.

The business plan enables forward planning. It provides guidance for the business to follow, outlining key activities such as promotion and pricing, and setting out expected cash flow and profit. Once the business is operational, the plan enables comparisons to be made between what actually happened and what was planned.

Summary table

What is a business plan?	A complete description of a business and its plans for the next 1–3 years
Who uses it?	The owner and his or her advisers, and lenders
What does it contain?	Executive summary, environmental outline, competition and market, marketing plan, operations plan, financial plan
How should it be set out?	In a concise and clear way to convey relevant information to potential users and to establish a clear 'to do' list for the owner

Summary questions

1 Why does Rohit need to create a business plan?

2 How is the business plan going to help Rohit to match the competition and provide a product that customers are willing to buy at the prices he charges?

3 Why is it important to include the following?
   a   A marketing plan   b   A financial plan

Specific objective

On completion of this section, you should be able to:

■ develop a business plan, with reference to the executive summary and the business description.

Executive summary

An executive summary is a brief outline of a business plan, set out at the start. Although it appears first, it may be the last item you write. The summary should give a very brief overview of the plan and include an introduction to the business owner, a clear outline of the major objectives and an overview of the market and business environment. It should cover marketing and sales, competition, the operation of the business, and key financial projections and plans.

One way of constructing the summary is to take one or two key sentences out of each section of your plan. The language used should be positive. It should only be a few paragraphs long, with a focus on the points most likely to concern readers.

CASE STUDY

Rohit's Rotis: executive summary

Across Trinidad the market for ready-made rotis has grown rapidly in recent years. Port of Spain is a bustling commercial area. Market research shows that five out of 10 factory and office workers there are prepared to buy fresh, ready-made rotis on a regular or semi-regular basis.

There are 12 other established businesses in Port of Spain providing ready-made rotis, but only one other firm delivers directly to factory and office outlets seven days a week.

Rohit's Rotis is an imaginary partnership. It offers made-to-order filled rotis delivered directly to business premises in the Port of Spain area. The basic ingredients are wheat, flour, salt and water, and there is a variety of meat and vegetable-based fillings. The objective of the business is to make a profit for the owners and provide a high-quality food delivery service to fill a market need in the area.

Customers are to be factory and office outlets without their own canteen facilities and located away from retail and restaurant areas of the city. The business also delivers for private lunchtime functions. The rotis are prepared to order on the day of delivery. Orders can be made through the website or by order form.

Initially the business will have one employee, paid $1,200 per month. The employee has a Culinary Arts qualification from the Trinidad and Tobago Hospitality and Tourism Institute and a clean driving licence. He or she will share the duties of making the rotis and delivering them with the owner. Rohit will take responsibility for taking and recording orders to prepare schedules for the following week.

The owners of Rohit's Rotis are Rohit Khurana and his partner Sumita Sarkar, who will be responsible for recording the financial affairs of the business and preparing budgets and financial statements. Rohit has worked as a restaurant manager for the last five years and Sumita works full time for an accountancy firm.

Sales projections for the first year of trading are $367,500. Rohit's salary will be $30,000 and Sumita's $6,000.

Rohit and Sumita have each invested $25,000 in the business to meet **working capital requirements**. Additionally, the partners have received an interest-free (in the first year) loan of $20,000 from a Government Enterprise Agency. The only condition is the production of a satisfactory business plan. The **estimated net profit** from the first year of trading is $174,200.

1   To what extent does the summary provide you with a snapshot of the business, its market and its competitors?

2   Does it tell you enough about the background and qualifications of the owners and employee?

3   At first glance, does the business look as if it will be viable? Give reasons for your answer.

Business description

The reader (including lenders) will want to know about the legal status of the company, and its plans for starting up.

Rohit's Rotis: business description

Business address

Rohit's Rotis,

Trinidad Industrial Park Unit Number 12,

Port of Spain Trading Estate,

Port of Spain

Legal status of business (establishment history)

The business will officially be formed as a partnership on 1 October 2015. The partnership will be registered with Charles and Majithia Solicitors in Port of Spain. Partners will each contribute $25,000 and be entitled to an equal share of the annual profits of the business. The partnership will officially be recognised through the creation of a Deed of Partnership, which establishes a procedure for the resolution of disputes and for the sharing of rewards on dissolution of the partnership. The partnership has unlimited liability. The registration of the partnership will cost $500.

Start-up of business

The business will start when a lease for the hire of the business premises becomes available on 1 October 2015. The partnership will also acquire kitchen units, including a cooking oven and freezer for $12,000. A van will be leased to enable the delivery of rotis to business premises.

Key products

The products of the business are ready-made rotis supplied to office and industrial units. The range of fillings will be subject to ongoing market research. Initially standard offerings will include:

- roti wraps, including curried chicken, beef, goat, shrimp and channa (chick pea)
- aloo roti
- Trinidad curried lamb
- Bajan curry
- stuffed roti with curried chick peas and one other filling.

1 Why would lenders want to know about the legal status of the business?

2 Why might the location of the business be of interest to potential lenders?

3 Why might the lenders want to know about the main items of capital required to set up the business?

Summary table

Executive summary	Brief description of a company, its objectives, its markets, its competitors and key aspects of its operations, including some key financial information
Business description	Outline of the business location, description of the owner, plans to start up the business, legal form, key products

Summary questions

1 Think of a business idea of your own and set out:
   a   the business idea
   b   the location (and address) of the business
   c   the main resources that you will need to start up the business
   d   your key products
   e   an outline of the legal status of your business.

2 Who will be interested in reading your business description? What can you do to make it clear and convincing?

KEY TERMS

Sales projections: estimates of future sales value.

Working capital requirements: finance required to meet pressing payments and short-term debts.

Estimated net profit: projection of the final end profit for a particular period of trading.

On completion of this section, you should be able to:

- develop a business plan, with a focus on producing a business environment analysis by setting out the target market for the business, customer needs and location.

In the food market, vegetarians make up a specific and substantial sector. Targeting this group can be rewarding.

Research for Rohit's Rotis revealed quite a strong demand from vegetarians. Options that would be popular for this target group include spinach, chickpea, potato and pumpkin.

The market environment

It is important to show that you have a clear picture of who your customers are and what their specific needs are likely to be. You need to do this in order to demonstrate that:

- there is a market for your product
- you understand this market
- you can come up with a product and/or service that will meet the specific needs of your targeted customers.

You learned in Module 2 that 'target market' refers to specific groups of customers who are the focus of a company's marketing activities and products. This market needs to be large enough that a company can sell at the prices identified as being suitable and make a profit. If these customers are going to buy the product, the company must be aware of their needs and requirements (see 3.16 on market analysis).

The environment analysis should also look at the location in which the business will take place. As you can see in the case study below, Rohit's Rotis has identified a target group of customers specific to the Port of Spain area in which it will be working.

CASE STUDY

Target market for Rohit's Rotis

Rohit's Rotis has identified specific target groups of customers. These are factory and office workers in the Port of Spain area, who are not currently catered for by a delivery service. The specific organisations to be targeted will employ a minimum of 20 employees so that Rohit's Rotis is able to benefit from scale economies in terms of distribution costs.

Market research has identified that there is sufficient demand and a number of companies looking for a quality supplier.

The research identified that the specific needs of targeted customers were for a range of fillings and a supply of drinks. Customers would like the rotis to be supplied in packaging that helps the food to remain hot, should the employee have some pressing task that takes them away from their lunch for a while. A range of fillings were identified as being particularly popular and likely to sell well, including curried chicken, channa, beef and shrimp. No specific age profile was identified by the research, although it was found that younger employees were likely to make more regular purchases. The gender profile identified a male : female ratio of 60 : 40 in terms of willingness to buy into the service. The research identified key factors that would give Rohit's Rotis a competitive advantage: freshness, variety of fillings, punctual delivery and price.

1 Explain the process by which Rohit identified his target market.
2 How does the process of identifying this target market enable Rohit to gain greater credibility for his business plan?
3 Summarise the characteristics of the target market. What are its specific needs?

Other aspects of the business environment

While market considerations are particularly important in setting up a business, there are also some other factors that you need to consider in the wider environment:

- **Social factors:** Rohit needs to consider changes that are taking place in wider society. Are more people changing to healthier eating patterns? Do busy working lives mean that they have less time to prepare food?

- **Legal factors:** setting up a food business requires particular consideration of health and safety laws and regulations, including handling of food, hygiene of premises and content of foods. Rohit would need to show that he has considered each of these factors.

- **Economic factors:** the success of business depends in some measure on the changing economic climate. When the economy is booming, businesses can flourish. In a time of recession, however, people cut back on spending and this can impact on the sales of a business. For a new business, the loss of a few extra sales could be the difference between success and failure.

- **Political factors:** these often relate to the attitudes of government to business, for example whether there is a low or high tax regime and whether the government will subsidise new enterprises.

- **Technological factors:** as society develops, so does technology. For example, competition for Rohit will take the form of companies selling rotis from travelling vans with onboard cooking and cooling facilities. If there are too many of these, they could erode Rohit's potential sales.

 Exam tip

You can use the mnemonic SLEPT to help you remember which additional factors in the business environment are important to consider when setting up a business.

Summary table

Term	Definition	Applied to Rohit's Rotis
Target market	Group(s) of customers that a business identifies as being a good focus for marketing activities and product offerings	Office and factory workers in the Port of Spain area, working in units of more than 20 employees
Customer needs	The requirements of specific groups of targeted customers	Fresh, affordable rotis and drinks delivered to the place of work
Location	Where the business will take place	Factories and offices in Port of Spain – best to target those that are not currently catered for by a delivery service

Summary questions

1 Identify the target market for a business idea of your choice. How would you go about finding out about its needs and requirements?

   a What do you see as being the main requirements of the target market that you have selected?

   b How could you back this up in order to convince someone to invest in your business or lend you funds?

On completion of this section, you should be able to:

- develop a business plan, with reference to industry background, market analysis and competitor analysis.

Market analysis

Module 2 explained the importance of using market research to find out about potential competitors and the size of the market. A new business is unlikely to be able to dominate the whole of a market, so it needs to set out the industry background and identify specific areas (locations) and market niches.

For Rohit, market analysis would enable him to identify:

- products in which potential customers are particularly interested
- customer requirements in addition to the basic product or service offering, such as delivery on time and the facility to pay at the end of the week or month.

CASE STUDY

Rohit's market research

Rohit carried out market research into his market and competitors. Research focused on identifying local offices (i.e. within a 5 mile radius) with no canteen facilites. Two-hundred potential sites were identified. Forty of these (20 per cent) were contacted by phone to explore interest in a delivdlery service. Twelve showed a significant interest. Two offices where chosen for pilot research. Trinidad Insurance (80 workers) and Co-operative Finance (22 workers). This inolved a trial period. Employees in these offices were provided with an order form for types of roti, roti fillings, drinks required and additional orders (e.g. samosas).

Findings from the research were that the average price consumers were willing to pay was $2.20.

There is a substantial market for lunchtime rotis in the area north of downtown. Based on the research figures, Rohit's Rotis could have a thriving market in about 25 per cent of factory and office premises in the area. However, it would be unrealistic to supply all these outlets.

The company has therefore decided to focus on 25 premises that are close to each other and to our central processing unit. The outlets chosen employ over 20 people (average e mployment is 28 per premises).

Assuming that we can sell one roti per day regularly to half the employees of these firms, this will give daily sales of:

25 (number of outlets) × 14 (average number of employees buying rotis) = 350 rotis

350 (rotis) × $2.20 (average revenue) = $770 per day

So weekly sales revenue is $770 × 5 = $3,850

Annual sales revenue *for 50 weeks = $3,850 × 50*
= $192,500

In addition, market research shows that a customer will spend an extra $2.00 on sweets, drinks and chocolate supplied per day.

350 (purchases of non-sandwich items) × $2.00 = $700 per day

So weekly sales revenue from non-roti items = $3,500

Annual sales revenue from non-roti items = $3,500 × 50
= $175,000

Total forecast sales revenue for Rohit's Rotis in Year 1 of trading = $367,500

1 Identify the assumptions on which these sales figures have been calculated.

2 What potential issues might there be if the sales figures have been overestimated? At which of the stages outlined might this be the case?

3 What problems might arise if demand is greater than expected?

4 How does carrying out a market analysis enable Rohit to plan ahead? What are the other benefits of carrying out a market analysis?

Competitor analysis

Competing businesses follow each other's actions closely. Although Rohit and Sumita believe that they have spotted a market niche, there is likely to be some direct competition in the area north of downtown, and indirect competition in the form of local restaurants, mobile roti vendors and street-corner sellers.

Table 3.16.1 shows a competitor analysis – an inventory (list) of direct and indirect competitors with main strengths and weaknesses identified.

KEY TERMS

Annual sales revenue: the physical number of sales made multiplied by the average price per sale. Alternatively, weekly sales revenue multiplied by the number of trading weeks in the year.

Table 3.16.1 A competitor analysis for Rohit's Rotis

Competitor	Strength	Weakness
Hosein's roti shops	Largest chain of roti retailers in Trinidad – offering high-quality products and many varieties	Not in close range of the area north of downtown
Local competitor selling from mobile van	Low-price rotis, freshly cooked in convenient locations	Only operates in the area north of downtown two days a week and is sometimes late arriving, so consumers have to look elsewhere
Consumers making their own rotis	Low cost, can choose their own variety	Cost of preparation not that different from commercially produced rotis, as lack of scale in manufacture Trouble of making one's own

Studying the competition indicates how Rohit can avoid direct clashes with rival businesses. Studying their weaknesses makes it possible to identify ways of building competitive advantage by being better than his rivals. The research explains Rohit's decision to target office and factory premises that are not located near to competitor outlets and where work starts before competitor outlets open.

Summary table

What is a market analysis?	Study of features of the market for a good or service to identify: ■ number of potential customers ■ average price they are willing to pay ■ number of purchases that they will make ■ other aspects that will help to shape buying patterns.
What is competitor analysis?	Study of what competitors are doing to identify: ■ their key strengths ■ their key weaknesses, in order to gain a competitive advantage.

Summary questions

1 Think of a good or service that you might seek to develop as a business idea. Identify the market research analysis that you should engage in to identify whether your idea is likely to be a success.

2 Carry out a competitor analysis for your business.

Specific objective

On completion of this section, you should be able to:

- develop a business plan, with a focus on setting out a marketing plan.

Marketing plan: a sub-component of the overall business plan, providing a detailed blueprint of marketing efforts, including marketing objectives, definition of the target market and an outline of the marketing mix (product, place, promotion and price).

The marketing plan

The **marketing plan** for a company like Rohit's Rotis might run to several pages in order to illustrate the depth of research that has gone into developing the idea. It should include the pricing, promotion and distribution strategies. Table 3.17.1 summarises the key components of the plan. Distribution strategies were discussed in 2.28–2.30; look back at these to remind yourself of the key points.

Table 3.17 1 Rohit's Rotis: summary of the marketing plan

Market definition and opportunity	Lunchtime rotis, snacks and other refreshments supplied directly to targeted business premises in the office area north of downtown in Port of Spain.
Proposed target market segments	Factory and office premises employing more than 20 employees, seeking Caribbean speciality foods at lunchtime; companies with no current canteen facility on the premises.
Demand for product/service	Research showed a sizeable market for freshly made rotis and snacks.
Competition	Only one competitor (providing an intermittent and unreliable service).
Other market influences	Published research shows demand for rotis and Caribbean snack food growing steadily in Trinidad.
Marketing tactics	See below for outline of the elements of the marketing mix (4 Ps).

Elements of the marketing mix

The four Ps, the elements of the mix, are closely integrated: a top-of-the-range product needs to be complemented by high pricing and expensive promotional activity.

Product

The core product is rotis, supported by other snacks and drinks to provide a complete meal offering. An important element is the packaging, in heat-retaining foil. Market research indicated the most popular roti fillings (Table 3.17.2).

Rohit will prepare rotis in line with these percentages and adjust according to changing preferences, festivals and seasonality. Drink and confectionery stocks will be bought in line with demand patterns, although they may be bought in bulk and stored.

Place

Fresh Rotis will be cooked daily at Rohit's Rotis kitchens and delivered by van to the premises of participating firms. Delivery is guaranteed before 11am. The rotis will be available in agreed locations within each premises, set out on a large paper tablecloth with names of purchasers.

Promotion

Rohit's Rotis products are promoted through advertising on company notice boards in the participating premises. Order forms with clear

Filling	Chicken	Channa	Goat	Beef	Lamb	Vegetarian	Other
Percentage	20	15	15	15	10	14	11

Table 3.17.2 Most popular roti fillings

CASE STUDY – *continued*

instructions are also delivered in batches to every employee at the selected locations. Each premises involved in the scheme will have a free trial in the first week that the company begins operating. Rohit's is also promoted through signs on its van and features in the local press.

Price

Strategy has been based on:

- cost-based pricing – to ensure a profit margin of 66 per cent on items sold. Prices reflect the cost

of ingredients, so beef curry fillings are more expensive than channa

- competitive pricing – prices have been competitively set to be similar to those offered by the nearest outlets.

Market research

Careful analysis has been made of secondary information provided by market research companies relating to consumption of food away from the home. The prime source of information is Business Monitor International's *Caribbean Food and Drink Report*, which shows changes in food consumption in the Caribbean. The research shows a steady growth in food consumption away from home in Trinidad.

Primary research was carried out in targeted outlets in the area north of downtown (see 3.16). This helped to provide a strong business case for developing Rohit's Rotis in 25 office outlets there.

Sales forecasts

Sales forecasts are based on: number of premises participating × numbers likely to place a definite
order × projected average spend per customer:

$25 \times 14 \times \$4.20 = \$1,470$ per day

Assuming that sales are made for 50 weeks in the year and that there are five working days in the week, this gives total sales revenue for the year of $367,500.

Table 3.17.3 sets this out in a sales forecast, which assumes that the lowest sales will be in the first month when interest is being built up. Highest sales will take place in the second and third months due to initial interest, then sales will establish a steady pattern.

> Statistics from the market research on product demand:
>
> - 50 per cent of employees likely to place a regular order
> - typical average spend of $4.20 per day
> - the range of rotis and complementary products preferred.

Summary questions

1 Set out a marketing plan for an organisation of your choice, using the headings outlined in this section.

2 Include a sales forecast for your product for a 12-month period.

Table 3.17.3 *Sales forecast for Rohit's Rotis*

Apr	May	Jun	Jul	Aug	Sep	Oct	Nov	Dec	Jan	Feb	Mar
20,000	40,000	37,500	30,000	30,000	30,000	30,000	30,000	30,000	30,000	30,000	30,000

Summary table

Marketing plan	Blueprint setting out marketing objectives and the marketing tactics that a company will employ
Marketing tactics	Integrated outline of the marketing mix (i.e. the products, place, promotion and pricing aspects of the marketing plan)
Market research	Research into the market that helps to structure the components of the marketing plan
Sales forecast	Forecast of future sales, based on market research conducted by the organisation

Specific objective

On completion of this section, you should be able to:

- develop a business plan, with a focus on setting out an operations plan and a managerial summary.

For Rohit's Rotis the operations plan focuses on:

- how orders will be taken for new rotis
- how supplies of ingredients will be purchased in order to be available just in time for manufacture
- how the rotis will be manufactured
- how employees will be organised to carry out their duties and responsibilities
- how rotis will be delivered to place of sale
- how rotis will be displayed
- how the company will interact with existing and new customers.

An operations plan

The operations of a business are the activities that it carries out. In the example of Rohit's Rotis, the operations relate to the cost of production: that is, manufacturing, distributing and selling rotis and other lunch foods. Rohit needs to be able to convince potential lenders and investors in the business that there is a sound operational plan in place. The plan will cover the following:

- purchase of machinery and the organisation of a production system: for example, for the storage of food in sanitary conditions, and an efficient cooking operation
- manufacturing – that is, cooking in the industrial unit using the roti oven
- distribution of the food on time, at the right temperatures, to the right places. Part of getting the distribution system right will be to have an effective system through which customers can make orders
- managing sales and after-sales: Rohit may want to take feedback from customers about how satisfied they are with the service and what improvements they would like to see
- setting out roles and responsibilities of employees in the organisation: what will they do and when?

Rohit's operations plan shows that the weekend is used to set out a schedule of orders for the coming week. The industrial unit will be cleaned and fresh supplies will be delivered. Rohit uses a small number of suppliers who are paid on a monthly basis. An inventory of stock is made out at the end of the week so that exactly the right amounts of new materials can be ordered for the week to come.

During the week, operations start at 7am when the fresh rotis are cooked. By 11am all the products need to be ready for delivery and placed in heat-retaining containers. A schedule of deliveries is organised to get to the premises in good time and place the items in appropriate storage positions. A system is in place to pick up orders and to input these into the production planning system.

Key considerations in establishing the operations plan are:

- Order the right quantities of materials for production.
- Organise production in a systematic pattern so that there is a regular production schedule for making the rotis and assembling the separate baskets of food for delivery.
- Get the products to the right places at the right time, with a strong focus on making sure that the food is still hot when customers come to eat it.
- Make sure that new orders are recorded and assembled as part of a well-focused production schedule.
- Always be polite to customers and attend to their requirements.

Managerial summary

To convince stakeholders in the company that it will be well run, it is important to include a brief managerial summary setting out the qualifications, experience and skills of the managers. Currently there are two managers at Rohit's Rotis: Rohit Khurana and Sumita Sarkar. The plan would also set out staffing plans for the business.

CASE STUDY

Managerial profile

	Role	Qualifications	Experience	Skills
Rohit Khurana	Managing director, operations director, marketing manager	MSc in Business and Management (UWI)	10 years' management in the hotel industry	Finance, operations, sales and marketing
Sumita Sarkar	Chief financial officer, purchasing manager	BSc in Accounting (UWI)	Chief financial officer in a telecommunications company	Finance and accounts, purchasing

1 To what extent do Rohit and Sumita appear to have the qualifications, skills and experience required to deliver the business plan?

2 What other qualifications, experience and skills appear to be missing that could impact on the effectiveness of the organisation?

Summary table

Key ingredients of an operations plan	■ How will goods be manufactured? ■ How and when will materials and components be delivered? Who will do what and when? ■ How will goods be displayed, packaged and delivered to customers? ■ Who will take responsibility for the operations plan?
Key ingredients of a managerial summary	■ Who are the managers? ■ What qualifications, experience and skills do they have, particularly in relation to running a specific company?

Did you know?

For a small business, key managerial roles are sales and marketing, administration and production. Of course, a single manager can perform more than one role: in many small businesses the owners and managers are the same people.

Summary questions

1 Set out an operations plan for a business of your choice.

2 Why is it important to construct an effective operations plan?

3 What problems might arise if the operations plan has not been carefully thought out? Relate your answer to Rohit's Rotis.

Specific objective

On completion of this section, you should be able to:

- develop a business plan, with a focus on the financial plan: sources of funds and cash flow.

Sections of a financial plan

There are six main sections in a financial plan:

1 sources of funds

2 cash flow forecast, or statement

3 profit and loss (income statement)

4 business ratios

5 break-even analysis

6 the assumptions on which sections 1–5 have been drawn up.

Sources of funds

Small businesses need to plan carefully to secure finance to set up, operate and expand the business. Look back to 3.10 to remind yourself of the main types of finance available for enterprises.

Look back to 3.10

CASE STUDY

Funding Rohit's Rotis

The following is an extract from Rohit's business plan. Sources of funds required for the business are:

- **Start-up capital:** *the business has $50,000 in the form of partners' capital – more than enough for hiring premises, leasing the van and buying the kitchen equipment. However, the owners have arranged an additional interest-free government loan of $20,000 to meet any unforeseen contingencies (for example, a second van or a move to a larger facility).*

- **Ongoing running costs:** *flour for the rotis is being sourced from Trinidad Flour Mills. They will supply on credit and require payment at*

the end of each week. Drink and potato chip stocks are to be purchased from cash-and-carry suppliers, using a store card, with payments either in cash or at the end of the month. To simplify accounting procedures, Rohit's Rotis will purchase stock for cash. In addition, Rohit's Rotis has arranged an overdraft facility of $2,000 with the bank – but it is highly unlikely that this facility will be used.

1 What start-up capital would you require to set up a business of your choice? What would be the main start-up costs?

2 What would be the main running costs of your business? How would you cover these?

Cash flow forecast

To prepare a cash flow forecast, a business must be able to estimate the cash inflows and outflows over a future period.

Pre-start-up income and expenditure

Before you start to construct your cash flow forecast you should calculate the pre-start income and expenditure. The pre-start up income is the start-up funds. For Rohit's Rotis this is $50,000 owners' capital and $20,000 of bank finance = $70,000. Subtract from this the pre-start up expenditure, which is shown in the calculation to the left.

The opening balance of cash in Rohit's Rotis bank account will therefore be $56,250 (start-up funds minus start-up costs).

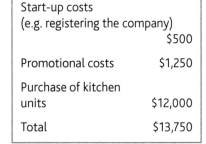

Start-up costs (e.g. registering the company)	
	$500
Promotional costs	$1,250
Purchase of kitchen units	$12,000
Total	$13,750

The cash flow statement

Figure 3.19.1 shows Rohit's cash flow statement for the first six months. It shows:

- opening balances at the start of each month
- receipts (money received from sales) during the month
- outgoings during the month – rent on the industrial unit, lease charges on van hire, payments for website hosting, staff wages, fuel (including petrol) and cooking bills, raw materials including all food and drink ingredients, additional items such as order forms (consumables) and business insurance
- closing balance (opening balance plus incomings minus outgoings).

The forecast shows that, given relatively low start-up costs and a high margin on items sold, the cash position will steadily improve over time – assuming that sales figures can be achieved and costs kept to budget.

Note that the cash flow statement does not show the profit of a business, only the timing and amounts of cash flowing in and out. The statement helps a new business owner to identify periods when cash balances are likely to be low and finance required.

Did you know?

Businesses with high start up-costs are unlikely to make a profit in the first year of trading. Cash outflows will also often exceed cash inflows, so it is important to make loan arrangements with a bank.

A bank will rarely lend more than 50 per cent of the capital required to set up a new enterprise. The owner is expected to bear most of the burden.

Summary questions

1 Create a cash flow statement for a business of your choice:
   a Make pre-start calculations to work out the opening balance.
   b Identify all the incomings and outgoings.

2 a Show how the balance changes each month.
   b Identify periods where you may need an additional loan to support you through cash flow difficulties.
   c What sources of finance could you use in these periods?

Figure 3.19.1 Rohit's cash flow statement

	Apr	May	Jun	Jul	Aug	Sep
Opening balance	56,250	63,684	84,452	103,552	117,652	131,752
Receipts	20,000	40,000	37,500	30,000	30,000	30,000
Outgoings						
Rent	600	600	600	600	600	600
Lease	400	400	400	400	400	400
Hosting	50	50	50	50	50	50
Wages	1,200	1,200	1,200	1,200	1,200	1,200
Fuel	450	450	450	450	450	450
Materials	6,666	13,332	12,500	10,000	10,000	10,000
Consumables	50	50	50	50	50	50
Insurance	150	150	150	150	150	150
Salaries	3,000	3,000	3,000	3,000	3,000	3,000
Total outgoings	12,566	19,232	18,400	15,900	15,900	15,900
Closing balance	63,684	84,452	103,552	117,652	131,752	145,852

Summary table

When an enterprise will require finance	For start-up capital and ongoing running costs
The purpose of a cash flow statement	To identify the timing and amount of incomings and outgoings, as well as the monthly balance
How to create a cash flow statement	1 Calculate the pre-start income and pre-start expenditure, to arrive at the starting balance. 2 Add incomings and subtract outgoings to give monthly balances.

Specific objective

On completion of this section, you should be able to:

■ develop a business plan, with a focus on the financial plan: profit and loss, profitability ratios and break-even analysis.

The income statement

Setting out a forecast income statement for the end of a first year of trading provides evidence that a company is able to make a profit, break even or at least not make a significant loss. This can help to convince potential lenders that they are not taking too big a risk in lending to the company. It also helps the business owner to plan ahead.

Rohit's Rotis: profit and loss calculation and the income statement

We saw in 3.14 that Rohit's sales forecast shows that the annual sales revenue will be $367,500.

This is based on marking up cost of sales by 200 per cent. For example, you can see from the cash flow statement in 3.19 that in April materials costs were $6,666 and Rohit was able to make sales of $20,000.

We can calculate mark-up on the cost at which Rohit bought his materials, where mark-up is the difference between Rohit's selling price and his buying price (total mark-up = $13,334). The mark-up is therefore double the cost of sales, i.e. 200 per cent.

Rohit's expenses of running his business come to $92,400 for the year (including owners' salaries of $36,000 for Sumita and Rohit).

Rohit's Rotis is thus able to set out the following predicted income statement for the first year of trading:

Income statement Rohit's Rotis Year x	
	$
Sales revenue	367,500
Cost of sales	(122,500)
Gross profit	245,000
Expenses	(34,800)
Owners' salaries	(36,000)
Net profit	174,200

1 How does the income statement help Rohit to have confidence that he has a sound business idea?

2 What is the source of the information used to calculate sales revenue? What is the relationship between sales revenue and cost of sales?

3 What would be the impact on net profit if Rohit were only to mark up his items at 100 per cent on cost of sales? Give the figure.

4 What would be included in the figures for expenses?

Did you know?

It would also be possible to include a depreciation charge in the income statement for Rohit's machinery and equipment. This would appear as a deduction from income. Additionally some or all of the start-up cost of setting up the business could be recorded in the first year.

Profitability ratios

It is possible to calculate profitability ratios from the figures outlined above.

Gross profit percentage shows how many cents of profit Rohit's Rotis is making for each $1 of sales.

$$\text{Gross profit margin} = \frac{\text{Gross profit}}{\text{Sales}} \times \frac{100}{1}$$

$$= \frac{245,000}{367,500} \times 100 = 66.7\%$$

The net profit margin shows the net profit as a percentage of sales.

$$\text{Net profit margin} = \frac{\text{Net profit}}{\text{Sales}} \times \frac{100}{1}$$

$$= \frac{174,200}{367,500} \times 100 = 47.4\%$$

Break-even

To calculate the break-even point for Rohit's Rotis, the first step is to calculate the contribution per customer.

Every time Rohit's serves a typical customer, the company receives $4.20. Rohit's has to pay out $1.40 for materials used to produce that order. Rohit's therefore earns a contribution of $2.80 per customer.

$$\text{Contribution} = \text{Sales income} - \text{Variable cost}$$

$$= \$4.20 - \$1.40$$
$$= \$2.80$$

The amount is called the contribution because it literally contributes towards the fixed costs, no matter how many customers are served. With one customer there would be a contribution of $2.80 to fixed costs. With two customers there would be a contribution of $5.60 and so on.

The break-even point will occur when there are sufficient contributions to pay off all the fixed costs of running the enterprise. At this point there will be no profit and no loss.

$$\text{Break-even point} = \frac{\text{Fixed costs}}{\text{Contribution per customer}}$$

The annual fixed costs for Rohit's are:

	$		$
Rent on premises	7,200	Fuel	5,400
Lease charges on vehicle	4,800	Consumables	600
Website hosting	600	Insurance	1,800
Computer/telephone cost	1,000	Salaries	36,000
Staff wages	14,400	Total fixed costs	71,800

To find the break-even point, we divide the total fixed cost by the contribution.
$$\frac{71,800}{2.80} = 25,643 \text{ customers to break even}$$

In the market analysis (3.16) we were able to see that, given the market research data, Rohit's was expecting to serve 350 customers a day, which is 1,750 in a five-day week and 87,500 in a 50-week year.

Summary questions

1   a   Set out an income statement for a business for which you have created a business plan.

     b   Calculate the break-even point.

     c   Calculate the estimated figure for gross profit and net profit (or loss).

2   Would there be a problem if the total contribution in the first year of trading was insufficient to cover the fixed costs? Give a reason for your answer.

Summary table

How do you set out the profit and loss?	1 Calculate sales revenue (average value of sales $\times$ number of sales). 2 Deduct cost of sales. 3 Deduct administrative expenses.
How do you set out profitability ratios?	Gross profit is calculated as a percentage of sales. Net profit is calculated as a percentage of sales.
How do you calculate the break-even?	Break-even is calculated by dividing the fixed cost by the contribution.

Specific objective

On completion of this section, you should be able to:

■ develop a business plan, with a focus on the financial plan: assumptions and financial (business) ratios.

Assumptions

Although assumptions are informed guesses, they form the basis for forecast inputs and outcomes in a financial plan (and other parts of a business plan). They should be the result of careful and thorough research: the better the research, the more accurate the assumptions are likely to be.

Key assumptions relate to:

■ sales forecasts, based on what the market research indicates will be the number of sales made at the price charged

■ cost of sales forecasts, based on current cost of purchasing stocks and materials, and more importantly, forecasts of likely future costs

■ administrative costs, needing careful projections

■ charges such as business taxes on profits.

CASE STUDY

Key assumptions made by Rohit's Rotis

Several assumptions have been made in the business plan:

Demand for rotis will average 350 per day in the first year and that the average spend will be $4.20 per day. This key assumption forms the basis for the excellent profit figures. If it proves to be incorrect in any way, sales could be much lower than the prediction.

The profit margin will be 66% on items sold. However, if costs are higher than expected (e.g. by 10%), this will severely impact on profits.

Various assumptions relating to fixed costs:

Monthly rental for the enterprise unit including charges for rates, electricity and water: $600.

Kitchen and refrigerated units – purchased directly and fitted: $12,000.

Cost of leasing a delivery van based on discussion with van leasing company: $400 per month.

Telephone, computer and internet connection: $1,000.

Hosting of website: $50 per month.

Employees' salary – including national insurance contributions: $1,200 per month.

Registration of company with registrar: $500.

Initial marketing costs (posters and order forms): $1,250.

By setting out these and other assumptions Rohit demonstrates that he has carried out the research around which the plan has been built. He will be sure to keep a folder containing each of the quotes and documents relating to these items.

1 How would Rohit have gathered the information for the assumptions that he is making?

2 Which of the assumptions is the most reliable? Which is the least reliable? Give reasons for your answers.

Did you know?

One of the assumptions that a company makes is about the level of competition. Rohit is assuming that he will not face significant competition, but he needs to show that he has researched potential competitors.

Financial ratios

To make a successful business case, it is also helpful to identify key financial ratios that show the business is likely to provide a return for investors.

Important business ratios include:

■ **Profit margin:** gross profit margin = gross profit as a percentage of sales; net profit margin = net profit as a percentage of sales (see 3.20).

- **Return on capital employed:** we saw that Rohit and Sumita had each put $25,000 into the business, and that there was a further business loan of $20,000, giving a total capital employed of $70,000 at the start of the first year. The return on capital employed is calculated as operating profit (before interest and tax) as a percentage of the capital employed. It is best to use the average capital employed, which is calculated by adding the start-out capital and the end capital, and dividing by 2.

- **Return on equity:** the return on the amount the shareholders have invested in the business can be calculated as profit after tax for ordinary equity holders (Sumita and Rohit) as a percentage of their share capital.

- **Gearing:** this measures the extent to which a company is exposed to high levels of external borrowing. It is found as a ratio of external borrowing to the total capital employed (external and internal) in the business.

> Rohit's Rotis is to be set up on external finance of $20,000 and internal finance of $50,000, so the gearing ratio is 20:70. This is a low gearing ratio, indicating that the company is not exposed by having to pay extensive interest repayments out of its revenues.

- **Liquidity ratios:** these measure the extent to which a company has liquid reserves available to pay pressing liabilities. The current ratio shows the relationship between stock, debtors and cash compared with pressing liabilities that a company has run up. Rohit's is a fast-moving catering business, generating new cash flows all the time from sales, and is unlikely to have pressing liquidity issues.

Table 3.21.1 highlights some of the key financial considerations that Rohit would incorporate in his business plan.

Table 3.21.1 *Rohit's key financial considerations*

Rohit's Rotis: summary	
Assumptions relating to sales (3.16)	Based on daily sales of 350 with average spend of $4.20, leading to annual sales figures of $367,500
Variable costs	Calculated as comprising 33% of the sales price
The cash flow forecast (3.19)	Shows healthy closing balance ($145,852) after six months
Gross profit margin (3.20)	Calculated at 66% with net profit margin of 47% for the first year of trading
Break-even (see 3.20)	Calculated to take place between the 14th and 15th week of trading
Assuming that the business generates revenues as expected, it is anticipated that there will be no liquidity issues.	

Summary table

Assumptions	Bases on which figures set out in a financial plan have been forecast and calculated. Key assumptions relate to sales estimates and estimates of costs.
Financial ratios	Financial ratios help to demonstrate viability of a business plan. Examples include gearing, gross and net profit, and liquidity ratios.

Summary questions

1 Identify some of the key assumptions that you have made in constructing the business plan for your chosen organisation.

2 Under what circumstances might the assumptions prove to be over-optimistic? How can the creator of a business plan guard against over-optimism in the planning process?

3.22 Practice exam-style questions: Small business management

Answers to all exam-style questions can be found on the accompanying CD.

Section 1: Multiple-choice questions

1 'Intrapreneurs' are persons who:

A establish their own business in order to make a profit for themselves

B show creativity and enterprise within an existing organisation

C invest finance in a new business enterprise

D carry out routine tasks within an existing large organisation.

2 Which of the following qualities is least likely to be a characteristic of a successful entrepreneur?

A Organised

B Hard working

C Inflexible

D Able to deal with failure

3 Using the World Bank definition of a micro enterprise, which of the following would be classified as a micro enterprise? (Figures are in US$.)

A A company employing 20 people

B A company that has only recently started

C A company with sales of $50,000

D A company with total assets of $110,000

4 An example of a technical economy of scale for a larger firm is being able to:

A employ specialist manufacturing equipment

B raise finance more cheaply than smaller companies

C buy goods in bulk from suppliers

D spread risks by providing a range of products.

5 Which of the following best illustrates the 'organic growth' of a business?

A Increasing the sales made by the company in a sustainable way

B Merging the company with a similar business

C The takeover of another business

D Reducing the scale of operations of the business

6 Which of the following means of sourcing capital for a small enterprise involves giving up some of the equity in the business to other owners?

A Government funding

B Trade credit

C Venture capital

D Loan finance

7 The best example of an e-preneur is someone who:

A employs an entrepreneurial approach to running a business

B sets up a business and employs others to work in that business

C develops new ideas in an existing business

D uses online electronic approaches to support enterprise.

8 The executive summary of a business plan should focus on:

A setting out details of the marketing plan

B outlining a summary cash flow for the coming year

C clarifying the main points included in the business plan

D establishing the strengths and weaknesses of the business.

9 A cash flow forecast set out in a business plan should concentrate on:

A identifying past situations where income has fallen short of expenditure

B projecting future incomings and outgoings of cash to and from the business

C establishing how much cash currently exists in the business

D setting out a statement of the cash flow position today.

10 The prime users of a business plan for a small business are:

A the owner and providers of finance

B competitors and government development agencies

C suppliers and customers

D the local community and business partners.

Section 2: Structured questions

11 a State TWO key differences between a 'private enterprise' and a 'social enterprise'. [4]

b Identify ONE example of a social enterprise with which you are familiar. Explain THREE of the key objectives of the enterprise. [7]

c What qualities would an individual need to have to become a successful entrepreneur? [10]

d How could an individual demonstrate 'intrapreneurship' within his or her current job role? [4]

12 A website designer operating from Barbados has set up a small company which designs websites for larger businesses.

a Identify THREE approaches that might be applied to defining the website design business as a small company. [6]

b If the business is successful and decides to grow, how might the company grow:
i organically
ii through external growth? [6]

c How can the small business benefit from operating in a country which has a free-market economy? [10]

d List THREE ways in which the company may be affected by government decisions in Barbados. [3]

13 Loretta is setting up a mobile hairdressing business that will go to people's homes to provide 'at home' hairdressing services. She will employ two other hair stylists to work alongside her and will purchase two motor vehicles to transport the stylists.

a Set out THREE reasons why Loretta should create a business plan for her new business. [6]

b What details should she include in the marketing section of the plan? [12]

c Identify THREE principal start-up costs for the business. [3]

d Why might the actual revenues from the business be lower than those predicted in the business plan? [4]

14 An agricultural cooperative in the eastern Caribbean markets the products of small farmers located in this area so that the crops produced by the cooperative can be sold throughout the Caribbean and in North America. It has recently produced a business plan in order to secure funding in the form of government grants, which it can channel into more marketing activities.

a Explain THREE reasons why it should set out the current sources and amounts of funds/finance that it is receiving in its business plan. [6]

b How might government grants help the marketing cooperative to expand its marketing activities? [4]

c As well as sources of funds, what other financial details should be included in the business plan? [9]

d Why might the marketing cooperative be considered a 'social enterprise'? List THREE reasons. [6]

15 Many of the Caribbean's largest companies, such as those engaged in food and drink manufacture, and retailing, started out as small enterprises run by an individual or family group. Over time these enterprises have grown through internal and external growth so that they now benefit from economies of scale.

a How do new business opportunities arise? Identify THREE sources of new business ideas. [6]

b Identify TWO sources of external growth for a business. [4]

c Define 'economy of scale'. [2]

d Show how FOUR different sources of economy of scale can benefit a large retailing organisation such as a supermarket chain. [8]

e Why do small businesses continue to flourish in retailing despite the benefits of economies of scale? Give FIVE reasons. [5]

Further exam questions and examples can be found on the accompanying CD.

Glossary

A

Absorption costing: the process by which fixed as well as variable overheads are charged to cost units.

Acquisition: the process of acquiring (i.e. gaining an interest in) another business.

Activities: operations (e.g. in a bottling plant, moulding bottles, filling, capping and packing).

Adding value: making goods and services more desirable for the end consumer.

Advertising: the promotion of a product using paid-for media (e.g. television).

Analysis: making a detailed examination of the results of research, in order to find patterns and structures.

Annual sales revenue: the physical number of sales made multiplied by the average price per sale. Alternatively, weekly sales revenue multiplied by the number of trading weeks in the year.

B

B2B: where a business sells industrial or other products to other businesses using the internet.

B2C: where a business sells goods to consumers using the internet.

Benchmarking: the continuous process of measuring products, services and practices against the toughest competitors of those companies, regarded as industry leaders.

Bottlenecks: hindrances to the flow of production, usually a point of congestion in the production process. Here workloads arrive more quickly than can be handled by that section of the system, resulting in the congestion. This causes the entire process to slow down or stop.

Brainstorming: discussion process whereby members of a group are encouraged to suggest ideas and solutions to problems based on the first ideas that come into their heads. These ideas are refined by working with ones that are useful and eliminating those that cannot be taken further.

Brand: a brand consists of elements such as a brand name (e.g. Nike), a logo (the distinctive Nike symbol) and a slogan ('Just do it').

Branding: all the processes involved in creating a unique name and image of a product in consumers' minds.

Break-even: to exactly match costs with revenues received.

Bricks and mortar: describes businesses that do not trade online (e.g. your local bakery).

Bulk-decreasing industry: an industry with output that is cheaper to transport than its input.

Bulk-increasing industry: an industry where the output is more expensive to transport than the raw materials.

C

Capacity: quantity of machinery × number of shifts × utilisation of machinery × efficiency. Output produced is determined by the amount of machinery (and/or labour) employed, the number of hours machinery is worked, the extent to which production capacity is used, and the efficiency with which equipment is used.

Capacity planning: the process used to make sure that a business is able to meet the changing demand for its products.

Capacity utilisation: the percentage of a firm's total production capacity actually being employed at a given time.

Capital: the funding put into a business or the physical machinery and equipment that the business purchases to carry out its activities.

Capital employed: the total value of the funds put into the business internally (by shareholders and other owners) and externally (by lenders and other external sources of funds).

Cause-and-effect diagrams: simple illustrations often showing how problems or successes have arisen, with the aim of achieving a fuller understanding of operational processes.

Cause-related marketing: a joint funding and promotional strategy by a company and a charity or good cause, in which a percentage of sales revenue is donated to the charity.

Cell: a group of workers, machines and resources focused on producing families of related components and products.

Change in contribution: marginal revenue minus marginal cost.

Clicks and mortar: describes businesses that cut their costs by using the internet as a shop window. Customers can browse for products and services from the comfort of their own home.

Collateral: property or goods belonging to a borrower which a lender can require to be sold in order to pay back a loan.

Commercialisation: full-scale launch of a product, to secure financial gain (after all testing has been carried out).

Competitive price: price perceived to offer better value for money (when combined with other elements of the marketing mix) than prices offered by rival firms.

Competitive pricing strategy: pricing plan designed to use pricing of goods as a means to attract and win customer purchases.

Consumer choices: purchasing decisions made by consumers (e.g. to buy Brand X rather than Brand Y).

Consumer survey: a consumer research technique in which a questionnaire is used to research a particular topic, such as consumers' opinions about a specific product or issue. The survey typically involves a sequence of questions.

Contribution: sales value less variable cost of sales. It is the contribution that an individual item makes to covering the fixed costs of a business.

Criteria (singular **criterion**): the means by which a distinction or categorisation of an object, or group of objects, is made.

Critical path: a path showing the network of activities that need to be completed on time if the whole project is to be completed on time.

Culture of quality: established patterns, values and norms focusing on meeting, exceeding and delighting internal and external customers.

D

Databases: stores of data gathered for particular purposes. Today they usually refer to computer programs designed for the storage of data.

Design capacity: maximum amount of work that an organisation is capable of completing in a given period of time.

Direct costs: costs that a management accountant can allocate easily and accurately to a specific unit of production (e.g. the cost of paper that went into manufacturing this book is a direct materials cost).

Discount: a reduction in the price charged per unit (or in the total bill) to reward bulk purchasing or early payment.

Diseconomies of scale: the disadvantages from having higher production capacity, resulting in rising unit costs of production.

Disintegration: in business and economics, breaking down into component parts. Disintegrated elements are usually smaller businesses that serve the needs of larger organisations at the heart of a particular industry.

Distribution channel: a set of independent organisations that help to make a product available for use by consumers or business units.

Distribution intensity: focuses on the number of intermediaries through which a producer distributes goods and the degree of market coverage required for a product. There are three levels of intensity: intensive, selective and exclusive distribution.

Downmarket: cheap and low-quality products designed for less well-off consumers.

E

Earliest start time: earliest time at which an activity can commence.

E-commerce: buying and selling goods online.

Economic order quantity: the number of units a company should add to stock with each order so as to minimise the total costs of inventory.

Economic system: the overall pattern of decision making within a society, which is based on who makes decisions related to areas such as buying, selling, production and price setting.

Economies of scale: benefits from operating on a larger scale that enable a business to produce at lower unit costs than smaller firms.

Effective capacity: maximum amount of work that a company can actually achieve in a particular period of time.

E-marketing: finding out about customers' needs and wants online in order to meet their requirements.

Entrepreneur: a person who sets up and runs an enterprise, and in the process takes a financial risk.

E-preneur: a person who develops an enterprise online and sells goods through a website.

Estimated net profit: projection of the final end profit for a particular period of trading.

Ethnic group: a socially defined category based on people sharing a common culture or nationality.

Exchange: the act of giving or taking one thing in place of another.

Expected value (EV): the expected financial return resulting from making a decision, calculated by multiplying potential financial outcomes by the probability of their being achieved.

External economies of scale: benefits from the growth of an industry that enable all (or most) firms in that industry to produce with lower unit costs.

F

Financial return: the financial outcome (e.g. profit) resulting from making a particular choice.

Fitness for purpose: when a good or service does what a customer wants it to do.

Fixed costs: costs of production that do not alter according to the level of output or sales.

Footloose industries: businesses that do not require a particular location.

Forecasting: making a prediction of what will happen in the future, usually based on identifying a pattern from past and current data.

Franchise: a larger company with an established business idea and brand (the franchisor) allows a smaller organisation (the franchisee) to sell its products, trade under its name and use its systems of manufacturing and selling, in return for an initial payment and royalty fees. Fees are usually based on a percentage of the franchisee's sales or profits.

Frequency: the number of times an event happens in a given period of time. Frequencies are often measured in market research (e.g. the frequency with which a particular individual or group of customers buys specific items).

H

Histogram: a form of bar chart in which the width of each bar relates to a numerical scale. The number of observations relating to each variable is represented by the area covered by the bar, not necessarily the height of the bar. In a histogram, there should be no gaps between bars on the horizontal axis.

Homogeneous: of the same kind.

I

Indirect costs: costs that a management accountant cannot allocate directly to a specific unit of production.

In-house production: producing goods and carrying out activities internally.

Innovation: the introduction of new ideas or methods.

Intermediaries: firms or individuals such as wholesalers, retailers and agents who help to move a product from the producer to the consumer or business user.

Internal economies of scale: benefits from the growth of an individual firm, resulting in lower unit costs for that firm.

Intrapreneur: an employee within a large enterprise who shows creativity and drive.

Inventory control: managing the amount of stock held in a business.

J

Just-in-case: producing to ensure that there is enough inventory to meet additional demand from consumers – typically by operating with inventories of finished goods, raw materials and work in progress.

Just-in-time: producing in response to demand from consumers, only supplying when demand is signalled and delivering just in time to meet the order.

L

Latest finish time: latest time by which an activity must be completed if the project is to be completed on time.

Lean production: concentrating on creating value in manufacturing by eliminating all forms of waste (e.g. wasted materials and time).

Least-cost location: a site where, after taking all costs into account, the cost of manufacturing or distribution is lowest.

Long-run average cost curve: a curve showing unit costs at different levels of output in the long term.

M

Marginal cost: change in total cost resulting from producing one additional unit of output.

Marginal cost of labour: cost in money terms of employing an additional employee.

Marginal physical product of labour: number of products that can be produced by an additional employee.

Marginal revenue: change in total revenue resulting from producing one additional unit of output.

Marginal revenue product of labour: value in money terms of the output of an additional employee.

Market (or free) economy: economic system where prices act as signals to sellers about which goods it is profitable to produce, and to consumers about which goods provide value for money. Buyers and sellers consider prices when making buying and selling decisions.

Market segment: a large, identifiable group within a market, with similar wants, purchasing power, geographical location, buying attitudes or buying habits.

Market share: proportion or percentage of total sales in a particular market held by a specific firm.

Marketers: people who work for the marketing department of a company, or for a specialist marketing company. Their job is to secure custom for a business by developing marketing tools and tactics that enable market research to be carried out to identify customer requirements.

Marketing: the anticipation and identification of consumer wants and needs in order to meet those needs, and to make a profit.

Marketing audit: a comprehensive, systematic evaluation by a company of its current marketing activities and markets.

Marketing mix: the four key elements that businesses must plan to attract customers: product, price, place and promotion (the four Ps). These are the things that customers focus on when making buying decisions.

Marketing plan: a sub-component of the overall business plan, providing a detailed blueprint of marketing efforts, including marketing objectives, definition of the target market and an outline of the marketing mix (product, place, promotion and price).

Marketing strategy: a process whereby the marketing goals of an organisation are built into a plan that includes the marketing mix.

Mass market: a widely defined group of target customers.

Maximum stock level: maximum acceptable level of stock to be held.

Merger: when two firms voluntarily join together to become a single entity.

Micromachines: machines that produce device components ranging from 1 micrometre to 1 millimetre (1 micrometre is about one-tenth of the diameter of a human hair). A nanometre is three orders of magnitude smaller than a micrometre.

Minimum stock level: minimum acceptable level of stock.

Mixed economy: an economy in which decisions are made by a combination of government decision making and the market.

Modules: bundles of product components that are mass-produced prior to installation in modular form. A module is physically coherent as a sub-assembly.

N

Niche market: a narrowly defined group of target customers.

Nodes: in a critical path diagram, points in time setting out when activities must start and be completed.

O

Operations: converting inputs into finished outputs.

Outsourcing: buying in supplies and work from suppliers outside the organisation.

Overcapacity: when a company has too much plant and production resources relative to the demand for its products.

P

Penetration pricing: charging a low price on a new good in order to enter a market.

Planned economy: an economy in which the government runs many industries and establishes planning targets – how many goods will be produced, what type, where they will be sold and what prices will be charged for them.

Plant: one or more buildings and production facilities used to carry out operations.

Pollution: the introduction of harmful substances or products into the natural environment.

Primary data: data that are collected for the first time by the researcher (e.g. through answers to a questionnaire).

Probability: how likely an event is to occur, measured by the ratio of the extent to which it is likely compared to the total number of cases possible.

Product benefits: actual features (e.g. size, colour, use) or perceived features (e.g. image, reputation) of a product that make a consumer feel that it will meet his or her needs.

Product development: all stages involved in the development of a new (or existing) product.

Production: the processes involved in providing goods and services.

Productivity: a measure of the output (or value of output) that can be obtained from using productive resources.

Promotion: the different methods of communicating with a business's target audience.

Public relations: deliberate, planned and sustained effort to establish and maintain mutual understanding between an organisation and its public.

Publicity: information about an individual, group, company, event or product that is spread through the media in order to attract public attention.

Q

Quality assurance: checking work in progress during the production process and final goods at the end in order to supply goods with zero defects.

Quality control: ensuring that goods meet the requirements of the end user.

Questionnaire: a structured set of questions that can be given to one or a number of people.

R

Randomised sampling of product units: examining what has been produced to identify strengths, weaknesses and areas for development.

Reference groups: groups that consumers look to as role models or influencers when making purchasing decisions.

Relocation: movement of employees, used by firms to acquire the skilled workers they need.

Reorder level: quantity of stock required to replenish stock from minimum to maximum stock level.

Response rate: the percentage of responses received in comparison to the number of questionnaires sent out or interviews requested.

S

Sales projections: estimates of future sales value.

Sampling frame: list of population by sampling units.

Sampling units: groups of people who are to be questioned as part of a marketing research strategy.

Scanning the environment: the process of examining and researching the macro-environment in order to identify changes that are taking place and develop a strategic response.

Screening: using predetermined criteria to eliminate options that are less likely to be effective.

Secondary data: data that are already published (e.g. in the form of existing market research reports).

Segment: in the context of marketing, a group of customers with similar characteristics.

Skimming: charging a high price for a new good to yield high returns when there is little competition.

Spare capacity: plant and other resources that are not being used but could be, to increase production.

Spillover effect: a secondary result of an activity that affects those who are not directly involved in it.

Stimulus–response: in the context of marketing, where particular marketing actions lead to buyer responses. Understanding customer characteristics helps marketers to predict the likely responses.

Sub-assemblies: component parts of the overall assembly of a product (e.g. the engine of a car).

Survey: research tool used to find out the general view of a large number of people on a particular topic.

Sustainable enterprise: a business that continues to flourish and grow over a long period.

Sustainable growth: growth of a business (e.g. by growing capacity) in such a way that growth can be maintained steadily over the long term.

T

Takeover: when one firm gains control of another by purchasing a minimum of 51 per cent of the shares of the other company.

Target audience: the specific group of viewers, listeners or readers who are the focus of appeal of advertisements.

Target market: a specific group of customers who are the focus of marketing efforts.

Test marketing: trying out a product in a smaller market that is representative of the main market, in order to trial marketing activities.

Think 'outside the box': come up with new and original ideas rather than tried-and-trusted approaches.

Total quality management: developing a quality culture within an organisation so that everyone inside the organisation sees themselves as having a responsibility for satisfying customers and for making improvements to quality.

U

Undercapacity: when a company has insufficient plant or other resources to meet the demand for its products.

Unique selling point (USP): key factors that differentiate a product from those of rivals. Marketers may focus on one or several differentiating factors.

Unit costs: the cost of producing one unit of output.

Upmarket: expensive goods and services designed for more affluent consumers.

V

Value chain: a series of integrated activities in which a firm in a specific industry engages, to provide a valuable product to the consumer.

W

Wait time: delays.

Work in progress: partly assembled goods and processed raw materials part way through the manufacturing process.

Working capital: capital that is available to a business to purchase stock and carry out current manufacturing and trading activities. It is sometimes defined as current assets minus current liabilities.

Working capital requirements: finance required to meet pressing payments and short-term debts.

Index

Key terms are in **bold** and are also listed in the glossary.

A

absorption costing 30–1
acquisitions 154–5
activities, **critical path method (CPM)** 54–5
actual product, product concept 95
adding value 62, 65
advertising 126–7
AIDA model, **promotion** 125
analysis, market research 84–5
annual sales revenue 168, 169
assistance, small business 137, 160–1
assumptions, financial planning 178
augmented product, product concept 95

B

B2B 130
B2C 130
batch production 6, 7
behavioural segmentation 90–1
benchmarking, quality management 46–7
Boston Matrix, product management 98–9
brainstorming, quality management 46
brand 104–5
branding 104–5
break-even 32–3, 177
bricks and mortar businesses 130
bulk-decreasing industries 10, 11
bulk-increasing industries 11
business description, business plans/planning 165
business ideas 138–45
    criteria (singular criterion) 156
business plans/planning 162–79
    see also financial planning
    business description 165
    competitor analysis 168
    components 162–3
    environment analysis 166–7
    executive summary 164, 165
    financial planning 174–9
    managerial summary 173
    market analysis 168
    market research 168, 171
    marketing plan 170–1
    operations plan 172
    target markets 166
business size 148–53
    criteria (singular criterion) 148
    measuring 148–51
    small firms vs large firms 152–3
buying behaviour, consumer *see* consumer buying behaviour

C

CAD *see* computer-aided design
CAM *see* computer-aided manufacturing

capacity 20–1
capacity planning 20–1
capacity utilisation 20–3
capital 152
capital employed 148
cash flow forecast, financial planning 174–5
cause-and-effect diagrams, quality management 46
cause-related marketing 67
cell 7
cell production 7
cellular layout 27
change in contribution 34–5
clicks and mortar businesses 130–3
collateral 156–7
commercialisation, **product development** 101
company, enterprise type 139, 157
competition pricing 112–13
competitive price 112–13
competitive pricing strategy 112–13
competitor analysis 168
competitors 70–1
computer-aided design (CAD) 18
computer-aided manufacturing (CAM) 18–19
consumer buying behaviour 92–3
    purchasing process 92–3
    reference groups 93
    seven stages of a buying decision 92
    stimulus-response approach 93
consumer choices, demographic segmentation 88
consumer surveys, **forecasting** 12, 13
contribution 30–1
cooperative, business type 157
core product, product concept 94–5
corporate entrepreneurship 140–1
cost considerations, production/business location 10–11
cost-plus pricing 114–15
costs of production 28–9
CPM *see* **critical path method**
criteria (singular criterion)
    business ideas 156
    business size 148
critical path 54
critical path method (CPM) 54–5
culture of quality, quality management 44–5
customer focus, **marketing** 69

D

databases, market research 82–3
decision trees 56–9
Delphi method, **forecasting** 12, 13
demand, price elasticity of demand 110–11
demographic segmentation
    consumer choices 88
    ethnic groups 88
design capacity 22

direct costs 28–9
discount, pricing 117
diseconomies of scale 24–5
disintegration 25
distribution 118–23
    distribution channels 118–23
    distribution intensity 122
    factors influencing 120–1
    logistics strategies 122–3
downmarket, goods and services 109

E

e-commerce 130–3
    small business 158
e-marketing 130–3
e-preneurs 136
earliest start time, **critical path method (CPM)** 54–5
economic order quantity (EOQ) 39
economic systems 136, 146–7
economies of scale 24–5
    large firms 152–3
effective capacity 22
elasticity, pricing 110–11
entrepreneurs 138
    characteristics 144–5
    successful 144–5
entrepreneurship 138–45
    corporate 140–1
    social 142–3
environment
    see also macro-marketing environment; micro-marketing environment
    production/business location 8–9
environment analysis, business plans/planning 166–7
EOQ *see* **economic order quantity**
estimated net profit 164, 165
ethnic groups, demographic segmentation 88
EV *see* **expected value**
exchange 65
executive summary 164, 165
expected value (EV), decision trees 58–9
external economies of scale 25
external sources, market research 82–3

F

finance, sourcing 156–7
financial planning 174–9
    see also business plans/planning
    assumptions 178
    break-even 177
    cash flow forecast 174–5
    financial ratios 178–9
    income statement 176
    profitability ratios 176–7
financial ratios, financial planning 178–9
financial return, decision trees 56
fitness for purpose 42
fixed costs 24, 28–9

fixed position layout 26–7
focus groups, market research 79, 80
footloose industries 11
forecasting 12–13
franchise 138, 157
frequency, market research 85

G
geographic segmentation 88–9
globalisation, small business 158
goods marketing 106–7
        see also pricing
growth opportunities, businesses 154–5

H
histograms, market research 85
homogeneous, goods 106
in-house production 36

I
ideas, business 138–45, 156
income/class segmentation 91
income statement, financial planning 176
indirect costs 28–9
infrastructure, production/business
        location 8
innovation 140–1
integration, product design 14, 15
intellectual property rights (IPRs), small
        business 158–9
intermediaries, distribution channels 118
internal economies of scale 24–5
internal sources, market research 82
internet marketing 130–3
internet marketing decisions 63
interviews, market research 81
intrapreneurship 136, 140–1
inventory control 38
inventory management 38–41
        just-in-time (JIT) 40–1
        order quantities 38–9
IPRs see intellectual property rights
ISO standards, quality management 46

J
JIT see **just-in-time**
job production 6, 7
jury of experts, **forecasting** 12, 13
just-in-case 40–1
just-in-time (JIT) 40–1

K
kaizen, quality management 45

L
labour productivity 51
**latest finish time, critical path method
        (CPM)** 54–5
layout strategies, **plant** 26–7
lean production 7, 48–9
least-cost location 10
life cycles, product 102–3
lifestyle segmentation 90
line extensions, product mix 97
line production 6–7

location of production/business see
        production/business location
logistics strategies, distribution 122–3
long-run average cost curve 24–5

M
macro-marketing environment 62, 72–3
        vs micro-marketing environment 71
        PESTLE analysis 73
        scanning the environment 72–3
        strategies 73
        SWOT analysis 73
make or buy 36–7
management preferences, production/
        business location 9
managerial summary 173
margin of safety 32–3
marginal cost 34–5
marginal cost of labour, productivity 51
**marginal physical product of labour,
        productivity** 51
marginal revenue 34–5
**marginal revenue product of labour,
        productivity** 51
market analysis, business plans/planning
        168
market economies 146–7
market research 62–3, 65, 68–71, 74–85
        analysis 84–5
        business plans/planning 168, 171
        data sources 77
        databases 82–3
        external sources 82–3
        focus groups 79, 80
        histograms 85
        internal sources 82
        interviews 81
        limitations 75, 85
        objectives 77
        observation 79, 80
        presentation of results 84–5
        primary data 77
        primary research techniques 80–1
        problem identification 76–7
        questionnaires 80–1
        reasons 74
        research plan 74–5
        response rate 80–1
        sampling 78–9
        sampling frame 78
        sampling units 78
        secondary data 77
        secondary research techniques 82–3
        surveys 80–1
        target markets 74
market segment 86
market segmentation 63, 86–91
        behavioural segmentation 90–1
        consumer buying behaviour 92–3
        demographic segmentation 88
        geographic segmentation 88–9
        income/class segmentation 91
        lifestyle segmentation 90
        mass markets 87
        niche markets 87
        psychographic segmentation 90–1

strategies 86–7
        target markets 86–93
market share 113
marketers 65
marketing 62–9
        customer focus 69
        defining 64
        goods and services 106–7
        role 68–9
marketing audit 68–9
marketing concepts 66–9
marketing management 62–3
marketing mix 63, 68–9
        marketing plan 170–1
        pricing 108–9
        services marketing 107
marketing plan
        business plans/planning 170–1
        marketing mix 170–1
marketing strategy, micro-marketing
        environment 71
mass markets, market segmentation 87
maximum stock level 38–9
mergers 154–5
micro-marketing environment 62, 70–1
        vs macro-marketing environment 71
        marketing strategy 71
micromachines, product design 14–15
minimum stock level 38–9
minituarisation, product design 14–15
mixed economies 146–7
modularisation, product design 14, 15
modules, product design 14, 15
moving averages, **forecasting** 13

N
nanotechnology, product design 14–15
new product development (NPD) 100–1
niche markets, market segmentation 87
nodes, critical path method (CPM) 54–5
non-probability sampling, market research
        78
NPD see new product development

O
observation, market research 79, 80
operations 2, 4–5
        operational decisions 5
        operations management 2–3
        operations plan 172
outsourcing 36–7
        quality management 47
overcapacity 20

P
packaging 105
partnership, enterprise type 139, 157
penetration pricing 117
personal selling 128
PESTLE analysis, macro-marketing
        environment 73
planned economies 146–7
planning
        see also business plans/planning;
                financial planning

capacity planning 20–1
marketing plan 170–1
production/business location 9
plant 20–1
layout strategies 26–7
plant productivity 50
pollution, production/business location 8
positioning, pricing 108–9
presentation of results, market research 84–5
pricing 108–17
competition pricing 112–13
cost-plus pricing 114–15
demand 110–11
discount 117
elasticity 110–11
factors influencing 110–11
marketing mix 108–9
penetration pricing 117
positioning 108–9
price elasticity of demand 110–11
skimming 116–17
primary data, market research 77
primary research techniques, market research 80–1
probability, decision trees 56–9
probability sampling, market research 78
process layout 26
product benefits 95
product concept 94–5
actual product 95
augmented product 95
core product 94–5
marketing 66
product design 14–15
computer-aided design (CAD) 18
computer-aided manufacturing (CAM) 18–19
integration 14, 15
minituarisation 14–15
modularisation 14, 15
nanotechnology 14–15
strategies 14–15
value analysis 16
value chain 16–17
product development
commercialisation 101
new product development (NPD) 100–1
screening 100
test marketing 100–1
product layout 26
product life cycles 102–3
product management, Boston Matrix 98–9
product mix 96–7
line extensions 97
strategies 96–7
production 50
production/business location 8–11, 158
cost considerations 10–11
environment 8–9
infrastructure 8
management preferences 9
planning 9
qualitative factors 8–9
quantitative factors 10–11
production concept, marketing 66

production methods 6–7
production process 2, 4–5
productivity 50–3
factors impacting 52–3
labour productivity 51
plant productivity 50
resources 50–1
strategies 53
waste, reducing 53
profitability ratios, financial planning 176–7
promotion 124–9
advertising 126–7
AIDA model 125
objectives 124
personal selling 128
public relations 128–9
publicity 128–9
sales promotion 63, 128
psychographic segmentation 90–1
public relations 128–9
publicity 128–9
purchasing process, consumer buying behaviour 92–3

Q
quality assurance 44–5
quality control 19, 44–5
quality management 42–7
benchmarking 46–7
culture of quality 44–5
dimensions of quality 42–3
ISO standards 46
kaizen 45
outsourcing 47
quality circles (QCs) 46
total quality management (TQM) 42, 44–5
questionnaires, market research 80–1

R
randomised sampling of product units, quality management 46
ratios, financial 178–9
reference groups, consumer buying behaviour 93
relocation 11
reorder level 38–9
resources, productivity 50–1
response rate, market research 80–1

S
sales force composite, forecasting 12, 13
sales projections 164, 165
sales promotion 63, 128
sampling, market research 78–9
sampling frame, market research 78
sampling units, market research 78
scanning the environment, macro-marketing environment 72–3
screening, product development 100
secondary data, market research 77
secondary research techniques, market research 82–3
segmentation see market segmentation
selling concept, marketing 66–7

services marketing 106–7
see also pricing
seven stages of a buying decision, consumer buying behaviour 92
size, business see business size
skimming, pricing 116–17
small business 148–53
assistance 137, 160–1
challenges 136–7, 156–9
defining 149
e-commerce 158
globalisation 158
intellectual property rights (IPRs) 158–9
opportunities 136–7, 156–9
small firms vs large firms 152–3
social entrepreneurship 142–3
societal marketing concept 67
sole trader, enterprise type 139, 157
spare capacity 36
spillover effect 8
stimulus-response approach, consumer buying behaviour 93
sub-assemblies, product design 14, 15
surveys, market research 80–1
sustainable enterprise 161
sustainable growth 22
SWOT analysis, macro-marketing environment 73

T
takeovers 154–5
target audience, advertising 126–7
target markets
business plans/planning 166
market research 74
market segmentation 86–93
test marketing, product development 100–1
thinking 'outside the box' 140–1
time-series analysis, forecasting 12–13
total quality management (TQM) 42, 44–5
TQM see total quality management

U
undercapacity 20
unique selling point (USP) 69, 71, 126
unit costs 24
upmarket, goods and services 108–9
USP see unique selling point

V
value, adding 62, 65
value analysis, product design 16
value chain, product design 16–17
variable costs 28–9

W
wait time, capacity utilisation 22, 23
waste, reducing 48
lean production 48–9
productivity 53
work in progress 7
working capital 152
working capital requirements 164, 165